Schooling, Society and Curriculum

D0220154

The Foundations and Futures of Education Series focuses on key emerging issues in education as well as continuing debates within the field. The series is interdisciplinary, and includes historical, philosophical, sociological, psychological and comparative perspectives on three major themes: the purposes and nature of education: increasing interdisciplinarity within the subject; and the theory–practice divide.

In recent years, much curriculum debate has focused less on wider issues related to the purposes of education and more on the content and 'delivery' of school curricula themselves, including new and revised *national* curricula.

Schooling Society and Curriculum seeks to return curriclum studies to critical, generic debates about formal education and its relationships to the wider society, reminding readers of the key curriculum debates that have been present since formal state education began and reassessing them in the context of current curricular trends and policies. The approach goes further, however, by placing such debates within a future-orientated perspective and focusing on some of the key emerging issues of the twenty-first century. These include:

- 'globalization' and reconstructed nationalism
- a revived interest and understanding of what it means to be a good citizen
- developments in the areas of cultural pluralism
- the rapid development of digital technology and its impact on learning
- changing relationships between the 'state' and the 'market' and their impact on formal education.

The book, part of the Foundations and Futures of Education Series, addresses these issues through eleven essays by prominent, nationally and internationally known experts. Centrally it looks at what it is that young people need from a school curriculum to help them develop as happy, socially responsible adults, capable of managing and making the most of a very unpredicatable future.

Alex Moore is Reader of Education and Head of the School of Curriculum, Pedagogy and Assessment at the Institute of Education, University of London, UK.

Foundations and Futures of Education

Education and the Family
Passing success across the generations
Leon Feinstein, Kathryn Duckworth & Ricardo Sabates

Education, Philosophy and the Ethical Environment
Graham Haydon

Educational Activity and the Psychology of Learning
Judith Ireson

Improving Schools
Using research to inform practice
Frank McNeil & Pamela Sammons

Schooling, Society and Curriculum
Alex Moore

Gender, Schooling and Social Justice
Elaine Unterhalter

Schooling, Society and Curriculum

Edited by Alex Moore

Routledge
Taylor & Francis Group

LONDON AND NEW YORK

First published 2006
by Routledge
2 Park Square, Milton Park, Abingdon, Oxon OX14 4RN

Simultaneously published in the USA and Canada
by Routledge
270 Madison Ave, New York, NY 10016

*Routledge is an imprint of the Taylor & Francis Group,
an informa business*

© 2006 Alex Moore, selection and editorial matter;
the contributors, their own chapters

Typeset in Galliard by
Newgen Imaging Systems (P) Ltd, Chennai, India
Printed and bound in Great Britain by
The Cromwell Press, Trowbridge, Wiltshire

British Library Cataloguing in Publication Data
A catalogue record for this book is available
from the British Library

Library of Congress Cataloging in Publication Data
A catalog record for this book has been requested

ISBN10: 0–415–36395–0 (hbk)
ISBN10: 0–415–36396–9 (pbk)
ISBN10: 0–203–01516–9 (ebk)

ISBN13: 978–0–415–36395–2 (hbk)
ISBN13: 978–0–415–36396–9 (pbk)
ISBN13: 978–0–203–01516–2 (ebk)

Contents

Figures

Contributors

David Halpin is Professor in Education in the School of Curriculum, Pedagogy and Assessment at the University of London's Institute of Education. Well known nationally and internationally for his research and writing on the effects of educational policy, David is founder editor of the *London Review of Education*, having previously been co-editor of the *British Journal of Educational Studies*. David's impressive array of publications includes the recent book *Hope and Education: The Role of the Utopian Imagination* (2003), whose sequel, *Romanticism and Education*, will be published in 2006.

David Hartley is Professor of Education (Professional Learning) at the University of Birmingham. A former co-convenor of the Teacher Education Research Network of the European Education Research Association, Programme Chair of the Teachers' Work/Teachers' Unions special interest group of the American Educational Research Association, and member of the General Teaching Council for Scotland and of the Scottish Council for Research in Education, David is currently a member of the editorial board of the *British Journal of Sociology of Education*. His prolific publications record includes the single-authored *Re-Schooling Society* (1997) and *Understanding the Primary School: A Sociological Analysis* (1985). He recently co-authored, with Anne Edwards and Peter Gilroy, *Rethinking Teacher Education: Collaborating for Uncertainty* (2002), and has just completed work, with Professor Maurice Whitehead, on the five-volume *Teacher Education*.

Gunther Kress is Professor of English and Head of the School of Culture, Language and Communication at the University of London's Institute of Education. A leading international figure in studies of the Culture of Education, Gunther's numerous publications include *Multimodal Discourse* (2001); *Before Writing: Rethinking Paths to Literacy* (1997); *Literacy in the New Media Age* (2003); and *Writing the Future* (1995).

Angela McFarlane is Professor in Education at the University of Bristol and Director of the TEEM (Teachers Evaluating Educational Multimedia) project on evaluation of digital content in the classroom. She is a member of the steering committee of the FutureLab project, and of the education committee of Nesta (National Endowment for Science, Technology and the Arts). Well known for her many radio and television appearances and for her column in the *TES Online* magazine, Angela has published widely and with distinction on ICT in Education, including *A Digitally Driven Curriculum?* (2001); and *Information Technology and Authentic Learning: Realising the Potential of Computers in the Primary Classroom* (1997).

Alex Moore is Reader of Education and Head of the School of Curriculum, Pedagogy and Assessment at the Institute of Education, University of London. His publications include numerous journal articles and book chapters, in addition to three single-authored books: *Teaching Multicultured Students: Culturism and Anti-culturism in School Classrooms* (1999); *Teaching and Learning: Pedagogy, Curriculum and Culture* (2000); and *'The Good Teacher': Dominant Discourses in Teaching and Teacher Education* (2004). He has particular interests in curriculum development and design, teachers' work and experience, and young people's experiences of schooling.

Audrey Osler is Professor of Education and Director of the Centre for Citizenship and Human Rights Education at the University of Leeds. Her research addresses education for human rights, equalities and democratic citizenship, children's rights and student participation. She is currently engaged in a European Commission Framework VI study on Citizenship and Intercultural Learning. Among her recent publications are *Teachers, Human Rights and Diversity: Educating Citizens in a Multicultural Society* (2005), *Changing Citizenship: Democracy and Inclusion in Education* (2005) and *Citizenship and Language Learning* (2005) both with Hugh Starkey.

Carrie Paechter is Professor of Education at Goldsmiths College, London. Her research interests, which have been developed out of her previous experience as a mathematics teacher in London secondary schools, include the intersection of gender, power and knowledge, the construction of identity, especially with regard to gender, space and embodiment in and outside schooling, and the processes of curriculum negotiation. She regards herself as a Foucaultian poststructuralist feminist in orientation and writes regularly on issues of research methodology in this context. Her most recent books are *Educating the Other: Gender, Power and Schooling* (1998) and *Changing School Subjects: Power, Gender and Curriculum* (2000).

David Scott is Professor of Educational Leadership and Learning at the University of Lincoln's *International Institute for Educational Leadership*, having previously been a senior lecturer in Curriculum and Learning at the Open University. From 1995–2001 David was editor of the *Curriculum Journal*. An expert in Curriculum Studies, he has published numerous books, book chapters and journal articles, including the edited *Curriculum Theory, Volumes 1–4* (2003) and *Assessment and Curriculum* (2000).

Bridget Somekh is Professor of Educational Research at Manchester Metropolitan University. Her research interests are in the process of change for individuals and organizations, particularly in relation to the use of technology in teaching and learning. Her books include *Action Research: A Methodology for Change and Development* (2006); *Research Methods in the Social Sciences* (with Cathy Lewin, 2005); and *Using ICT Effectively in Teaching and Learning* (with Niki Davis, 1997).

John White is Emeritus Professor of Philosophy of Education at the University of London's Institute of Education. A very well-known figure nationally and internationally for his work on curriculum values and rationales, John's books, which have variously been translated into Greek, Japanese and Chinese, include *Education and the End of Work: Philosophical Perspectives on Work and Learning* (1997); *Education and the Good Life: Beyond the National Curriculum* (1990); *A National Curriculum for All: Laying the Foundations of Success* (1991) (with Philip O'Hear); and *The Aims of Education Restated* (1982). More recently, John has edited the highly acclaimed *Rethinking the School Curriculum* (2004) and is author of *The Curriculum and the Child* (2005).

Michael F.D. Young is Emeritus Professor of Education at the University of London's Institute of Education, and has been a leading figure for many years in the Sociology of Education. Michael's numerous publications include *The Curriculum of the Future: From the 'New Sociology of Education' to a Critical Theory of Learning* (1998); *Education in Retrospect: Policy and Implementation Since 1990* (2001); and *Knowledge and Learning in Specialist and Non-Specialist Organisations* (1996).

Series editors' foreword

One of the most remarkable transformations over the last 200 years has been the universal development of mass education. With each successive decade, provision has expanded to encompass more learners at more stages in their lives. The ambitions for education systems have also expanded to encompass objectives as diverse as personal fulfillment and wellbeing, cultural transmission, active citizenship, social cohesion and, increasingly, international economic competitiveness.

The broad range of ambitions and the sheer pace of change have created a climate in which it is sometimes difficult to stand back and make sense of what education is for and where it should be going. *Foundations and Futures of Education* provides an opportunity to engage with these fundamental issues in new and exciting ways. The series adopts a broad and interdisciplinary stance, including historical, philosophical, sociological, psychological and comparative approaches as well as those from within the fields of media and cultural studies. The series also reflects wider conceptions of education embedded in concepts such as 'the knowledge economy', 'the learning society' and 'lifelong learning'.

In each volume, the academic rigour of the arguments is balanced with accessible writing which we hope will engage the interest of those working in and for education, as well as a wide range of undergraduate and post-graduate students. Although it will be clear that there are few 'easy answers' to many of the questions currently being asked, we hope that you will find the debates and dialogues exciting and thought-provoking.

In this volume, *Schooling, Society and Curriculum*, a group of distinguished education academics deliberate different aspects of the school curriculum. They seek to revitalize discussions of its form and content and purposes and prospects at a time when many national governments, having intervened directly to impose on teachers the requirement to 'deliver' prescribed programmes of study, have inhibited enquiries of a fundamental nature about what is being taught, and how, and with what effects.

These enquiries embrace a wide spectrum of intellectual perspectives, including contributions from the foundation disciplines of education, notably sociology and philosophy, as well as analyses written by scholars operating out of such diverse fields as gender and cultural studies in education and educational history and learning theory. They also identify and engage with issues that are globally rather than merely locally consequential – such as how better to define the curriculum in the wake of worldwide advances in digital technologies; and how better to reflect on what the curriculum is for in the light of current debates about what counts as worthwhile knowledge, including the degree to which it is possible to identify some subject matter as having inherent and enduring value.

Finally, these enquiries meet head-on the dilemmas created by marketized versions of the curriculum, especially those that stress competition and instrumentalism at the expense of alternative visions which prioritize its contribution to maintaining a moral economy of sociality.

Peter Aggleton
Institute of Education, University of London, UK

David Halpin
Institute of Education, University of London, UK

Sally Power
Cardiff University, UK

Acknowledgements

The chapters in this book represent, through the collective eyes of a particular group of British experts in the field, an attempt to revisit abiding curriculum issues in new contexts and to discuss new curriculum issues related to rapid developments in communications technology, changing attitudes concerning individuals and society, and new understandings of learning and knowledge. Each contributor belonged to a core membership for the seminar series 'New Directions For Curriculum Studies' that I had the privilege of chairing between January 2003 and January 2005, several being present at all seminars and most attending more than their own particular presentations. The eleven papers that comprise this book were originally presented at the series, and have been modified in the light of discussions arising out of the presentations. In addition to the presenters, the seminar series attracted substantial numbers of teachers, university students and lecturers and researchers at the Institute of Education and elsewhere, whose invaluable contributions have in no small part shaped the overall and specific contents of the book. With reference to this, I am particularly indebted to the contributions of my colleagues Denis Lawton, Paddy Walsh, Dennis Atkinson and Val Klenowski, and to those members of the Institute's research student community who attended the seminars and contributed so powerfully to them. Though they did not submit papers for the series, their voices and wisdom are never far from the arguments being put forward.

Other acknowledgements are due as follows:

Earlier versions of Michael Young's chapter were presented at the Institute of Education, University of London, Oslo University College, Norway, the Department of Sociology and Education, University of Joensuu, Finland and the School of Post Compulsory Education, University of Huddersfield. I am grateful to colleagues at these seminars who raised questions and criticisms

An earlier version of David Scott's chapter has appeared as Scott, D. (2003) 'Four Curriculum Discourses: A Genealogy of the Field', in D. Scott (ed.), *Curriculum Studies: Major Themes in Education*, London: RoutledgeFalmer.

John White's chapter is a modified version of chapter 5 of his forthcoming book *Intelligence, Destiny and Education: The Ideological Roots of Intelligence Testing*, London: Routledge.

David Hartley's chapter originally appeared as 'The Instrumentalisation of the Expressive in Education' in the *British Journal of Educational Studies* 51(1): 6–19.

Introduction

Alex Moore

Studying the curriculum

The collection of essays in this book have all emerged from the seminar series 'New Directions for Curriculum Studies' hosted by the School of Curriculum, Pedagogy and Assessment at the Institute of Education, University of London between March 2003 and January 2005. The series, comprising eleven seminars, each introduced by an internationally respected specialist in the field, was intended from its inception to respond to what many of us saw at the time as something of a crisis for the discipline of Curriculum Studies. Though the discipline seemed to be alive and well in some parts of the world – most notably, in the United States – in England and elsewhere its scope and breadth, indeed its politics, seemed to have become overly constrained by the immediate matter of responding to a recent spate of government policy directives in public education and a particularly heavy governmental hand in the area of the school curriculum.

In England in particular, some of the more fundamental debates about curriculum selection, modes of assessment, models of learning and pedagogy, issues of cultural inclusion and exclusion, indeed the very purposes of public schooling and curriculum, had seemed in danger of becoming overly focused on government interventions that had produced a prescriptive national curriculum, an outcomes-driven system of school inspection, a rapid and heavy increase in a very narrow but very high stakes system of national testing, and the development of national literacy and numeracy strategies and detailed training programmes for beginning teachers that had begun to tell schoolteachers not just what to teach but how they should teach it.

While these were clearly important developments that demanded a response, and while our reactions to them as curriculum theorists inevitably and deliberately sought to draw debates back from contingent issues to more fundamental ones, too often, we felt, our voices were becoming overly focused on the detail of the specific content and implementation of existing curricula, rather than being directed to more fundamental and global questions of curriculum purposes and effects, or of the wider relationships between curriculum, society, culture and the (official and unofficial) purposes of public schooling. It was becoming increasingly clear, too, from our work in schools and with our schoolteacher students participating in professional development programmes or undertaking research degrees, that we were not alone in this situation, and that classroom practitioners were also being encouraged away from discussions of curriculum principles towards acquiring often very routine skills in curriculum implementation. Nowhere was this in sharper evidence than on the bookshelves of one of the leading retail outlets for educational materials in the United Kingdom, situated close by our institution. Whereas once this bookshop, widely used by our masters, research and beginning teacher students, had organized its copious volumes under discipline headings that had included 'Curriculum Studies', this category, along with several others, had long since disappeared to be replaced by a bewildering plethora of books of teaching materials and revision exercises, aimed not at promoting understandings of curriculum issues but at preparing teachers and students to make the best (in terms of end results) of an existing curriculum that was, by implication, beyond debate.

'New Directions'

The title of the seminar series through which we intended to contribute to a principled reoccupation of the Curriculum Studies ground – 'New Directions for Curriculum Studies' – was a conscious borrowing from Philip Taylor's earlier collection 'New Directions *in* Curriculum Studies'. In that volume, published in 1979, Taylor had described the discipline of Curriculum Studies as being, at the time, 'at a point of departure' (Taylor, 1979: xii). That departure, he had suggested, concerned a general movement away from 'scientific', 'technical', 'applied' approaches to the field (1979: 3) to a mode of enquiry 'seen more and more as the study of human practical problems': one, in short, that had begun to take on a much more sociological orientation.

One of the central concerns in our own series was to consider the extent to which such an orientation had (a) established itself inside and beyond the theoretical field (including, centrally, in schoolteachers' understandings of curriculum issues), (b) influenced wider policy decision-making related to curriculum development, particularly in light of the plethora of national curricula now being designed and redesigned around the globe. We were also conscious of the fact that much had changed in the social, economic and cultural world since 1979 that had impacted very considerably on public education everywhere – specifically, 'globalization' in its various guises; the very rapid development of the Internet and other information and communications technologies; the redrawing of many national boundaries; related developments concerning understandings of nationhood, citizenship and governance; and – though we may be forgiven for having failed to notice them – increasingly sophisticated understandings of human thinking and learning, and of the possible positive and negative effects of formalized education. As Kelly argued (1991: 1):

> education has changed drastically in the last twenty or thirty years...
> [b]oth in the United Kingdom and elsewhere. [Consequently it is] the
> need to ensure that [education] continues to develop, and that it
> responds appropriately not only to other changes in society but also to
> our increasing understanding of the educational process itself, which is,
> or should be, the central concern of educational studies and especially of
> curriculum studies.

In line with Kelly's suggestion that education and curriculum always
have the multiple – of not always easily compatible – functions 'to keep pace
with and match changes in society' while at the same time 'to
maintain...those standards and values which may be seen as transcending
particular times and societies' and 'to respond to that increased *understanding of education* and curriculum which has come from extensive work
in the field of curriculum studies' (my emphasis), we knew that many of the
issues and 'new directions' identified in Taylor's earlier book would still be
highly relevant and central to our current concerns. We were also aware,
however, that they were in very real need of recasting in light both of
those subsequent social developments to which I have referred and of those
developed understandings referred to by Kelly, and that some genuinely
new issues and concerns had also emerged in the intervening period. In
particular, we were interested to assess the impact on Kelly's multifunctional
curriculum of the very rapid pace of social, political and technological
change in addition to the change *per se*, and, within that, of dramatic changes
in local and world economic activities and the 'downward' impact on
curriculum of what has come to be regarded both as 'knowledge' and 'useful
knowledge'.

There was one other thing that concerned us, however, and that related
to what Eisner – one of the contributors to Taylor's book – described as a
tension or mismatch between, on the one hand, modes of educational
enquiry and their underpinning epistemological and ontological rationales
and, on the other, recent policy imperatives and their underpinning
epistemological and ontological rationales. Eisner (1979: 6) had suggested
that in tension with increasing government emphases around the world on
technicist modes of pedagogy, off-the-peg knowledge and easily measurable
learning outcomes as evaluative tools and success-indicators, academic
enquiry into schooling and curriculum had moved in a seemingly counter
direction, central to which had been a shift from quantitative to qualitative
modes of enquiry. While central governments and their policy-forming
agencies appeared to remain locked into 'old' understandings of knowledge,
of learning, and of evaluative practice, 'What we see emerging in the
university is the epistemological and methodological *opposite* of what is being
advocated as desirable for the schools' (Eisner 1979: 6). This new research

movement:

> represents one of the most radical and promising developments in education since the turn of the [19th–20th] century, since it aims to explore and exploit a fundamentally different set of assumptions about the nature of knowledge than the view that has dominated in education since 1900, at least in the United States.

Today, this mismatch between the educational understandings of central governments and those of many researchers and theorists in the field have not only not gone away, they have, arguably, given rise to another situation – one which itself fuelled our sense of urgency in constructing the seminar series. This concerns the conscious or unconscious erosion by central governments of those new modes of enquiry elaborated so enthusiastically by Eisner, and their replacement with approaches more akin to those that underpin policy itself: a not surprising circumstance, perhaps, since governments may feel that Eisner-style evaluation of and research into outputs-driven reform would necessarily be counterproductive and irrelevant to their own purposes. One of the contributors to this current collection, Michael Young, has expressed particular concern, both here and elsewhere, at this attempted 'hijacking' of serious, potentially more influential and longer-lasting educational research, suggesting that, in the United Kingdom at least:

> Successive... governments have introduced various strategies which aim to make educational research more useful, in the sense of helping teachers and others improve student learning. The strategies seek to link educational research to political and wider social goals and, at least by implication, move it away from the criteria and priorities of individual researchers working within disciplines. One example of such a strategy is the extent to which research funding has been shifted from funding bids from individual researchers towards national programmes... which have a specific policy focus. Other examples are the requirement on those bidding for research funds to take account of 'users'... and the encouragement of universities to bid for government tenders and the inevitable priorities that they involve.... [I]n weakening the discipline-based autonomy of educational research (and, by implication, the conditions for knowledge production), government strategies are in danger of undermining the scope for real advances in educational knowledge that might, in the longer term, contribute to improvements in policy.
>
> (Young, Chapter 1, this volume)

One of the common elements of the papers that make up this book is that all the authors locate themselves within the drive to contribute to the 'real advances in educational knowledge' referred to by Young and to the broad mode of enquiry celebrated by Eisner – either implicitly or explicitly critiquing outcomes-driven policy developments from the perspective of the deeper understandings of people, of society, and of 'the nature of knowledge'.

Curriculum theorizing: local and global issues

From out of the seminar series, a number of key issues and concerns emerged. These – along with a note on the general content and organization of the book – are outlined below. First, however, it is important to say something about what might be called the 'internal dynamics' of the work.

In particular, it is essential that (despite the observation with which I concluded the previous sub-section) readers do not come to this book expecting consensus. If they do, they may merely end up experiencing theoretical debate as conceptual confusion. As David Scott points out in Chapter 2, curriculum theorizing, no less than curriculum policy making, is, like any other discipline, concerned with matters 'foundational': contested territory, which inevitably produces argument and debate among its practitioners, often related to differing philosophical, epistemological or political starting-points. From the outset, it was important to us that both the book and the seminar series from which it arose reflected at least some of this diversity of positions and views, as well as including a range of specialist interests within the field. Our aim was not to present a 'united front' (which in any event would have seriously undermined the rationale for a series of seminars in the first place), but rather to produce a set of authentic discussions and debates that included a variety of perspectives. The series, then, was more conversation than collective assertion, and that conversation, including some of its more significant disagreements and contestations (e.g., about the nature and meaning of knowledge), has also been reproduced in the book. In some instances, these disagreements are at root philosophical or epistemological in nature, reflecting the different 'takes' and priorities of the contributors on schooling, society and curriculum; in other cases, they may reflect differing interpretations of key texts or theories, or – more accurately perhaps – differing uses of such texts or theories in the support of the particular argument being put forward. (In my own chapter, for example, I have cited Basil Bernstein's 'collection code' of curriculum organization, comprising 'strong classification and framing' [Bernstein, 1971a,b], as an undesirable mode of operation for the secondary-school English teachers I worked with in the 1980s, who preferred his 'integrated code' model comprising 'weak classification and framing' – a point not dissimilar to one made by Bridget Somekh in her chapter, who suggests that strong framing and classification in the traditional English curriculum work against the effective incorporation of Information and Communication Technology (ICT) into school learning. By contrast, Michael Young, in his analysis of the difficulties confronting Curriculum Studies and curriculum development and design in the United Kingdom and elsewhere, makes a different use of Bernstein's theory, citing the collection code in support of his argument for a strengthening of the boundaries – via a stronger classification between learning domains – between disciplinary knowledge on the one hand and knowledge selections that are essentially economically or socially driven on the other. Elsewhere in the book, knowledge itself becomes a contestable and contested concept, revealing sharp differences in opinion and approach.)

If the opinions and understandings of the book's contributors do not always chime (a positive characteristic, I hope it will be agreed, which has the added benefit and intention of drawing readers into the various debates), nor do their 'angles of approach' or their chosen communicative styles. As David Halpin argues in his chapter:

> many of us in the academy have sought intellectual asylum in the Curriculum Studies field which, historically, has acted as both the siphon for and the melting pot of our ideas about schooling, many of which were first developed within specialist areas of enquiry…the abstract aspects of which are rendered practically significant in our work through their attachment to arguments about what subject matter schools should teach and how they should teach it, and to whom.
>
> (Halpin, Chapter 10, in this volume)

As has already been indicated, the perspectives in this book cover a wide spectrum, including contributions from the disciplines and subject areas of sociology, philosophy, feminism, cultural studies, educational history and learning studies. They also reflect the range of registers apparent in the series from which they have been drawn. While some are deliberately academic or formal in style, others are more 'conversational' and exploratory (I am thinking, for example, of Gunther Kress's chapter, with which I have chosen to conclude the collection: a chapter which focuses on Kress's particular take on examples of young people's language and learning drawn from his own research). For all these differences, however, there are a number of key themes and concerns that chime regularly and insistently throughout the volume's pages. They are not the only themes and concerns that might have been given prominence in a series based around Curriculum Studies (readers will find little specific – though, I would suggest, much implicit – reference, for example, to issues and theory related to curriculum design and modeling), but they do express common and fundamental interests as to what curriculum and schooling are or should be about, and in particular what they are or should be about in relation to the rapidly evolving societies in which we now find ourselves living.

Some of these themes will be identified by readers themselves. All I intend to do now, in the short space I have allowed myself, is to identify five that have struck me with particular force during the process of re-reading the eleven contributions. These, like the six curriculum discourses identified by David Scott in Chapter 2, are neither discrete nor exclusive but inextricably inter-connected, each offering merely an entry-point – though a potentially very helpful one – into considerations of school curricula and of the theories of knowledge and society that underpin them. They are also, I hope, themes which, though often explored by the contributors in the context of recent education policies in England and Wales, will resonate strongly with the recent experiences of readers more familiar with educational and curricular issues in other settings. This is more, I think, than just hope. Ross (2000: 8) has recently argued that 'global manifestations of curriculum form ... suggest that an international curriculum form is emerging that is perhaps related to the near-ubiquity of a liberal education culture.' In terms of broad curriculum content, for example, curricula tend to comprise, as a minimum, at least one national language; mathematics; science; social science; and (usually) aesthetic and physical education. Citing Meyer *et al.*'s (1992) work on global curricula, Ross reminds us (2000: 14–15) that:

> John Meyer's team at Stanford University has looked at the curricular categories used in primary education in over seventy countries since the 1920s. Instead of diversity, they discovered 'an extraordinary homogeneity across the extraordinarily variable countries of the world'
> (Meyer *et al.*, 1992: 6)

Ross is wisely sceptical about making too strong a set of claims from these findings, suggesting that '[g]eneral world conceptions of curricula are not ... as hegemonic as Meyer's team seems to suggest, and more local forces still have a pervasive influence on the forms and purpose of the curriculum' (Ross, 2000: 17). Nevertheless, the ubiquitous general patterns observed by Meyer and his team, the proliferation of the development or revision of national curricula around the globe, the strong involvement of central governments in this latter trend, and the oral contributions to our seminar series of our many overseas students, have led us to suggest that the issues we have identified as central will be of global rather than merely local significance.

Key issues for Curriculum Studies

The impact of digital technologies

One of the more obvious developments to have impacted on our educational lives (in-school, out-of-school and in concert) and, relatedly, our working lives is one to which I have already alluded: that is, the recent, rapid and pretty much worldwide advances in digital technologies – arguably, as radical and far-reaching a development as that of the printing press. Increasingly, young people are accessing information – and perspectives on information – not only inside school but outside it as well: sometimes the same kinds of information and perspective, but often very different kinds too. Schools, meanwhile, as Angela McFarlane and Bridget Somekh indicate in their chapters, often remain strapped by funding difficulties, resulting in a failing struggle to keep pace with the quality of communications systems available to their young students privately.

The potential mismatch between in and out school learning practices is further emphasized, as Kress argues in his chapter, by the wide choice over learning available to young people outside the school, where there is no requirement to follow the priorities – or indeed the top-down 'delivery' – of a national curriculum; by an apparently widening gap between pupil knowledge and expertise in relation to ICT and that of many of their teachers (Moore and Klenowski, 2003); by continuing inequalities in private access to computers and other new forms of communication; by erratic relationships between schools and the producers of educational software; and by the increasing need to be ICT-literate in order to thrive in modern societies. Each of these circumstances poses very demanding questions both to curriculum designers and to curriculum students, not least the extent to which some existent, very 'fixed', body-of-knowledge-and culture-based curricula can survive in a social world in which the manipulation, 'creation' and informed access to information and knowledge appears to be becoming at least as important as the information and knowledge itself.

Defining curriculum

These issues concerning developments in digital technologies and students' access to them outside the formal school context (not to mention the growth of educational television programmes, from quizzes to televised 'lessons' to historical and nature documentaries) resurrect important questions about what counts as curriculum, and where we set our boundaries in discussing it. In effect, it forces us back to definitions of curriculum and to ask whether these continue to be helpful. Kelly (1999: 5) has argued that 'Our definition [of curriculum] must embrace all the learning that goes on in schools whether it is expressly planned and intended or is a by-product of our planning and/or practice', going on to offer a definition of curriculum as 'the totality of the experience the pupil has as a result of the provision made' (ibid.: 7). Such a definition is not very far from Kerr's earlier (1968: 16) definition of curriculum as 'all the learning which is planned and guided by the school, whether it is carried on in groups or individually, inside or outside the school'.

Such definitions are fine as far as they go, but do seem to limit curriculum – and therefore curriculum study – to what happens in or is initiated and controlled by formal educational establishments such as schools. The kinds and amounts of learning that take place outside school (not only via the Internet, but in the form of workbooks and national curriculum readers bought by parents increasingly concerned with their children's Students' Aptitude Test (SAT) and examination results) suggests that we may need to expand somewhat the boundaries by which curriculum is defined and studied – perhaps even (to modify Kerr's definition) to consider curriculum in terms of 'all the learning which is planned and guided – consciously and overtly or unconsciously and covertly – *by the wider society*'. (See also, however, Bridget Somekh's re-definition, in her chapter, of curriculum as 'the learning, both planned and unplanned, that results from interactions between teachers, learners *and tools* within an educational setting *capable of maximizing their transformative potential*'.) I am aware that such a suggestion, which also brings into question Vygotskyan distinctions between 'scientific' and 'everyday' learning, is not popular with many curriculum theorists. On the other hand, there are others (e.g. Kress, 1982) who have regularly drawn comparisons between curriculum content and broader societal manners and preferences, and we might even suggest that there have always been national curricula of sorts, the only difference being that now they are getting formalized in programmes of study. Others, too, have pointed out that a wider social curriculum has always existed and continues to operate in a relatively autonomous way 'outside' the school curriculum *per se*. Ross, for instance, suggests connections between the 'hidden curriculum' of schools (the way the adults treat the children, the kinds of behaviour that are accepted as normal, the ways in which learning is organized and so forth) and the wider curriculum that young people continue to experience beyond the school walls:

> Beyond this, curriculum exists in much wider domains, and it can – and perhaps should – include any socially constructed or prescribed activities, selected in some way from the culture of that society, that result in the transformation of the individual....[In relation to parenting, for example] [t]hough such a curriculum appears to be purely voluntary and informal, it is in fact governed not only by the socially accepted view of what constitutes 'good parenting', but through a series of laws such as the Children Act and Education Acts....
>
> (Ross, 2000: 8)

Ross's reference to 'the culture of that society', of course, raises further questions concerning cultural norms and differences within societies and the extent to which young people may be travelers within and between various curricula – each with its own cultural 'borders'.

Curriculum, the market and the state

This last point raises another very important set of questions for curriculum planners and theorists. Do we take the view that we are 'born into a curriculum' (or curricula), which is merely repackaged, recontextualized, modified and re-presented in a variety of sites including the school classroom – that this has always been thus but that it is now, typically, more formalized than ever before? Or does the school curriculum comprise something that stands, as it were, in counterbalance to wider social values, trends, and preferred knowledge and learning styles, supporting some while resisting others? Implicit in these questions are very large issues concerning education and the role of the state – or more specifically, perhaps, education, the 'market' and the state.

While over-involvement by the state can, depending on its nature, result in an overcrowded and partial national curriculum that reduces opportunities for pluralism and (Skilbeck, 1984) clips the wings of school-based curriculum development (as is the case, I suggest in my own chapter, in England), there is a clear danger, recognized by others, that under-involvement might critically undermine the school curriculum's defence mechanisms against some of the less palatable values of the marketplace: values such as selfishness, over-competitiveness, and instrumentalism. In other words, the curriculum, supported and controlled by the state, serves as a buffer against potentially antisocial, self-serving values and protects more 'enduring' social values such as pleasure in learning, collaboration and tolerance. Not surprisingly, perhaps, the issue of the nature and extent of state involvement in – or control of – public education is taken up explicitly or implicitly in several of the chapters in this book: most obviously, by Young and Hartley. The insidious involvement of the market, including its relationship with the state, also features prominently, particularly in the chapters by Hartley and Kress, both of whom frame educational and curricular policy within wider socioeconomic shifts that prioritize the development of consumers over producers. To quote Kress, for whom the school and the school curriculum remain 'special and essential in relation to maintaining and building sociality, social cohesion, the possibility of community and society':

> A state which is becoming the servant of the market, and an economy based on consumption, have an entirely different relation to the 'educational system' than those of before. [. . .] In [an] environment where the market is increasingly the dominant social, cultural and economic force, a no doubt old question needs to be posed newly and urgently; what is the curriculum for, and what [in relation to academic subjects] is this subject for?
>
> (Kress, Chapter 11, in this volume)

The question of knowledge

Finally, though clearly inseparable from these other issues, there is the matter of curriculum design and knowledge: What goes into a curriculum? What are its bases and rationales? Should it be content/knowledge led or skills led? Should it focus on the perpetuation of 'valued' knowledge, beliefs and cultural practices, or on the development of lifelong skills geared towards the (increasingly unpredictable) future – or indeed on both of these?

Closely linked to this set of questions is another question that will not easily go away, and which, in common with all the other issues I have picked out, is underpinned by probably the biggest questions for curriculum theory and design: What – and who – is the curriculum for? Why do we have it? This is the question of knowledge. How do we define knowledge? What 'counts' as knowledge? Do we need to construct educational curricula around an identified 'body of knowledge'? If so, where does that body come from? To what extent is it self-evident? Does it inevitably reflect existing power relations and support power differentials? Or is it, as Michael Young suggests in his chapter, rather more complicated than that? Is there knowledge which endures because it does, genuinely, have some kind of inherent value? To what extent can we have a discussion about the curriculum if we do not initially agree that it must comprise, essentially, a body of knowledge? What alternatives might there be to the 'knowledge-based' curriculum? Do different people have different understandings of what knowledge is in the context of the educational curriculum because of their different subject specialisms? And do we need to adjust our understandings of knowledge – as McFarlane, Somekh and Kress suggest in their chapters – in light of rapid developments in digital technologies and their increasing in- and out-school use for knowledge and information accessing by young people?

These challenging questions are never far from the surface of what follows in this book, in some chapters – for instance those by Scott, Young, White, Hartley, Paechter and McFarlane – occupying centre stage. Of particular interest, as I have already suggested, are the book's internal debates and disagreements concerning these contentious matters: the different 'takes' on knowledge that the different contributors have, but also the differing concerns they identify. In her chapter, for example, which draws our attention to issues around ICT in the curriculum, McFarlane, after Bereiter, describes knowledge as 'something to be worked on and with, not an entity to be passively consumed or even individually constructed': in other words, an oppositional understanding to that of 'reified' knowledge, whether 'received' or 'produced'. Such an understanding questions the very function(s) of knowledge, seeming to suggest that we should treat it not so much an end in itself, nor as a means to some often tenuously connected end, but rather as a way of supporting and promoting the overall creative-cognitive development of the learner.

Structure and content of the book

With an eye to these major issues, I have organized the book into four sections plus this Introduction. Part I – 'Issues and Contexts' – introduces and elaborates generic issues to be developed in subsequent chapters, acting as a 'mapping out of the territory'. Part II – 'Values and Learners' – focuses on questions of curricular values and rationales, and of the kinds of learner and citizen that may be perceived, promoted and constructed via the curriculum experience. Part III – 'School Curricula in the Digital Age' – concentrates on the use and impact of the new technologies on teaching, learning, assessment and curriculum content and implementation, suggesting new ways of understanding knowledge, education and curriculum in a rapidly evolving 'techno-society'. Finally, Part IV – 'Foundations and Futures: Exploring the Possible' – provides an analysis of current curricular arrangements and difficulties in the United Kingdom and elsewhere, and suggests a continuing role for curriculum studies in envisioning 'alternative' school curricula underpinned by different rationales and values than those currently in favour in many countries around the globe, that are more appropriate in terms of the wider changes occurring in our societies.

At the heart of all four sections, further details of which are given at the start of each, are the abiding questions: How should the discipline of Curriculum Studies (re)define itself in the current conjuncture? What should be its priorities? What does it have to offer wider debates related to educational policy? In response to these questions, we are, I think, agreed, as authors, that whatever else Curriculum Studies needs to do it is vital that it continues to critique and to 'uncover': in particular, to find out what we think is 'really going on' in curriculum design and development rather than limiting ourselves, as some governments would no doubt prefer us to do, merely to commenting on its implementation and easily quantifiable effects. Such a project takes us well beyond Illich's notion of the hidden curriculum, towards considerations of espoused and repressed intentionalities in relation to curriculum design – suggesting a need to explore curriculum effects (on individuals, on societies, on social, cultural and economic groups within societies) other than those claimed through analyses of examination results, truancy levels, SAT results and the like. As Kelly (1999: 5–6) has argued in this respect, with a nod to Stenhouse (1975):

> What is actually received by pupils must be an equally important, or even more important, concern [than what is planned]....[C]urriculum studies must ultimately be concerned with the relationship between...intention and reality, and, indeed, with closing the gap between them, if it is to succeed in linking the theory and the practice of curriculum.

Theory and practice: 'Back to the Future'?

As part of a particularly intriguing contribution to Philip Taylor's *New Directions in Curriculum Studies* Frank Musgrove (1979: 57) suggests that:

> There was once a time when the most powerful influence on thinking about the curriculum was John Dewey. Even Durkheim had his day. But in the mid-1970s it is Karl Marx and Althusser. The curriculum maintains, reproduces or replicates the power structure of society either because its cultural discontinuities prevent working-class children from learning,

or because its ideological potency does not. In any event classroom knowledge, whether learnt or rejected, legitimates the inequalities and reproduces the consciousness that an overripe capitalist society requires. [Marxist criticism of schooling and curriculum provide] probably the dominant perspective on the curriculum.

I want to suggest that such a situation no longer prevails (if it ever really did) – in the United Kingdom or, indeed, anywhere – but that a return to this particular critical orientation might not be such a bad thing. This is partly because an abiding issue for Curriculum Studies, and one that I outline in my own chapter, concerns the tensions implicit in constructing curricula that are both inclusive and common: in particular, in what ways and at what points does the desire for commonality cramp and subsequently destroy the drive towards inclusion? Arguably (Pinar, 1979: 14) 'traditionalist' approaches to curriculum studies have had very little to contribute to this issue. (In 'traditionalist', I include the 'scientific', 'technical' and 'applied' approaches to the field, whose waning influence Taylor [1979: 3] may have been a little too optimistic in declaring.)

Earlier, I made two observations that I think are very important and that perhaps I should make a little more of. The first concerns the fact that one of our major retailers of educational books in England has its shelves currently filled with guides, practice booklets and 'cribs' at the expense of books which seek to examine and discuss different models and intentions of curriculum design. The second takes me back to a place and a time when I was Head of the English Department of a large inner-city comprehensive school in England in the 1970s. To the best of my recollection, none of the core members of my Department then (myself included) were following an MA in Education course, or studying for a Doctorate in Education. All, however, were very familiar with a wide range of current critical thinking on issues of teaching, language and learning (e.g. the work of Barnes, 1969, 1976, and of Britton, 1972); on cultural differences between home and school and their implications for curriculum, pedagogy and learning (for instance, the work of Kress, 1982, Brice Heath, 1983, Tizard and Hughes, 1984); on the over-inflation of the 'inherent' values of standard English and a corresponding under-estimation of the values of non-standard English (including the work of Labov, 1972; Stubbs, 1976; Trudgill, 1983); of appropriate orientations towards and understandings of bilingualism and bidialectalism (most notably, the work of Cummins, 1984 and Levine, 1990); and of how English lessons could be used to explore the ways in which existing relations of power are perpetuated through language, including language which is 'invisibly' racist or sexist (in particular, work coming out of the Inner London Education Authority's *English Centre*, such as *The Languages Book*, 1981).

The critical eye that this team of teachers was able to direct towards the curriculum had come about not purely though their own initiatives, but largely via professional development sessions put on by their school and by their local education authority: that is to say, it was considered very important at the time for the professional development of teachers of English (and not only teachers of English) to continue to explore fundamental issues of curriculum development and design in addition to developing classroom techniques in relation to curriculum coverage (indeed, it was typically very difficult – and not considered at all necessary or desirable – to draw a distinction between the two: i.e. between 'curriculum' and 'pedagogy'). As Hewitson (2004) has argued in relation to professional development for Australian teachers, professional development nowadays (clearly, not just in the United Kingdom) is far more likely to prioritize instrumental matters (how to 'deliver' – or perhaps we should say, bearing in mind its wholesale production and distribution, how to 'retail' – the curriculum) at the expense of exploring core questions and issues. (Hewitson's account of professional development for teachers increasingly comprising imposed agendas for whole staffs at specified times led by invited 'expert speakers' providing useful tips on curriculum implementation will resonate, I suspect, with the experiences of many teachers, regardless of what national education system they work within.)

Major questions like this – including hugely important ones about a curriculum's inherent fairness or unfairness – have not entirely gone away from officially sanctioned debates; however, in England they have certainly been marginalized by a central government apparently capable of seeing no further than simplistic correlations between everyone following (roughly) the same curriculum (i.e. a 'national curriculum') and the curriculum consequently being fair and equitable. It is arguable that these questions will only ever return to the political arena if Curriculum Studies itself goes forward by going back to its theoretical, critical, philosophical and sociological – but also its helpfully constructive – roots and, backed by the force of rigorous empirical and statistical research, impels them back there. This will only happen if academics, including teacher educators, can continue to find ways of working together with curriculum practitioners – centrally, teachers – in the articulation and promulgation of sophisticated (re)conceptualizations of school and other curricula that return again and again to the core purposes of education, refusing to allow these to be overly constrained by local economic imperatives or by a perceived need to maintain the socioeconomic status quo.

Part I

Issues and contexts

Writing about Curriculum Studies in the late 1970s, William Pinar suggested that the discipline was, then, at the point of departure after what he referred to as a lengthy period of stagnation. 'By the summer of 1978', he wrote, 'there will have been six conferences and five books in the past six years which are indications of a socio-intellectual phenomenon in this field'. If what he identified as a process of 'reconceptualization' of the field 'continues at its present rate, the field of curriculum studies will be profoundly different in twenty years time than it has been during the first fifty years of its existence' (ibid.: 13). Highly significantly, Pinar contrasted a certain liberation of curriculum studies (from earlier 'traditional' and 'conceptual empiricist' orientations to include more critical, sociological, 'emancipatory' approaches) with serious concerns about what was happening in the broader education field which, in the United States of America and elsewhere, had 'lost whatever (and it was never complete of course) intellectual autonomy it possessed in earlier years, and now is nearly tantamount to a colony of superior, imperialistic powers' (ibid.: 16).

Pinar's identification of a tension between an increasing (self-)liberation and developing critical edge in the field of Curriculum Studies and a corresponding narrowing of possibilities in the field of Education generally was echoed at the same time by Elliot Eisner's suggestion (referred to in my general Introduction) that an increase in critical, qualitative educational studies in the universities, that aimed to 'explore and exploit a fundamentally different set of assumptions about the nature of knowledge than the view that has dominated in education since 1900', existed in tension with increasing government concerns about 'standards', accompanied by burgeoning 'back to basic' policy interventions, which perpetuated much narrower perceptions and understandings of knowledge and indeed of what should 'count' as knowledge in school curricula.

In 2006, this all sounds oddly familiar! So, too, do the following observations made by Alistair Ross six years ago in his helpful account of current curriculum issues, 'Curriculum: construction and critique' (Ross, 2000). Comparing central governments' economic imperatives with those concerned more with education's intrinsic value, Ross refers to what has recently resurfaced as a dominant curriculum debate in England and elsewhere concerning the relative weightings given to strictly 'vocational' and strictly 'non-vocational' curriculum content, and the extent to which different kinds of curriculum should or should not be followed at some point in their school careers by different students assessed as having different aptitudes. (This set of issues, which has recently erupted quite controversially in England through the publication of the *Tomlinson Report* on 14–19 education, is commented on in more detail by Michael Young and David Scott in the opening two chapters of this section.) In a passage very reminiscent of Eisner's analysis a quarter of a century earlier, Ross argues: 'The comparative economic decline of the United Kingdom, over the past twenty years in particular...has been analyzed as a consequence of inappropriate schooling, that prefers "academic" non-industrial, or even anti-industrial, values over the acquisition of "useful" skills' (Ross, 2000: 5–6).

Likening the current National Curriculum in England to 'a cottage garden', Ross highlights another tension – also explored by Michael Young in the first chapter of this section – between the economy-driven policies of central government on the one hand and that same government's apparent predilection for the past on the other. For all the government's apparent obsession with the changing needs of business and industry, the contemporary curriculum, Ross argues, comprises 'a preservation of cultural forms achieved through time-honoured processes, resistant to challenge or criticism' (ibid.). As Scott points out in Chapter 2, though such a curriculum may appear to be – or be presented as – self-evident and timeless in its choice of content and style, it is, in reality 'socially constructed' and 'the result of competing claims to truth, of bargaining and negotiation'.

The commentaries of Pinar, Eisner, Ross and others raise very important questions concerning the differing and sometimes overlapping roles and positionings of the state and of the academy in relation to curriculum and indeed to wider educational concerns and issues. Most of the contributors to this current book would agree, I think, that there is a growing tendency for the state to become a little too involved in such matters and to become involved in the wrong ways – and perhaps that the academy is not involving itself enough, or in the right ways. While on the one hand there is a recognition that state involvement in education is both necessary and desirable (in relation, for example, to ensuring equitable funding and curriculum provision for all students, comparable standards of teaching across schools, and the preservation of some traditional social values that may be threatened by the invasiveness of some market values) concerns do arise when such involvement threatens teacher professionalism (in, for instance, undermining school-based curriculum development and teacher assessments of students' work) and focuses overly much on economic imperatives tied to particular contingencies (e.g. the need to produce a workforce for the growing Information and Communication Technology (ICT) and media industries).

The academy, meanwhile, needs to be careful of over-directing its own involvement in curriculum and education to specific criticisms of specific policies, or to undertaking research that is tied to government and (in whatever form) government-sponsored agendas rather than exploring educational issues of its own identification. While it is, of course, important for academics to be centrally involved in the assessment and critique of policy initiatives, bringing an alternative and relatively independent voice to such activity, it is equally important that our work does not become entirely sidetracked in this process and that we do not stop debating those very fundamental issues concerning curriculum content and the nature of knowledge and learning that I have earlier identified as being at the heart of our seminar discussions: that is, to ensure that we keep such issues *open*. This relates to a much larger point concerning the role of the academy in free societies. That role is not merely to contribute to the development of critical, knowledgeable lifelong learners – important and central though that imperative clearly is – but to provide, and to invite people into, an alternative, critical voice in relation both to some of the commonsense voices that we may hear in the wider society and to some of the opinions and imperatives of our politicians. My own understanding is that in a healthy democracy (such as we are often told we have in the United Kingdom), governments and government agencies will welcome and want to preserve such a function for the academy, even though they might not always like what the academy has to say or always want to reflect it in policy. In light of this, it is a great pity that the critical voices of the academy appear, often, to be less than welcome by governments and their agencies, and that attempts to return to still-key debates are too often pathologized on the grounds of their being 'irrelevant' to practitioners.

Each of the four chapters with which this book opens, all very differently from one another, impel us insistently back to questions that still lie mysteriously unresolved despite everything we now know about teaching, learning, and the functionings and effects of formal education. They do this critically and at times in the 'emancipatory' way advocated by Pinar (1979), in each case seeking to get beneath the surface of what is happening so that we may better understand curriculum and policy processes and meanings. That they do this in the context of current or new concerns (the increasing focus on vocational education, central to Michael Young's discussion, for example, or a relatively new interest in emotionality as described by David Hartley) is no contradiction, in that, to borrow an expression from Freud, there is inevitably an extent to which these concerns and initiatives will provide 'new sites for old conflicts'. This is partly what Young is getting at when he talks about need to go back in order to go forward: it involves the reconsideration of abiding questions and concerns in new contexts. In particular, it involves key questions – addressed in each of these opening chapters and examined in particular contexts in those that follow – concerning state-education relationships and our understandings and views about the very purposes of formal, state-provided education.

1 Education, knowledge and the role of the state

The 'nationalization' of educational knowledge?

Michael F.D. Young

I have chosen to open this book with a contribution from Michael Young that raises many of its key themes and issues: What is knowledge and what 'forms' of knowledge should or should not be included in curriculum design? What is and should be the role of the state in public education? To what extent are espoused notions of educational and curricular inclusion genuine or merely rhetorical? Anticipating David Hartley's account of how even the 'expressive' in education (one aspect of 'education for its own sake') is becoming marketized and instrumentalized within current UK policy initiatives, Young contrasts new drives towards 'excessive instrumentalism' in curriculum policy and design in all phases of education with purposes that are 'specifically educational'. Young argues that current polarized debates about education and curriculum, that tend to adopt either a fundamentalist acceptance of 'the existing orderings of knowledge and the social structures that they serve' or an endlessly contingent approach whereby knowledge selections are justified in terms of specific 'social and political goals', both overlook key questions concerning the necessary 'conditions for the acquisition of knowledge'. In developing this argument, Young invokes Bernstein's notions of classification and framing and of genericism, arguing for a return to stronger distinctions between formal and everyday knowledge, and a re-prioritizing of expert-led disciplinary knowledge over knowledge whose curricular inclusion and status is essentially policy-driven. This particular argument, apart from providing an interesting context for subsequent chapters by Bridget Somekh and Angela McFarlane (and an important counter-point to the position I have adopted in my own chapter, where I invoke Bernstein's theory in support of a somewhat different argument), suggests that we should be concerned about a 'nationalization' of education on the part of regulatory bodies, whereby institutions and curricula are increasingly reduced to the role of 'delivery agencies'. In his concluding remarks, during which he draws on the ideas of Michael Polanyi relating to the relationship between the creation of scientific knowledge and the science-related demands of the state, Young effectively reminds us of the important independent and critical role of education within wider social systems and the particular importance of university disciplines (including, we might add,

Curriculum Studies) not allowing themselves to be drawn away from essentially educational issues into dealing with those in which knowledge follows political and economic imperatives.

Introduction

This chapter is concerned with the role of central government in education and the interventionist trend in educational policy which is in danger of undermining the purpose of schools, colleges and universities to provide access to knowledge not available to most people in their work and everyday lives. I am primarily concerned with two issues. The first is the question of knowledge, the importance of distinguishing between different types of knowledge and what role they have or should have in education. The second issue relates to recent efforts by government to raise standards and how this takes the form of an excessive instrumentalism, where education is increasingly directed to political and economic goals and justified by them. I shall argue that this instrumentalism necessarily reduces the space and autonomy for the work of specialist professionals, both teachers and researchers. The implicit and sometimes explicit assumption of instrumentalism is that specific educational purposes – what in the English tradition is often referred to as 'education for its own sake' – is little more that a mask for preserving privileges. This scepticism about 'education for its own sake' is not a feature of all national cultures. It is perhaps not surprising to find it so dominant in England, where the idea of 'education for its own sake' has been so closely associated with the elitist liberal education tradition of Newman, Arnold, Leavis and Eliot. To what extent 'education for its own sake' can be other than in some sense elitist is a point that needs discussion but is beyond the scope of this chapter.

The main expressions of instrumentalism in current educational policy are the growing marketization and regulation of the work undertaken by schools, colleges and universities. In public debate the possible alternatives appear limited to what amounts to two forms of nostalgia – one from the political right and one from the left. The one from the right argues against regulation *per se*. It invokes a return to the idea of the 'scholar professional'; at the same time it invariably avoids (or accepts) the elitist implications of the old system within which the scholar/professional was assumed to play a central part. The nostalgia associated with the left goes back to the ideas of the Italian Communist, Antonio Gramsci (1971), but has few voices today. It sees (or used to see) specialist professionals as potentially the organic intellectuals of a truly democratic society. However as far as I am aware the left long since gave up trying to think through either the kind of society in which this might be possible or the role of the state in such a society.

In opening up these issues, I draw on two critical traditions within the sociology of education; the sociology of educational knowledge and, although

I do not deal with it in detail in this chapter, the research on privatization and choice associated with scholars such as Stephen Ball, Sally Power and Geoff Whitty. I shall argue for a reformulated version of the former that focuses on *the conditions for the acquisition of knowledge* as the key educational research issue. With regard to the critique of privatization and the central role given to parent choice, I shall argue that we need to re-think our use of the categories public and private at a time when government is seeking not just to privatize the public sector but to use the private sector as a model for the public. Finally, I shall turn to the political philosopher Michael Polanyi and suggest that his idea of a 'republic of science' may give us a more realistic alternative for the future role of government in education and professional work generally.

Theoretical background

Some readers will be familiar with my early work in the sociology of educational knowledge that began with the book *Knowledge and Control* (Young, 1971). The primary purpose of that book was to unmask the ideological assumptions of the official curriculum and to argue that it always expresses some interests. Interests in the sense it was used then referred to social class and dominant power relations; however the argument is equally applicable to the more specific cases of power and dominance associated with gender or ethnic relations. Despite its strengths in reminding us always to question official versions of the world, however embedded and taken for granted, this approach to knowledge in education had a fundamental flaw. In arguing from the premise that all knowledge is social (an inescapable truth if you do not give authority to divine revelation) it was either trivial (Hacking, 1999) or led to the position that curricula are never more than a reflection of the interests of those in power. In other words it is power not knowledge that counts in education as elsewhere: an intellectual relativism and a reductionism that is of little help in debates about the future of the curriculum.

More recently a radically different approach to the sociology of educational knowledge has been developed that is concerned not just with a social critique of knowledge but with identifying *the conditions for knowledge*. In contrast to the earlier sociology of educational knowledge this approach takes a *social realist* rather than a *social constructivist* approach to knowledge. It is realist in the sense that it recognizes that knowledge cannot be reduced to the activities and interests or activities of those who produce or transmit it. It draws on the later work of Basil Bernstein and is associated with that of Rob Moore (2004) in Cambridge and Joe Muller (2000) in Capetown among others.

My interpretation of social realism (the meaning here is quite distinct from its use in art and literary criticism) rests on a number of assumptions which are crucial to the rest of this chapter. They are:

1   The question of knowledge (what it is that people need to have the opportunity to learn in the school, college or university curriculum) must be central to any educational policy.
2   Knowledge about the world, if it is to be the basis of the curriculum, involves concepts that take us beyond both the contexts in which learners find themselves and those in which knowledge is acquired or produced.
3   The crucial implication of this idea of knowledge for the curriculum is that a distinction is essential between the theoretical knowledge produced by scientists and other specialists, usually within disciplines, and the everyday practical knowledge that people acquire through their experience in families, communities and workplaces. It is the former not the latter that must be at the heart of the curriculum. This, however is not to denigrate the latter which is essential and superior to theoretical knowledge for everyday living in all societies.
4   The primary but not only purpose of educational institutions is to take people beyond their everyday knowledge and enable them to make sense of the world and their lives and explore alternatives; the purpose of educational institutions is not to celebrate, amplify or reproduce people's experience.

Two contemporary fallacies

I want to illustrate why these rather abstract issues about knowledge are important and have a practical relevance, especially in relation to how knowledge is pedagogized in curricula and disciplined in research, by referring to two fallacies in current educational thinking. I will call them *internalist* and *externalist*.

The *internalist fallacy* is typical of the approach adopted by those on the political Right. They take an a-social view of knowledge as a taken for granted given and that it has to be acquired by anyone who wants to see themselves as educated. For them, knowledge changes only occur as internal features of the knowledge itself. This enables them to defend existing orderings of knowledge and the social structures that they serve. A good representative of the political Right is Chris Woodhead, the former Chief Inspector of Schools for England and Wales. In 2004 he wrote a pamphlet (Woodhead, 2004) for the Think Tank 'Politeia' criticizing the proposals in a report on the 14–19 curriculum (DFES, 2004a) of a Working Group chaired by his successor as Chief Inspector, Mike Tomlinson (the *Tomlinson Report*). The report recommended the phasing out of distinct academic examinations (in England known as A levels) and vocational programmes and their replacement by a single four-level unitized diploma structure.

Views such as Woodhead's are correct in one sense; they recognize that there is something special about knowledge, and distinct subject-based programmes like A levels at least are expressions of this. However they are mistaken in seeing this specialness of knowledge as a given and being tied to a particular form of examination which has been in existence for just over fifty years; the specialness of knowledge and the conditions for its acquisition are both social and historical in origin. One result of the limitations of Woodhead's type of critique is that it can only shore up existing knowledge structures and the social inequalities associated with them. In his policy recommendations Woodhead does little more than plead for a return to the 1950s and earlier when the 95% not going to university were either apprentices or, far more likely, manual workers.

What I refer to as the *externalist fallacy* is far more common today and takes the opposite position. Rather than treating knowledge as given and only characterized by internal changes, it sees nothing special about any particular ordering of knowledge: all are contingent. It follows that there are no pedagogic or epistemological reasons why the curriculum or research should not be determined as far as possible by social and political goals. This *externalism* can take a variety of forms: the currently fashionable approach is to identify broad political goals such as promoting social inclusion, widening participation or economic competitiveness and using these goals as the basis for developing targets to drive the curriculum and research priorities. My point is not to argue against these broad political goals, but that, as currently envisaged in educational policy, they take no account of the specifically educational conditions under which they might be realized. Despite their fundamental differences, both positions have one thing in common. They fail to take account of the conditions for producing and transmitting knowledge (Moore and Young, 2001). Whereas the *internalists* treat the existing knowledge structures as a-historical givens, the *externalists* treat knowledge as just another instrumentality which can be manipulated to serve the goals of whatever government is in power.

It was the English sociologist, Basil Bernstein who began at the end of the 1960s to theorize the conditions for knowledge acquisition and production and hence to provide a way of moving beyond the two fallacies that I have described. He saw school and university curricula developing on the basis of what he referred to as the *strong classification* of different fields of knowledge and *strong framing* between educational and everyday knowledge structures. The key condition for the acquisition and production of knowledge for Bernstein was *insulation*: insulation between disciplinary fields and insulation between educational and everyday knowledge. This is obviously a highly contentious argument, but it provides a useful starting point and leads to two questions:

1　Can these conditions survive as further and higher education continue to expand and be made subject to greater external regulation?

2   How far do current innovations designed to promote greater participation (e.g. work-based learning, e-learning, recognition of prior learning, foundation degrees and modularization) undermine (or preclude) the conditions for acquiring and producing knowledge that Bernstein identified?

With these broad issues in mind, I turn briefly and by way of illustration to three specific policy issues.

Three policy issues

The role of disciplines in educational research

As a result of many criticisms and a number of reviews, successive UK governments have introduced various strategies which aim to make educational research more useful, in the sense of helping teachers and others improve student learning. The strategies seek to link educational research to political and wider social goals and, at least by implication, move it away from the criteria and priorities of individual researchers working within disciplines. One example of such a strategy is the extent to which research funding has been shifted from funding bids for individual researchers towards national programmes like the ESRC's (Economic and Social Research Council's) *Learning Society* and the *Teaching and Learning* research programmes, both of which have a specific policy focus. Other examples are the requirement on those bidding for research funds to take account of 'users', and hence pay less attention to disciplinary criteria, and the encouragement of universities to bid for government tenders and the inevitable priorities that they involve. My argument in an earlier paper (Young, 2004) was that in weakening the discipline-based autonomy of educational research (and, by implication the conditions for knowledge production), government strategies are in danger of undermining the scope for real advances in educational knowledge that might, in the longer term, contribute to improvements in policy.

The crisis in the professions

In another recent paper with John Beck (Beck and Young, 2005) we applied a Bernsteinian conceptual framework to the crisis faced by professions – assailed, in the case of teachers and medical professionals by ever greater state regulation, and in the case of law and accountancy, by the encroachment of the market. Bernstein suggests that professional knowledge emerged in the tension between the 'inwardness' of academic disciplines and the 'outwardness' of practical demands (e.g. for better health, legal advice and new roads and railways etc.). This tension has led both to new professional fields such as accountancy and new disciplines such as molecular biology and mechatronics.

By the mid- or late twentieth century, we argued, the balance between inwardness and outwardness was shifting towards the latter and was leading to a new form of control of professionals – what Bernstein refers to as genericism. Genericism refers to the process of giving precedence to procedures and criteria that are not specific to individual occupations, disciplines or fields of study. Generic criteria invoke the needs of consumers and customers; however, in practice generic procedures and criteria always tend to be generated by governments and their agents. In the form of quality assurance measures they involve a shift in power away from specific professional and discipline-based and other specialist organizations towards generic criteria formulated by regulatory agencies. Generic modes of regulation are likely to weaken the basis for the development and application of new specialist knowledge by professionals and undermine their autonomy.

Reforming 14–19 curriculum

From the point of view of the two fallacies that I referred to above, recent attempts to reform the 14–19 curriculum in England and Wales represent a contradictory case. In proposing a four-level Diploma to replace all current vocational programmes, GCSEs and A levels, the Tomlinson Report gave precedence to generic criteria as the basis for a single Diploma structure (each student would be required to complete a specific number of core and specialist units) over the content-specific criteria of subjects, both academic and vocational. The proposed Diploma is an example of the *externalist fallacy* which assumes that common external criteria are more important than the content-specific criteria of subjects. The British government, however, has rejected the report's proposals for a Diploma structure and re-asserted the claims of distinct subject-based A levels and a single vocational diploma. This is an educationally contradictory but politically understandable position of adopting one position on A levels that is indistinguishable from that taken by Chris Woodhead and already referred to, but accepting a generic position on a vocational diploma. Where the Tomlinson Report and the government have similarities is that neither consider *the conditions for knowledge acquisition or progression*, whether in academic or in vocational pathways.

Implications of the three cases: the nationalization of education?

In each of the cases I have referred to we can note a shift from a reliance on *generalizing principles* associated with specialist professionals to a reliance on *procedural principles* associated with regulatory agencies. To put it another way, it is a shift from an *epistemological* form of accountability (which is concerned with notions of truth and objectivity shared within disciplinary communities) to an *administrative* form of accountability which relies on generic criteria that are applicable to all professional and research fields. I want to consider two implications of this shift.

First, I want to suggest that the shift in forms of accountability is an expression of a tendency to 'nationalize' the provision of public education. The term nationalization is not entirely satisfactory. Colin Crouch (Crouch, 2004) in a recent Fabian pamphlet suggests 'commercialization' to describe similar processes, and my colleague, Frank Coffield, when I presented this chapter as a paper at a seminar, suggested 'centralization'. My case for retaining the term nationalization is that it dramatizes an important and little discussed issue and that centralization has more neutral associations. In using the term nationalization, I do not mean it in the sense that the term has been traditionally used to refer to the public ownership of privately owned businesses. I am referring to how activities such as education, research and some professional work, which traditionally have had significant autonomy from state intervention whether in the public or private sectors, increasingly have to comply with goals specified by government or its regulatory bodies. The examples that I have referred to were the discipline-base of educational researchers, the autonomy of members of professions and the specialist knowledge-base of subject and vocational teachers in schools and colleges. Each is being constrained in the interests of making their activities more accountable to regulatory bodies and their procedural principles. What follows from my earlier argument from the sociology of knowledge is that these new forms of accountability will weaken the classification and framing of knowledge (in Bernstein's terms) and therefore the insulation which he argued was a key condition for the knowledge production and acquisition that might lead to rigorous educational research and high quality professional work. The balance is being shifted from strong classification associated with internal criteria defined by specialists to weak classification expressed in external criteria defined by regulatory bodies (and indirectly by government).

I do not want to imply that members of professions, subject specialists or educational researchers should be beyond public criticism; their practices may sometimes involve little more than preserving privileges or maintaining out of date practices. In the specific fields discussed, a high proportion of student drop-out at 16+ and 17+, weak educational research and medical malpractice are real enough issues. It follows that my concern is not with the role of the state, *per se*; some role is inevitable: it is with the form and extent of state intervention and the over-instrumental view of knowledge and education that such an interventionist approach to policy implies.

Second, I want to suggest that the issue we need to debate is not only that education is being privatized (as in cases where 'failing' Local Education Authorities (LEAs) have been handed over to engineering companies such as Jarvis) but *more generally the form of state intervention, which may or may not involve privatization*. What I am searching for is a way of describing the shift from a view of public education as a professional practice with significant autonomy from state intervention, to the present situation when public education is increasingly a state-directed practice under national rules and accountability procedures.

I am aware that many of the processes I am referring to as *nationalization* borrow the language and strategies of the private sector. However the power of intervention remains the power of the state and, more specifically, that of the elected government. It is state power being used to bring education into line with government goals. My own view, therefore, is that privatization is only one part of a wider process of weakening the boundaries between what should and what should not be open to central government intervention.

How, then, should we describe what such processes involve? I suggest that educational institutions (and in a not dissimilar way, other public sector institutions such as hospitals) are becoming *delivery agencies*, whether of research results, overseas students, qualified teachers, exam passes, higher rates of participation or whatever the government identifies as its preferred outcome. It is not that I am arguing we should oppose these outcomes – far from it. It is rather the consequences that may follow when they come to drive educational institutions and policy that I am concerned with. The combination of regulation, quantitative targets and tight funding associated with the emergence of the delivery agency model of education means that the specificity of what it is to be an educational institution is reduced; the dominating priority becomes delivering targets and outcomes – not what the targets are or how they are achieved.

A new and distinctive feature of this 'nationalizing' process under the present Labour government has been the substitution of the goal of promoting greater equality associated with earlier Labour governments by the new goal of overcoming social exclusion. The rhetorical power of social inclusion as a slogan is indicated by how difficult it is to challenge it without appearing to be conservative or elitist; who could be opposed to social inclusion except an old elitist? This is of course a classic 'third way' or New Labour strategy for pre-empting debate about alternatives. The problem with giving priority to overcoming social exclusion is that a focus on inclusion can easily preclude debates about what people are being *included in* and about the possibility that more social inclusion might be associated with greater inequality.

We are dealing, I suggest, with a new stage in the expansion and development of public education and we may need new concepts for understanding it. The history of this expansion up to now has involved two struggles: one over extending access to education to an ever wider public and one over the nature of the education that was provided. In England most of the efforts of the left and labour movements and indeed Labour governments in the past, have been directed to the former struggle. However, the present government is not driven by a popular movement demanding expansion, let alone one that challenges the nature of the education provided; it is driven largely by its own goal of overcoming what it sees as the 'conservatism' of educational institutions – another form of social inclusion! What is obscured by seeing educational institutions as 'conservative' is an important distinction between two kinds of conservatism which I will loosely call 'political' and 'educational'. 'Political' conservatism takes a variety of forms. Some are reflections of the conservatism of the wider society; the preferential funding treatment of Oxford and Cambridge universities and the charitable status of the Public Schools are the most obvious examples. Other examples of a more internal conservatism might be expressions of inertia within subject fields and the capacities of new types of learners. However there are forms of 'Educational' conservatism that have origins in the culture-conserving and -transmitting role of educational institutions and the need to defend those specific structures that are the inescapable conditions for knowledge acquisition and production. Examples of such forms of conservatism may be support for disciplines and forms of pedagogic authority, and opposition to the modularizing of the curriculum into 'bite sized' chunks supposedly more accessible for slow learners. My argument is that there is a danger that the excessive instrumentalism underpinning the delivery model of education and research and the commitment to doing away with anything deemed to be conservative may be undermining the conditions for access to knowledge which is the historic purpose of educational expansion.

Let me summarize my main argument. In so far as educational institutions are forced into delivery models based on administrative principles, the specificity of education and the epistemological basis of good research and professional work and genuine progression are undermined. In the three cases referred to I have suggested that the conditions that may be crucial to each – the disciplinary basis of educational research, the specialist knowledge of subject and vocational teachers in the 14–19 curriculum and the autonomy of professional expertise – may be threatened, not primarily by privatization, but by new forms of government intervention. In each case we have examples of a *centralizing or interventionist state* not a *privatizing state*. Furthermore, it is a direction that could be even more likely to undermine the conditions for knowledge production and acquisition than one based more directly on the market. For all its negative features and the great inequalities found in the United States of America, the protection of scholarship by the 'private' Ivy League universities cannot be ignored.

If we consider current policy solely through the lens of opposition to privatization, we may get trapped into thinking that what is needed is a larger role for the state. On recent evidence, at least in the English case, this could even accentuate the dominance of what I have referred to as the delivery model. It follows that both the state/private dichotomy and the trend to privatization in educational policy may have outlived their usefulness – at least analytically. It is the state that is intervening into professional and academic domains, not the private sector. We are in new circumstances and we may need new tools for critique and for thinking about alternatives. New Labour's election slogan for 2005 was *Forward Not Back*. My suggestion is that we may need to go back if we want to go forward. In the final section therefore, I turn to the possibilities of Michael Polanyi's essay *The Republic of Science*, first written in 1962, as a way of thinking about the role of the state in relation to the role of knowledge in education.

The state and knowledge: Michael Polanyi's *The Republic of Science*

In 1962 Polanyi faced a similar problem in relation to science to the one that I have suggested we are facing today in schools, colleges and universities. He refers to a state interventionist approach to science that was popular at the time but which many would think crude today. It involved setting specific political goals for scientific research and was expressed in its most extreme form in the Soviet Union with Lysenko's environmentalist biology; an example of the externalist fallacy taken to its limits. Of course in the Lysenko case the massive reality of the natural world undermined his ideology, as it was bound to in the end. In contrast, education as a set of social institutions has a less straightforward role in undermining the ideologies that underpin both policies and social theories, not the least because in the fields of social and educational policy we are involved in creating ideologies as well as in undermining them. Flawed and one-sided educational 'theories' such as 'learner-centredness' and competence-based approaches to vocational education keep being 're-discovered' despite the substantial body of research documenting their weaknesses.

Polanyi did not argue that state intervention in science was unquestionably wrong and that scientists should be left to themselves – the internalist fallacy. He takes a more subtle approach to science by seeing it as rooted in a form of market for ideas and by contrasting the relative unboundedness of economic markets with the boundedness of 'markets for ideas' in the sciences and other fields of knowledge. Science was not, for Polanyi, just a collection of bodies of powerful knowledge; it consisted of sets of institutions with their rules, codes, traditions and core values. The distinctiveness of the sciences as institutions is the unique value they place on innovation and the creation and defence of new knowledge. It is this value that distributes rewards, shapes research priorities and, albeit indirectly, influences school and university science curricula. This does not mean that science is beyond public criticism; it is a public institution, funded largely by the public as taxpayers. Polanyi argued that the role of the state is not to try and direct scientific priorities but to support the sciences in realizing their core value – the creation of new and reliable knowledge. Despite pressures for a more externally or user-driven approach this model still largely applies in the case of the Science Research Councils, although, as I have argued earlier, much less so for the Economic and Social Research Council (ESRC).

In a parallel way we can envisage education as an institution or set of institutions: like science with its rules, codes and traditions, but with a different core value – *the acquisition and transmission of knowledge* as well as its creation. We have, then, in the Polanyi-related idea of education and knowledge as institutions, the basis of an alternative role for the state in supporting both educational research and the professions in promoting the acquisition, application and creation of new knowledge. This would involve less state intervention and regulation and more self-regulation. It would, I am sure, require the professional education community to re-assess its commitment to its core value of promoting the acquisition of knowledge, and how far, in following political and economic goals, it has lost sight of it.

2 Six curriculum discourses
Contestation and edification

David Scott

In this chapter, David Scott identifies and describes six curriculum discourses or ideologies through which decisions about curriculum content and organization are made. These are: Foundationalism, Conventionalism, Instrumentalism, Technical Rationality, Critical Pedagogy and Postmodernism. These are not presented as definitive or mutually exclusive but rather in terms of a particular heuristic for critical explorations of curriculum theorizing and construction. (Readers may notice that in his chapter David Hartley refers to 'the discourse of instrumental rationality', and may wish to consider the extent to which this represents a conflation of Scott's 'instrumentalism' and 'technical rationality' discourses). Underpinning Scott's approach is a view of the role of the curriculum genealogist as (1) uncovering or deciphering the rules that constitute particular formations of power, (2) doing so without becoming embroiled in logo-centric discourses that assume originary knowledge structures. Apart from providing a useful heuristic for re-visiting Young's opening chapter and evaluating subsequent ones, the issues explicitly and implicitly raised in Scott's account – concerning curriculum content and design in relation both to particular understandings of knowledge and to particular understandings of power relations within the wider society – may be seen as abiding themes of the book as a whole, and are returned to in different ways and with different emphases and perspectives by succeeding contributors. (See, for example, the chapters by John White and David Hartley that conclude this opening section, and the chapters by Carrie Paechter and myself in Part II.) Scott's implication is that each of the six discourses or ideologies he identifies has its own formal structure, and each, in its different way and at different historical moments, has had a profound influence not just in academic understandings and critiques of curriculum but in terms of policy and practice in the field of curriculum design and development as a whole.

Curriculum theory and policy

At the risk of being thought unoriginal, the notion that curriculum-making is a contested activity can still provide a starting point for what follows.

In this chapter, I will sketch out six different versions of the curriculum or at least six different justifications for determining what should be included in a curriculum. It would be perverse to suggest that curriculum theorists and policy makers charged with developing curricula in real-life settings operate through one of these discourses without reference to the others. Indeed, curriculum-making is always embedded in policy-making processes and may be understood as a series of negotiations and compromises between different interests rather than as the creation of a comprehensive, perfectly formed and coherent set of prescriptions. Notwithstanding this, it is still worth examining attempts made by curriculum theorists to provide rationales or justifications for the form, logical relations between items and contents of a curriculum. This chapter therefore identifies and critically appraises six curriculum discourses: Foundationalism, Conventionalism, Instrumentalism, Technical rationality, Critical pedagogy and Postmodernism.

Foundationalism

Foundationalist curriculum rationales seek to provide a trans-epistemic justification for both the contents of a curriculum and the form that it should take. This type of justification may be philosophical, psychological or socio-logical. If the justification is philosophical then curriculum frameworks are understood as logically necessary; examples of which are Hirst's (1974) seven forms of knowledge; Phenix's (1964) six realms; and Schwab's (1962) three kinds of discipline: investigative, appreciative and decisive. Psychological frameworks are justified through observations of the brain; human beings have certain distinctive mental modules and this therefore underpins the blueprint for a curriculum. Gardner's (1983) recent work on types of intelligence falls into this category. Finally, there are trans-social explanations in which the justification for inclusion in the curriculum is that all non-pathological societies can be understood as having several domains of practice, and this provides sufficient reason for incorporating these domains and the boundaries between them into the curriculum (cf. Lawton, 1989).

In considering these types of justification, it is worth concentrating briefly on Hirst's seven forms of knowledge (or at least early rather than later Hirst [1993], who now seems to have abandoned this form of epistemological foundationalism), and in particular his contention that these represent discrete forms of knowledge and rationality. If it is possible to identify distinct forms of knowledge, then this provides a justification for what should be represented in a curriculum and what should be left out. An educated pupil should have been exposed to these different forms of knowledge, and his or her education should be considered insufficient or inadequate if this exposure had not taken place.

Though on the surface Hirst provides a rationale for the traditional form of the curriculum and in effect offers a means for dividing up that curriculum into discrete subjects, he was clear that this was not what was intended.

What he sought to do was to provide a logical foundation for a rational curriculum so that such a curriculum was 'based on the nature and significance of knowledge itself, and not on the predelictions of pupils, the demands of society, or the whims of politicians' (Hirst, 1974: 32). Even given this, however, there are serious philosophical problems with his seven logical forms. These principally rest with the argument that correct reasoning within one of these forms implies not that there are alternative forms of reasoning which can be accommodated in another of the forms, but that these alternative forms of reasoning are in fact wrong *per se*. So for example, religious judgements are not alternative forms of rationality but misguided attempts to determine the existence of phenomena that cannot be rationally proved. Further to this, the epistemological claims made for each form by Hirst have been disputed by various post-positivist philosophers, so that, for example, there is now a serious doubt as to whether empirical observations can be made which are not theory-laden (cf. Quine, 1953). Finally, doubts can be cast on Hirst's entire project, which implies an essentialist view of knowledge and its divisions and a neglect of the transitivity inherent in the development of the disciplines. Hirst's later philosophy would suggest that disciplines or traditions of knowledge *cannot* be construed as universal, transcendental and constitutive of rationality *per se*, which may be read as an acknowledgement that the original project has failed.

As I have indicated above, Hirst's approach may be seen as essentially philosophical. *Psychological* frameworks may be exemplified by the work of Gardner (1983). He identifies seven types of intelligence: linguistic, logico-mathematical, musical, bodily kinesthetic, spatial interpersonal and intrapersonal (later to be supplemented by naturalist, spiritual and existential intelligencies [Gardner, 1999]). Gardner's justification for these types (Gardner, 1983) rests on the identification of eight criteria or signs of intelligence: evidence from brain damaged individuals which isolated particular types of intelligence; the existence of exceptional individuals; the identification of a set of core operations in the brain; a distinctive development history in 'normal' individuals; empirical evidence from experimental task completion; support from psychometric findings; and the potentiality to be encoded in some form of symbolic system. This range of evidence, as White (1998) suggests, makes it difficult to develop a set of reasons for representing certain forms of intelligence in the curriculum and excluding others, and Gardner seems to have provided a plausible but ultimately unconvincing logo-centric version of the curriculum.

The third type of foundationalist rationale is exemplified by Lawton's (1989) contention that since all non-pathological societies share a common framework for dividing up their activities, this provides sufficient justification for inclusion of these discrete activities within the curriculum. The problem this argument has to confront is that social forms vary across cultures, historical periods and with different groups of people within the same culture. It would be false to infer from this that there are no universal social forms, as one of these might be right and all the others wrong. However, in the absence of contrary evidence or argument, conceptual relativists who deny the possibility of universal social forms are on more secure ground. Indeed, even if most or indeed every society shared some set of beliefs, this in turn would not prove the existence of social absolutes, since all of them might be wrong. Furthermore, distinguishing between pathological and non-pathological societies requires a set of universal criteria, which suggests that as an argument trans-sociality cannot provide a complete justification in its own right. A further justification therefore needs to be provided with regard to the possibility of identifying and applying these universal criteria.

Conventionalism

The issue of relativism is taken up by Rob Moore and Michael Young (2001) with particular reference to the curriculum, in their article: *Knowledge and the Curriculum in the Sociology of Education: Towards a Reconceptualisation*. It is worth considering their argument for one moment. For them, the curriculum debate has been structured in terms of two competing traditions. The first of these is what they call 'neo-conservative traditionalism' and the second is 'technical-instrumentalism'. Neo-conservative traditionalism represents the curriculum as a given body of knowledge that should be preserved through its institutionalizing in schools. Within this model, pedagogy is understood as contemplation on the canonical texts that constitute the various disciplinary traditions. The emphasis is on a respect for tradition and authority, expressed through a particular view of knowledge. The second ideology places itself in opposition to this view of knowledge. Technical instrumentalists are concerned to construct the curriculum around the needs of the economy. For them, the curriculum is understood as a means to an end, the end being a successful, efficient and competitive knowledge-based economy. The dispositions that education is meant to nurture are flexibility, entrepreneurship, trainability and a willingness to take part in a market economy. Whereas previously vocationalism was reflected in a work-related, practically orientated curriculum for those who were not considered to be academic, more recently the technical-instrumentalist curriculum has embraced employability for all students. Moore and Young (2001: 448) suggest that this ideology is congruent with 'a style of managerial regulation that is integrated with the broader apparatus of performance indicators, target setting and league tables.'

Postmodern critiques of both neoconservative traditionalism and technical-instrumentalism start from a basic assumption that knowledge is embedded in particular interest perspectives, which furthermore are concealed under the guise of a spurious objectivity. The implication for the curriculum is that epistemologically its contents are bound to be arbitrary (since postmodernists do not accept any foundational principles that underpin knowledge), but that in effect the knowledge base of the curriculum is so constructed that some groups in society are disadvantaged and others advantaged. It is here that the argument has to confront the difficult issue of relativism. For if knowledge is essentially arbitrary, then all knowledge is determined by social and political arrangements; or to use Foucauldian (1977) terminology, power and knowledge are inseparable. For postmodernists, there are no absolute grounds for determining that particular forms of knowledge should be curricularized and others not – a conclusion that Moore and Young are not prepared to accept.

Moore and Young, indeed, argue against this postmodern position, and their resolution of the debate is crucial to understanding whether a non-arbitrary view of knowledge can prevail that would constitute a curriculum. Their first argument is that postmodernists polarize and trivialize the two positions, neo-conservatism and technical-instrumentalism. The neoconservative position, they suggest, is not just about preserving an arbitrary standard, but also about understanding education as an end in itself. This places knowledge as central to any discussion of the curriculum. Furthermore, though it may preserve entrenched and partial interest positions, the neoconservative curriculum is also crucial for maintaining and developing standards and conditions for the development of new knowledge (see also Young's chapter earlier). Moore and Young's disagreement with neoconservatism rests on its tendency to reify knowledge, which ignores the way knowledge evolves in response to changing conditions and innovations. In like fashion, instrumentalism is criticized because it prioritizes economism at the expense of other worthwhile justifications for education and, furthermore, does not address the proper conditions for new knowledge.

It is the second argument that they make against postmodernism that goes to the heart of their critique. Postmodernism implies relativism and therefore arbitrariness; the denial in other words that knowledge can be objective. The implication is that if knowledge can be shown to be objective then this provides the basis for determining what should be included in the curriculum and what should not. For Moore and Young, it is the very social nature of knowledge that provides good grounds for objectivity.

Moore and Young may be seen as effectively redefining knowledge so as to preclude accusations that it is relativistic in character. Knowledge cannot be rooted in universalistic and trans-social categories but is constructed by historical agents, operating within determinate historical periods, and therefore any current version of knowledge has evolved from the efforts of many human agents, some long since dead. This is a different argument from the one which suggests that all knowledge is rooted in particular interests. Knowledge, though it may have been constructed originally by particular human agents with particular interests, has this enduring quality which may (though not always) transcend the particular interests of present day agents. Independent criteria are literally independent of standpoints and should not be equated with them. As Moore and Young argue, some knowledge can transcend the immediate conditions of its production. They therefore posit three arguments: first, knowledge is intrinsically social and collective; second, intellectual fields implicated in the construction of new knowledge are characterized by a complexity that postmodernists unjustly reduce to power relations; and third, there is an asymmetry between cognitive and other interests and the two should not and cannot be equated. Power and knowledge in Foucauldian terms are not inextricably tied together; and it is therefore possible to understand and develop the latter without reference to the former.

I want to suggest that ultimately, this is not a convincing argument. It rests on the possibility of distinguishing between those forms of knowledge which are interest-bound and those forms of knowledge which transcend the interests of human agents. However, to determine which is which demands a form of reasoning that transcends both the historical genesis of the particular and presently conceived idea of knowledge (see in this respect John White's chapter, which follows this one), and, more importantly perhaps, the past conception of knowledge which has provided the grounds for Moore and Young to argue that some types of knowledge can be objective. In order to show that knowledge is objective, it is necessary to argue not just that the form of knowledge transcends the particular interests and circumstances of the particular knowledge constructor, but, more importantly, that the criteria for determining whether it is true or false are not rooted in social arrangements made by human agents, but have transcendental attributes. The argument that Moore and Young have advanced renegotiates the meaning of objectivity so that it embraces the social and the historical, and yet classical definitions of relativism do just this. Their argument consequently may be seen as based on attacking a straw person; postmodernists would accept the social nature of the categories that underpin knowledge.

Instrumentalism

A different type of justification for the inclusion of items in a curriculum eschews foundationalism and epistemic conventionalism, and argues that it is possible to provide a justification for the contents of a curriculum in terms of certain virtues or experiences that children should have in order to lead a fulfilled life. The project is therefore definitively normative and redefines the notion of instrumentalism away from mere economism. It is a distinctive approach in that the curriculum is constructed in terms of whether the experiences undergone by students contribute to the development of dispositions that allow them to lead 'the good life'. There are two principal problems with this approach: first, there is a difficulty with establishing what the good life is; and second, there is an equal difficulty with identifying experiences for children in school which will lead to the development of dispositions so as to allow the individual to lead the good life when they leave school (cf. Callan, 1988; Clayton, 1993).

White (1982) is one of the leading exponents of this type of curriculum-making. He argues for a notion of autonomy, or the capacity to reflect on and make choices which allow the possibility of leading the good life and argues that if children do not develop such a capacity they cannot distinguish between projects which contribute towards the good life and projects which do not. Further, if they do not develop such a capacity, they are liable to be in thrall to arbitrary authority. Thus the autonomous individual is treated as an ethical absolute (though again there are problems with identifying such an individual because it is difficult to distinguish between actions that have been motivated by conformity to an arbitrary authority, and actions that have genuinely resulted from the exercise of autonomy, not least by the person themselves!).

This dilemma for White reflects the tension between leading an autonomous life and leading a fulfilled one, and the fact that the two are not necessarily the same. Indeed, a person who indulges their appetites may not be considered to be autonomous, though clearly there is a sense in which they have chosen to indulge their appetites and have thus exercised their autonomy. It is here that the problem is at its starkest, because autonomy as a concept cannot carry the weight attached to it and there are implicit and normative meanings attached to it. Certainly, autonomy means more than making choices or even having the capacity to make choices. There is a sense in which it is used to indicate the making of *good or right choices* and this is reflected in White's distinction between self-regarding reasons for choosing one form of life over another and other-regarding reasons in which the person also contributes to the welfare of others. Inevitably, instrumentalist views of curriculum-making are future-orientated, and can therefore only be justified with reference to political and social arrangements that are considered to be ideal. This ideal in turn needs to be argued for, and is likely to be contested.

Technical rationality: a science of pedagogy

Whereas essentialist or logo-centric discourses act to prescribe the contents and form of a curriculum, technicist epistemologies are indifferent to curriculum content and form *per se*. Proponents adopt, rather, a form of technical rationality with regard to knowledge and knowledge creation. Within this approach, practitioners are required to set to one side their own considered and experience-based ways of conducting themselves at work because these are partial, incomplete and subjective; by contrast they incorporate into their practice scientific knowledge which transcends the local and the particular. Practitioner knowledge is therefore considered to be inferior and incomplete because it is context-dependent, problem-solving, contingent, non-generalizable and is judged not by objective criteria but by whether it contributes to the achievement of short-term goals and problems encountered *in situ*. An assumption is made that the objective knowledge which is produced about programmes, activities and institutions binds the practitioner in certain ways; those ways being the following of rules which can be deduced from that knowledge. Knowledge produced by outsiders, or practitioners behaving as outsiders, is superior to the knowledge produced by practitioners working *in situ*.

The implication of such an approach for practitioners is that they should divest themselves of their prior incorrect and incomplete knowledge and adopt precepts based on the objective study of practical activities. Usher *et al.* (1996) describe the role of the practitioner in this mode as a technical and problem-solving activity. It is a view which is concerned with determining a measure of technical efficiency that will necessarily lead to the achievement of predetermined ends and these are separate from the determination of means *per se*. Lyotard (1984) has argued that knowledge is now constructed and legitimated in terms of its capacity to enhance the efficiency and effectiveness of the economic and social system. Disciplinary modes of knowledge rooted in epistemological foundations no longer have credibility in society, and have been replaced, in the current conditions of postmodernity, by knowledge as the optimizing of efficient performance.

Knowledge in this mode is applied to the practice setting, and indeed its rationale is whether it makes the workplace a more efficient and a more productive place. There is no desire here to examine the various contexts of the work, whether they are political, ethical or consequential. Knowledge is therefore non-critical, and blind to the way the curriculum is structured so that some groups of people may be favoured at the expense of others. Indeed, the curriculum is treated as unproblematic and marginalized as a knowledge-producing activity.

Since this discourse is typically marked by an emphasis on a notion of effectiveness, it is important to address whether proponents have satisfied or failed to satisfy their self-professed desire for value-free knowledge of schooling by using this notion. White (1997) suggests that they have not. His argument is that the notion of effectiveness carries with it two separate but often blurred or elided meanings. The first is a purely instrumental function; that is, regardless of what a person seeks to do, effectiveness refers to whether they have achieved their purpose. The second meaning is more significant. This is that it is impossible to separate out means and ends in any convincing way, especially with regards to education. Indeed, White (1997: 42–43) argues that 'the fact that measures to make less effective schools more effective are labelled "school improvement" blurs the distinction still further between "good as a means" and "good more generally."' He goes on to suggest that 'while both "improvement" and "progress" could be understood in a value-neutral, means-end sense, as implying getting closer to the ends in question, however good or bad they were, they usually have more global connotations' (ibid.). In using the phrase 'global connotations', White is suggesting that while specific aims may be achieved by the adoption of a neutral and value-free mechanism, the operation of that mechanism may indeed have other consequences, both easily foreseen and also unpredictable.

An example will bring out the force of the argument. If the goal of the teacher is simply the teaching of the ten times table, then though with the majority of children this can be achieved using benign and humane methods, in some cases it may be necessary (as it was considered to be in the past) to employ coercive measures. The end is now efficiently achieved, but the use of these coercive measures with some pupils may have far reaching consequences for their development. So we can see here that the means–end distinction inherent in the definition of school effectiveness is not quite as simple as it seems. It is the relationship between a variety of ends – and ends which, as educators, we may not foresee – which determines the precise means we employ. Furthermore, the means we employ embody particular value perspectives. It is not just that we have to decide about appropriate means for value-impregnated ends; we also have to decide about the appropriate balance, as we understand it, between ends and means. This can only be determined by our conception of how society should be structured, and this is an ideological or value-laden enterprise.

Critical pedagogy

As a reaction to technicist and essentialist forms of knowledge, a critical pedagogic framework was developed. This is best exemplified by feminist and anti-racist perspectives, and embraces the idea that curriculum-makers bring with them to the practice setting not only a theory or theories about the world, but also a desire to change it so that it conforms better to their view of what the world should be like. In particular, they argue that the curriculum should be enacted so as to identify and unmask those human beliefs and practices that limit freedom, justice and democracy. For feminists these practices comprise patriarchal discourses and practices. For anti-racists they are ethnically and racially discriminating. Critical theorists would also argue that much curriculum-making, especially when conducted within a positivist framework, acts to *conceal* its real purpose and effects, albeit that this may be unintentional (cf. Usher *et al.*, 1996; McLaren, 1989). Essentially, for critical theorists, conventional forms of knowledge act to oppress and discriminate: critical pedagogy is underpinned by a belief that schooling and the curriculum 'always represents an introduction to, preparation for, and legitimation of particular forms of life' (McLaren, 1989: 160). It thus seeks, through pedagogic means, to surface and in the process disrupt conventional forms of understanding which serve to reproduce undemocratic, racist, sexist and unequal social relations. As Lankshear, Peters and Knobel (1996: 150) make clear:

> (t)he task of critical pedagogy . . . is to unmask hegemonies and critique ideologies with the political and ethical intent of helping to empower students and more generally, the social groups to which they belong: by fostering awareness of conditions that limit possibilities for human becoming and legitimate the unequal distribution of social goods.

Unlike some postmodernist viewpoints, critical pedagogy adopts a clear *ethical* position with regard to society and with regard to the way in which society reproduces itself, though (as Young has implied in his chapter, earlier) some versions of critical pedagogy emphasize the need to disrupt conventional school knowledge structures and the reproductive processes that accompany them without specifying *alternative* frames of reference for students. The end-point, then, becomes the disruptive process rather than the re-forming of schooling and society in a particular way.

Lankshear, Peters and Knobel (1996) suggest that critical pedagogy has had to wrestle with a number of serious problems. First, though implicit within it is a notion of student-centredness and student empowerment, all too frequently teachers have found it difficult to forgo their role as orchestrator of proceedings, so that in effect critical pedagogy becomes a means by which one ideological viewpoint is simply replaced by another. Second, structural constraints on the implementation of critical pedagogic processes have proved to be difficult to negotiate around, and indeed the state may seek to reinforce the power of those structural constraints so that alternative pedagogic means prove difficult to enact (an example in the United Kingdom is the way the state imposed a national curriculum and appropriate methods for teaching it by strengthening inspection, evaluation and assessment arrangements). Third, students themselves have found it difficult to give voice to their own localized and immediately available experiential knowledge within the constraints of (what continues to be) a formal curriculum and a formal process of schooling. Fourth, the concentration on class, gender and race has led to an essentialized, reductionist and, as a consequence, over-simplified view of identity formation. Fifth, the political ideals that underpin critical pedagogy are frequently abstracted and decontextualized so that the movement itself has lost impetus. Finally, critical pedagogy has never developed beyond a system of ideas, so that the relationship between culture and practice has never been adequately operationalized.

To these problems and issues should be added the inability of critical pedagogy to confront the postmodern attack on *foundationalism*, both epistemological and, more importantly, ethical. In turn, critical pedagogy has lost ground to technicist frameworks of understanding, which have allowed governments round the world to set in place organizational and pedagogic structures that are antithetical to critical pedagogy.

Transgression: a postmodern dialogue

The sixth curriculum discourse – or indeed tradition of knowledge – is postmodernism which, strictly speaking, is not an epistemology as such, since postmodernists seek to subvert all foundational knowledge. What postmodernism does is attempt to undermine and surface those power–knowledge relations that it understands as underpinning conventional curriculum-making. Lather's (1991) postmodern approach seeks to displace orthodoxy and in the process reconfigure curriculum knowledge in new ways. It attempts to:

- provide a space for alternative voices and undermine the priority usually given to the agendas held by powerful people in society;
- surface the textual devices used in conventional curriculum texts, and as a result attempt to show how powerful discourses are constructed;
- question how authors construct these texts and organize meanings, and again in the process show how language works to construct certain types of truths;
- challenge realist assumptions that there is a world 'out there' waiting to be discovered;
- explore the various possible ways of constructing alternative realities and identities;
- and be concerned with power and the politics of knowledge-construction.

A postmodern approach would seek to deconstruct these linguistic and curricular forms (the use of binary oppositions which marginalize some forms of life at the expense of others; the attachment of evaluative connotations to particular words or phrases; the alignment of some ideas with others; the construction of boundaries round forms of thinking which act to exclude and marginalize) without at the same time putting in their place reified alternatives. Burbules (1995) suggests that the postmodern story may best be understood in relation to three narrative tropes: the ironic, the tragic and the parodic. The ironic trope is an attempt to indicate to the reader that meaning is never fixed or essentialized, and that the position one can take up can never be definitive or natural. The tragic trope is an acknowledgement that any attempt to speak outside the comforting modernist assumptions enshrined in everyday and commonsense discourses is bound to be ambiguous, unsettling and incomplete. The third narrative trope is the parodic, whereby the only option is to 'play the game' without at any time taking up foundationalist or fixed positions about the curriculum. In effect, a postmodernist position is an extension of critical theory in so far as it acknowledges the concealed ideological position taken up by much modernist curriculum-making, but at the same time refuses to accept that there are credible foundational alternatives.

This discursive frame is underpinned by a HyperTextual model of representation, in which the introduction of new media, in particular the World Wide Web, is acting to reconfigure discursive arrangements and the place of the reader within them. Conventional models of textual production and consumption have always tended to privilege the writer over the reader. The World Wide Web, however, has given us the possibility of (though it is as yet hardly a revolution) a more democratic relationship to the power of textual production which works on us and not through us. Landow (1992: 70–71) coins the phrase 'this HyperTextual dissolution of centrality', meaning that new media allow the possibility of conversation rather than instruction so that no one ideology or agenda dominates any other: '[T]he figure of the HyperText author approaches, even if it does not entirely merge with, that of the reader; [and] the functions of reader and writer become more deeply intertwined with each other than ever before' (ibid.).

Landow (1992: 70) suggests that this comprises the merging of what have historically been two very different processes: 'Today when we consider reading and writing, we probably think of them as serial processes or as procedures carried out intermittently by the same person: first one reads, then one writes, and then one reads some more' (ibid.).

HyperText, which allows the possibility of having access to an almost infinite number of different texts produced by different authors 'creates an active, even intrusive reader, carries this convergence of activities one step closer to completion; but in so doing, it infringes on the power of the writer, removing some of it and granting it to the reader' (ibid.).

This understanding ties HyperText more closely to what Rorty (1979: 70) has called an *edifying philosophy*, the point of which 'is to keep the conversation going rather than to find objective truth'. He goes on to suggest that this edifying philosophy makes sense:

> only as a protest against attempts to close off conversation by proposals for universal commensuration through the hypostatization of some privileged set of descriptors. The danger which edifying discourse tries to avert is that some given vocabulary, some way in which people might come to think of themselves, will deceive them into thinking that from now on all discourse could be, or should be, normal discourse. The resulting freezing-over of culture would be, in the eyes of edifying philosophers, the dehumanization of human beings.
>
> (ibid.)

Concluding remarks

In this chapter I have identified six curriculum ideologies: foundationalism, conventionalism, instrumentalism, technical rationality, critical pedagogy and postmodernism. I am suggesting that these should not be understood as relating to particular time-periods or to particular people. Indeed, individual theorists and policy makers work from within them and move between them. However, they do represent discursive positions, each with their own formal structure and relations between their parts, which have had and continue to have influence in the academy and on policy and practice in the field of curriculum. As such, they have the potential to serve, I suggest, as a useful heuristic device for understanding, comparing and critiquing not just different curriculum models but also different – often competing – rationales, values and epistemological positions *within* individual models and histories of curriculum.

3 The Puritan origins of the 1988 school curriculum in England

John White

Developing Scott's notion of curricular discourses, John White sets out to trace the development of modern school curricula through explorations of curriculum models and rationales whose origins lie in a time long before the advent of compulsory education. Through exploration of the influential ideas of the sixteenth-century logician Petrus Ramus and their impact on the early dissenting academies, White indicates how the current vogue for discipline-based curricula and the organization of learning from concrete to abstract thought are both rooted in earlier conceptualizations of knowledge and in curriculum choices based largely on religious views and imperatives. White maintains that while the theological rationales for classifying and dividing areas of knowledge and human beings has long since receded, the secular age experienced by many Western cultures is still left with ways of thinking about schooling which remain deeply embedded in Puritan culture: in short, the original reasons for curriculum choices have disappeared, but the curriculum originally chosen remains largely intact and therefore without current justification. White concludes by arguing for an aims-based rather than a discipline-based school curriculum, suggesting that England's current 'eighteenth century curriculum' needs to be replaced by one more fitting for the twenty-first century.

The Dissenting Academies and the roots of the traditional academic curriculum

In 1988 all state schools in England were obliged to follow a statutory curriculum based on traditional school subjects. As Richard Aldrich (1988: 22) has pointed out, these subjects were almost identical to those prescribed by Robert Morant in the 1904 Regulations for new state secondary schools. In this chapter, I shall examine the origins of this academic subject-based curriculum which has proved so resilient over the past century. The claim has often been made (Clarke, 1940; Williams, 1961) that these origins are to be found in the Dissenting Academies of the eighteenth century set up for teaching the sons of members of dissenting religious sects. But how far is this claim reliable?

In *The Long Revolution* Raymond Williams (1961: 133–134) writes of the Dissenting Academies:

> These varied considerably in quality, but it can fairly be claimed that in the best of them, in the eighteenth century, a new definition of the content of a general education was worked out and put into practice. Here, for the first time, the curriculum begins to take its modern shape, with the addition of mathematics, geography, modern languages, and crucially the physical sciences.

We know from the history of the Academies that, as well as preparing students for the ministry, they also provided a general higher education – in our terms an upper secondary/university education – for sons of dissenters from Puritan communities prevented by law after 1662 from attending universities. Boys usually began to attend the academies at fifteen, sixteen or seventeen, staying for four or five years (McLachlan, 1931: 26). As many of the English dissenters grew richer through commerce and industry throughout the eighteenth century, more and more of them must have had the wealth needed to prolong their sons' general education in this way, enabling them later to choose some 'liberal', non-manual calling on the basis of a wider knowledge of God's world and of their own capabilities.

The early Academies, which had to rely on teachers from Oxford and Cambridge, followed the traditional classical curriculum of those universities. With the founding of Philip Doddridge's academy at Northampton in 1729, English finally replaced Latin as the medium of instruction. Without this, the new subjects which began to appear on the curriculum would have been far more difficult to teach. At Northampton the full list of subjects of study for the four-year course was as follows:

First Year: logic, rhetoric, geography, metaphysics, geometry, algebra
Second Year: trigonometry, conic sections, celestial mechanics, natural and experimental philosophy, divinity, orations
Third Year: natural and civil history, anatomy, Jewish antiquities, divinity, orations
Fourth Year: civil law, mythology and hieroglyphics, English history, history of nonconformity, divinity, preaching and pastoral care

In addition, French was an optional subject and Hebrew, Greek and Latin, besides being used in prayers, were also taught in evening tutorials. In the first two years there were also required disputations in Latin and English (McLachlan, 1931: 147). A similar pattern of subjects, with some variations, spread from Northampton to other academies as the eighteenth century progressed.

A word about English. Its only mention in the 1729 account is in connection with required disputations in the first two years. In addition, divinity courses at the Academies standardly included practice in sermon writing; and according to McLachlan (1931: 28), this marked the origin of the English composition which has since become a staple of English lessons. In some later academies English began to become a subject in itself, as, at the end of the eighteenth century, did 'Belles Lettres', in which literary works were studied largely for the 'truths' they contained (ibid.).

Art, with the aesthetic connotations the term has for us today, had little or no place in the academies, their emphasis being on knowledge. The early Puritan belief in the need to acquire knowledge as a requisite of salvation had persisted into the age of the academies. There was no tension in Puritan thinking between acquiring knowledge on the one hand and faith on the other: philosophy, science, mathematics, history, geography and other subjects were held to be vehicles of the latter as they revealed the varied features of God's created world. Imagination and emotion, however, the sources of so much art, were thought of – in Watts's *Logic*, for instance – as tempters into error, as a 'fruitful source of false judgments' (Watts, 1792: 181). The 'pursuit of truth', in short, was the all-encompassing aim.

Others besides Raymond Williams have noticed, or thought they have noticed, the revolutionary importance of the academies for the content of education. Some years before Williams, the educationalist Fred Clarke, for instance, wrote:

> The Dissenting Academies are thus of importance in English educational history as representing a vigorous and sustained effort to think out a 'modern' curriculum and apply it in practice. While not departing from the dominant idea of education for culture, and while remaining thoroughly English in temper, they cut loose from the prevailing tradition of classical training and aristocratic accomplishments, looked at their own actual world with open eyes, and worked out a curriculum which would prepare for effective living in such a world.
>
> (Clarke, 1940: 16)

In this curriculum, as it evolved, 'classics and the customary linguistic studies had no great place; instead, we find English, history and modern languages with a good deal of mathematics and science' (ibid.).

Although Clarke's last sentence, like Williams's own account, may exaggerate the extent of the change – modern languages, for instance, actually being optional and so more peripheral than he implies – his reference to 'the dominant idea of education for culture' touches something really important. The dissenters' curriculum was not intended to provide specialist training. Here and there it included 'commerce' (McLachlan, 1931: 331), but overwhelmingly its interest was in pure rather than applied knowledge. Theoretical rationality rather than practical application was the substance. We know that alumni of the academies did go on to apply what they had learnt to build the new industrial and commercial England of the late eighteenth and early nineteenth centuries, and it is true that if such items as mechanics, trigonometry, chemistry and hydrostatics had not been part of their programme they could never have used them to create the new world. However, the main purpose of teaching these subjects was not to help the process of industrialization; rather, as has already been indicated, it was to reveal the world as it truly is. At a higher-order level, this still had a practical purpose behind it in the shape of a religious, salvationist, aim. For Puritan communities, the acquisition of knowledge was a necessary route to salvation. The new curriculum was intended to acquaint students with the manifold glories of God's created world. It had something of the same religious aim as Fred Clarke himself believed in, when he wrote in an earlier work that 'the ultimate reason for teaching Long Division to little Johnny is that he is an immortal soul' (Clarke, 1923: 2).

How accurate is the picture of the Dissenting Academies as catalysts of curricular revolution that we find in Clarke and Williams, as well as in full-length academic works on the Academies published by Parker (1914) and McLachlan (1931) earlier in the last century? There are things to be said on the other side. Hans (1951) provides a more global account of 'new trends in education in the eighteenth century', and, while not denying the contribution that the Academies made, locates them as just one of several types of institution responsible for curricular modernization. These included Oxford and Cambridge, grammar schools and private academies. Mercer (2001) also claims that Parker and McLachlan exaggerated the role played by the Academies in providing a progressive education for lay students. Although this was true of a handful of liberal academies like Warrington, Manchester College and Hackney New College, 'after 1750 the vast majority of academies were small orthodox seminaries for the training of Nonconformist ministers' (p. 35).

These doubts would appear to count against the bold thesis that the Dissenting Academies originated the modern subject-based curriculum that we find in English schools today. At the very least, this may require considerable qualification. A more circumspect claim would be the broader one, that Puritan/Dissenting educational ideas and practices had a major, if not the only, role in the story.

This latter thesis broadens horizons beyond the Academies and enables us to take into account other dissenting institutions and ways of thinking. These include, in England, schools set up for dissenters from the end of the eighteenth century, and, in eighteenth-century Presbyterian Scotland, both grammar schools and universities. This more accommodating thesis also allows us to go back to the world of Puritan education in the sixteenth and seventeenth centuries, before the first Academies appeared towards the end of the seventeenth century.

Ramus and the Puritan curriculum

The sixteenth-century logician Pierre de la Ramée (Petrus Ramus) has been seen as a major figure in the history of the curriculum. This comes out forcibly in David Hamilton's (1990) book *Curriculum History*. Ramus's logic consisted of a branching scheme of dichotomies (see Figures 3.1 and 3.2), from the most general categories to the most specific, within which the heterogeneity of God's created world could be systematically arranged. Following Plato, Ramus held that this world was to be understood as a 'material counterpart of an ordered series of ideas existing in the mind of God' (quoted in Morgan, J., 1986: 107, see also Miller, 1939: 126 for Ramus's curricular 'maps').

Hamilton relates Ramus to a wider group of humanist educationalists who preceded him and who were preoccupied with how teaching could best be organized. He quotes from Grafton and Jardine (1986: 124):

> 'Method' was the catchword of promoters of humanist education from the 1510s onwards. This practical emphasis on procedure signals a shift in intellectual focus on the part of pedagogical reformers, from the ideal end-product of a classical education (the perfect orator...) to classroom aids (textbooks, manuals and teaching drills).

Ramus was, in Hamilton's words (1990: 23), 'the high priest of method'. His logical maps were about both what to teach and how to teach it (ibid.: 26). They enabled the content of learning to be systematically arranged in discrete 'branches' of knowledge. As Mack (1998, vol. 8: 52–53) says: 'Ramus's method obliged him to avoid overlaps between subjects.... He emphasised the need to select material, according to what we would now call disciplinary boundaries.' The logic maps also gave teachers clear routes through the material, moving especially from more abstract to less abstract, experience-related components, but also vice-versa.

It is easy to understand the attractiveness of the Ramist method to Puritan or allied sect preachers, schoolmasters and textbook writers in the late sixteenth and early seventeenth centuries – Comenius (1592–1670), for instance (Triche and McKnight, 2004: 53) – given their interest in transmitting to their audiences huge quantities of orthodox information rather than encouraging them to think for themselves. (See Comenius (1907) on the possibility of mass education once one finds the one right method for teaching any subject matter (XIII: 15; XIX: 14–54); on teaching from the abstract and general towards the concrete and the detailed (XVI: 38–45; XX: 19); and on items learnt forming an encyclopaedic whole (XVIII: 34–35; XIX: 6).) In addition – and it is hard to know how much weight to put on the point – Ramist maps contain (see Figure 3.2), according to Hamilton, the first recorded use of the word 'curriculum' in an academic context (see Hamilton, 1990: 27). Hamilton suggests that this might be linked with the Calvinist predilection for the use of the term in the phrase '*vitae curriculum*', allied with the common presentation of human life as an obstacle course on the way to salvation (ibid.: 26–28). Certainly, Ramist

P. RAMI DIALECTICA.
TABVLA GENERALIS.

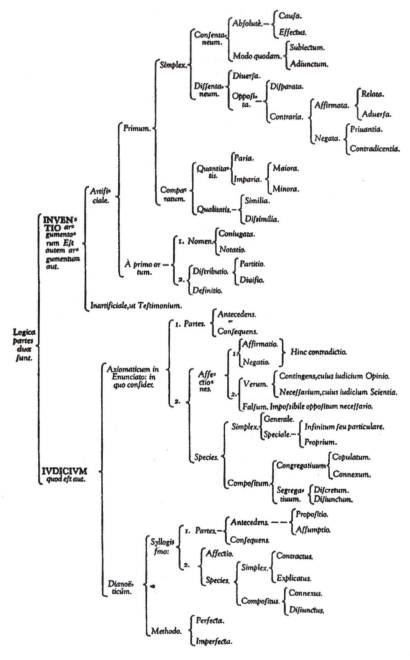

Figure 3.1 Ramus map (1): P. Rami dialectica: tabvla generalis. From Miller 1939: 126.

TABVLA ARTIVM, QVAS IN
hoc Volumine coniunximus.

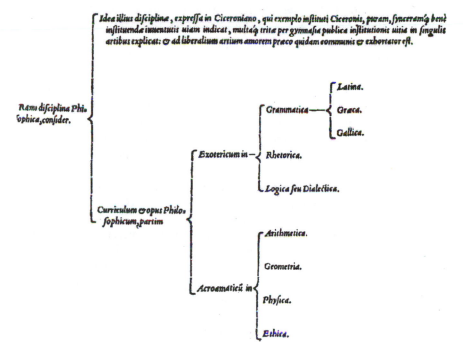

Figure 3.2 Ramus map (2): Tabvla artivm, qvas in hoc volumine coniunximus.
Source: P. Ramus, *Professio regia* Basle, 1576.

learning was far from detached from everyday preoccupations. It provided spiritual security. As McKnight (2003: 54–55) argues

> Uncertainty was the bane of Puritan existence, as in the well-reported psychological anxiety produced by nagging doubt of whether one was to undergo conversion or not. Ramist method provided not only psychological comfort but a 'form' by which to place over, understand, and so control the world.

The fact that Puritans used Ramist logic not to promote free thought but to show the one true path that understanding must take (see Morgan, J., 1986: 111) is a counterweight to an interpretation of Puritan educational activity in the seventeenth century aligning it with cutting-edge educational reform in the sciences and in the humanities, associated with the ideas of Bacon (Parker, 1914: chap. 1; Greaves, 1969). If one concentrates, as

Morgan does, on the *intentions* of Puritan educationalists, these were far from embracing the new Enlightenment world that was beginning to emerge. They sought 'not man's intellectual dominion in a rational universe, but rather a subordination of human reason to the demands of an enthusiastic faith' (1986: 309). *Consequences*, however, are a different story. As we have seen, Ramus's logic was anchored at its non-abstract end in experience of the world. This gave it a point of contact with the Baconians. As Morgan (1986: 111) writes

> Ramus' insistence that logic should agree with nature may have meant that puritan educators conditioned an era of students to see 'truth' in an empirically approached natural world, even though the puritans themselves had no such intention of diverting scholarly attention, or of shifting the bedrock of 'reality', from the Word to the world.

All this provides background to the fact that by the late eighteenth century at least some of the Dissenting Academies were the site of advanced scientific teaching and crucibles of industrial progress.

Ramus's logic, with the priority it gives to more abstract subjects and to teaching from the abstract to the concrete, and with its insistence on sharp, non-overlapping divisions between branches of knowledge, had an influence on the early formation of the 'modern' upper secondary school/higher education curriculum, in which logic, often Ramist logic, was indeed one of the components. It also has more than faint echoes, however, in the traditional school subject-based curriculum we know today. (More on both these points follows.)

Doubts about the role of the Dissenting Academies

Turning more globally from the seventeenth to the eighteenth century, we have seen reason to doubt the strong thesis that the modern curriculum was born in the Academies. Between 1750 and 1850 the Academies had little hand in the education of the laity, being predominantly, as Mercer tells us, theological colleges for the preparation of ministers; and other institutions from grammar schools to private academies were teaching a wide range of modern subjects.

But these two types of evidence are not conclusive. Mercer's thesis is only about what happened after 1750. He also states (2001: 35) that 'at the beginning of the eighteenth century at least half the academies were open to students who intended following careers other than in the ministry'. There is a plausible reason, which he does not mention, why the proportion of academies with lay students diminished after 1750 – from half to about an eighth (pp. 35–36). From 1779 Dissenters were allowed by law to follow the teaching profession (although dissenting schools also existed outside the law before this time, Hans [1951: 58–62] describing several examples of these). Many Dissenters moved from the Academies, as pupils and as tutors, into other institutions. One example of this is Mill Hill School (see also Roach (1986: 176–177) for details of its 'full and varied curriculum for the time'). This line of thinking strengthens the case for the influence of the Academies on the modern curriculum, either directly, via their own teaching, or via their staff teaching elsewhere.

There is more to be said, too, about Hans's thesis about the widespread presence of modern subjects in other eighteenth-century institutions. Although Hans (1951: 38–41) shows that these subjects were taught in two or three of the leading grammar schools, he does nothing to suggest that, by and large, grammar school education was not centred virtually exclusively on the classics. His evidence for modern subjects in private schools and academies is much more extensive, but he admits that 'very few of them published a detailed curriculum of studies' (p. 63). Students were organized into groups according to their intended destinations (e.g. the universities, the navy, the army, business and law, some technical professions) and their curricula varied accordingly. But all students 'would study English, Arithmetic, Geography, Geometry, History; most of the pupils would take French and Drawing, and all would participate in Sports' (pp. 64–65).

The curricular philosophy of these institutions was very different from that experienced by lay students in the Dissenting Academies. In most of the latter, lay students generally followed the first half of a four- or five-year divinity course (Mercer, 2001: 38). In the post-1729 Northampton course outlined logic, mathematics, natural philosophy and divinity were prominent in the first two years of a four-year course. At Warrington Academy in 1780 discussed later, the first three years of a five-year course covered theology, ethics, logic, mathematics, theoretical and experimental natural philosophy, geography, history, commerce, theory of language, elocution and composition (Mercer, 2001: 39–40). In the Dissenting Academies, virtually the whole of the curriculum was common to all students in the first two or three years. *It was planned – for the most part – as a unified whole*: religious considerations were uppermost in framing it. It was meant to equip the believer, lay as well as clerical, with those forms of knowledge which would help him to understand the nature of God and of his world – to see both the big picture and also how the mass of details fitted into it. There is little evidence, according to Mercer (p. 40), to support the belief that the leading Dissenting businessmen and manufacturers who sent their sons to the Academies after 1750 were primarily guided by *utilitarian* motives.

In one important way, the English secondary school curriculum introduced in 1904 and reinforced in 1988 is closer to that of the dissenting than that of the private academy. It *is a unity, not fragmented according to intended destinations*. It is wholly common for all students, not common only in subjects seen as basic. Its elements are to be studied largely for non-instrumental reasons.

This is one reason why Hans's thesis does not undermine, as much as it perhaps appeared to, the claim that the Dissenting Academies had a major role in originating the modern subject-based curriculum. Another is this. In his conclusion, Hans (1951: 210) states that in the middle of the nineteenth century 'all the achievements and pioneering ideas of the eighteenth century were forgotten'. Why this should be so he saw as a 'problem worthy of deeper investigation'. His own provisional thought on this is that the industrial revolution in the latter part of the eighteenth century produced a gulf between employers and labourers which was reflected in diverging forms of education for each, the new industrial middle class blocking the way for newcomers from below (p. 211). This eroded the eighteenth-century pattern, in which young people of lower social origin were more likely to enter the institutions Hans describes. Science, which had become prominent in eighteenth-century curricula, was henceforth demoted, as 'the social cleavage between employers of labour and employed labourers was reflected in the differentiation of social prestige, between the "classical" and "scientific" curriculum' (p. 212).

Hans's thesis is that although the great variety of schools and institutions with which he deals successfully introduced new subjects and new methods and so 'started modern education in England' (p. 209), the history of their influence is not continuous, there having been a major breach in this story caused by the industrial revolution. He does not say how the breach was healed. Neither is his claim that the 'scientific' curriculum became associated with employed labourers rather than employers plausible, science having been kept out of working class curricula throughout the nineteenth century, as well as in the Morant reforms of 1904 which set a pattern which lasted well into the second half of the twentieth century.

The Puritan curriculum in Scotland

The Dissenting Academies were not the only eighteenth-century institutions in which Puritan origins foreshadowed a modern curriculum. Scottish schools and universities also played a significant part, not only in the Scottish, but also in the English story. Again, we are talking about upper secondary/higher education.

Presbyterian Scotland had its own educational system for its élite. As early as 1574–80, the Principal of Glasgow University, Andrew Melville, established a curriculum which became the basis of the university's work for two centuries. As Smith (1955: 68) notes, his system was similar to that in many of the Dissenting Academies:

    Year 1: Humanities (Greek and Latin) and Ramus's dialectic
    Year 2: Mathematics, Cosmography, Astronomy
    Year 3: Moral and Political Science
    Year 4: Natural Philosophy and History

By the beginning of the eighteenth century, despite variations, its four universities, all dating from the fifteen and sixteenth centuries, tended towards a common pattern. This was to award MA degrees after a four-year course in theology, medicine or the arts. The latter was the staple curriculum; and its bent towards philosophy is again reminiscent of the Dissenting Academies, Greek tending to be taught in the first year; logic and meta-physics in the second; ethics and pneumatics ('covering such abstruse ques-tions as the nature of angels, the human soul, and the one true God') in the third; and natural philosophy probably including some mathematics in the fourth (Knox, 1953: 16–17).

A tilt was given to this curriculum in a more practical direction when, following Perth's example in 1761, a number of Scottish towns set up Academies offering a two-year higher secondary/university level course. In Perth's case

> [t]he scheme of study included in the first year Natural Science, Mathematics, Navigation, Astronomy, and English; in the second, Natural Philosophy, Practical Geometry, Civil History, Logic and the Principles of Religion. All teaching and exercises were to be in English. In course of time, Fine Writing, Drawing, Painting, and Chemistry were included in the curriculum.
>
> (Strong, 1909: 161)

Later in the century a further attempt was made to bring more order into the 'chaotic medley' of Scottish schools, which were rapidly increasing. Confusingly, the new type of school – which covered a wider age-group than the Academies, including the whole secondary age-group – was also called an 'academy'. One of the first, founded in 1793 for upper class boys, was Inverness Academy. It taught 'English grammatically' in the first year; Latin and Greek in the second; Writing, Arithmetic, and Bookkeeping in the third; Mathematics, Geography, Navigation, Drawing and Fortification in the fourth; and Civil and Natural History, Natural Philosophy, Chemistry and Astronomy in the fifth (ibid.: 164–165). In the first half of the nineteenth century the curricula of these academies, which were erected all over the country, was copied by some of the grammar schools, although the classical tradition remained strong in others (ibid.: 168–169).

In the eighteenth century Scottish educational institutions had close links with the English dissenting communities. From the end of the seventeenth century, many dissenter students, who were barred from Oxford and Cambridge, went for their higher education to Glasgow and Edinburgh univer-sities. Several of these students became tutors in the Dissenting Academies, and occasionally some Scottish graduates, not trained in the Academies, also became tutors there (McLachlan, 1931: 29–30). The replacement of Latin by English as medium of instruction in the Academies probably owed something to the Scottish influence (Smith, 1955: 70).

The story through to 1988

By the eighteenth century the dissenting communities in England had become a prominent part of the 'middling sort' of people (Gunn and Bell, 2002: 17), cut off as they were from the life and livelihoods of the Anglican establishment, and demarcated from the poor below. Their religiosity, as Weber (1930), Tawney (1926) and others have taught us, brought them not only the conviction of salvation, but also worldly success. Hard work in dedication to a vocation chosen in line with God-given talents paid off in financial terms. The dissenters' success in commerce, banking and manufacture, spurred by a desire for social improvement as they interpreted this, played a major part in the industrialization of the country in the late eighteenth century, some of them rising to great wealth. By the early nineteenth century, the dissenting middle classes, swelled now by many Methodists and evangelical Anglicans, were beginning to grow in political power and influence, and were merging, at their top end, with the old landed class of aristocrats and gentry.

In education, the emphasis on a broad range of discrete disciplines which we found in the Dissenting Academies and in the Scottish institutions is mirrored in the secondary education provided for Dissenters' sons. We saw above that after 1779 Dissenters were legally allowed to become school teachers. Over the next sixty years middle-class nonconformists had their sons educated in new private and proprietary schools, as well as some reformed grammar schools. They pressed for the same kind of broad curriculum that had been found in the Academies, in opposition to the narrow classical education of the grammar schools. Brian Simon (1960: 102–125; see also Roach (1986: 237)) gives a good account of these developments. He refers, for instance, to a report of 1834 about private schools in Manchester. Most had been established since 1820 and

> a high proportion of teachers were dissenters. An analysis of the curricula showed that the average boys' school provided teaching in reading, writing, grammar, arithmetic, geography, history, mathematics and languages, up to the age of about fifteen. A few schools taught natural history and drawing and in some there was a little moral and religious teaching.
>
> (Simon, 1960: 113)

The onward progress of the middle classes in wealth and now political influence continued through the nineteenth century, fuelled by the evangelical revival, and facilitated by the repeal of the laws excluding Dissenters from public life. Soon after mid-century, official action was taken to tidy up the raggedness of what schools across the nation were offering, and to fit the content of the curriculum explicitly to a three-fold social class division. In the late 1850s and 1860s, while the Clarendon Commission pressed for the retention of the classical curriculum in the leading public schools, and the Newcastle Commission urged a 'three-Rs' (reading, writing and 'rithmetic) based education for the masses, the Taunton Commission of 1864–8 recommended the general modern curriculum for second and third grade endowed and private schools, that is, largely for middle and lower ranks of the middle classes, among which dissenters were a prominent group. While 'second-grade' schools, for boys leaving at sixteen, were to have a curriculum based on Latin (but not Greek), English literature, political economy, mathematics and science, that of the 'third grade' ones, stopping at about fourteen, 'should include the elements of Latin or a modern language, English, history, elementary mathematics, geography and science' (op.cit.: 324).

The modern curriculum of the Prussian *Realschule* influenced the thinking of the Commission, as did the curricular desires of different sections of the English middle classes. It is significant that Prussia was a Protestant state (its Lutheran and Calvinist churches had been brought together in a unified Evangelical Church in 1817) and that its modern curriculum in the *Realschule* had been created in line with the wishes of the same commercial and industrial groups as were central to the English middle class – who had been pressing governments for many years but with little success to improve schooling for their children along modern lines.

Thus, while the Clarendon Commission of 1861–4 decided that the education of the upper classes (including now many of the upper middle classes) in the major public schools should continue to be devoted largely to classics, the plan for the bulk of the middle classes continued to be based on the traditional broad curriculum deriving originally from the dissenting tradition. Although the Taunton proposals were not put into effect, the pull of this curriculum was so great by the 1860s that it had begun to make inroads into the great public schools themselves (Roach, 1986: 239). The Clarendon Report itself suggested that although classics (with history and divinity) was to have over 50% of curricular time, there should also be room for mathematics, natural science, French or German, and music or drawing (ibid.: 240).

By the end of the nineteenth century the so-called 'traditional' (i.e. Nonconformist) middle class had been joined by new middle class members from Anglican or secular backgrounds, although the two groups often kept apart in fairly self-contained social networks and remained so until the 1950s McKibbin, 1998: 91). The twentieth century entrenched the middle classes – increasingly diverse, as we have seen, in their composition, and increasingly secular after mid-century – in the political influence which they were beginning to attain during its early years. The 1906 election had returned 185 Nonconformist MPs, nearly all sympathetic to the new Liberal government (Binfield, 1977: 207); with the decline of the Liberal Party after the First World War, the middle classes gravitated largely to the Conservatives. The old Puritan notion of belonging to an elect destined for salvation had by then lost most of its force, but vestiges of it may have remained in the notion of an academic élite identified by mechanisms of selection.

In 1904 Morant created a gulf between the new local authority secondary schools and elementary schools. The secondary schools, as under the Taunton proposals, had to follow a broad subject-based curriculum, consisting in the 1904 case of 'English language and literature, at least one language other than English, geography, history, mathematics, science, drawing, manual instruction (boys), domestic subjects (girls), physical exercise and organised games.'

Elementary schools, catering for some 75% of children, were obliged to follow a less intellectual curriculum, which included no science (only nature study), no foreign language, and more manual subjects (Board of Education, 1929). The core of the middle class was thus able to differentiate itself more adequately from those below it, scholarships for the more able of the latter providing no more than a frail ladder upwards.

A similar academic curriculum, based on a by now traditional list of curriculum subjects, lived on vigorously through the twentieth century, at first in the selective secondary sector and then in much of the secondary comprehensive system which largely replaced this from the 1960s. From mid-century onwards many egalitarian educational thinkers wanted the working classes to enjoy the same curricular advantages as those from the élite. In some cases – as in my own – this desire was intensified by personal experience of upward social mobility via the 'ladder' of scholarships into élite schooling. Comprehensive schools were also the home of innumerable attempts to move away from a totally subject-based curriculum towards new forms of curricular arrangement with more appeal and relevance to the mass of children. (The Schools Council played an important role here, e.g. after 1964: see Bell and Prescott 1975.)

In 1988 all innovation was blocked by the new National Curriculum, its ten compulsory subjects almost identical to Morant's in 1904, the only divergences being the inclusion of manual work/housewifery in 1904 and of technology and music in 1988 (Aldrich, 1988: 22). Unlike in 1904, the broad compulsory curriculum was now for all children, not only for a tiny élite. The subject-based curriculum was also extended from the secondary to primary schools. What began in the eighteenth century as a university/upper secondary level curriculum had percolated by 1988 into the infant school. What had grown up in the eighteenth century as a curriculum suited to the religious beliefs of the minority community of Old Dissenters had become, three centuries later and through various transformations, the taken-for-granted curriculum of the whole nation.

The traditional academic curriculum today

Many of us tend to take today's traditional school curriculum for granted, as we do ideas about pedagogy, timetabling and assessment which have become associated with it over the last three centuries.

On timetabling, the following example from Warrington Academy *c*.1778 is interesting:

Warrington academy: time table[a] (*c*.1778)

Hours	Monday	Tuesday	Wednesday	Thursday	Friday	Saturday	Sunday
7	Prayers	Prayers	Prayers	Prayers	Prayers	Prayers	Prayers
8	Arithmetic, Bookkeeping, Breakfast	Arithmetic, Bookkeeping, Breakfast	Arithmetic, Bookkeeping, Breakfast	Arithmetic, Bookkeeping, Breakfast	Arithmetic, Bookkeeping, Breakfast	Ancient Geography	— Breakfast
9	Algebra	Trigonometry	Algebra	Trigonometry	Algebra	Public Lecture	—
10	Greek Testament	Logic, Ethics, etc.	Theology	Logic, Ethics, etc.	Theology	Scheme Lecture	—
11	Geometry 1 2 3	English / — / Conic secs	Geometry 1 2 3	Conic Secs. / — / English	Geometry 1 2 3	Geography	Divine service
12	Writing	Drawing	Writing	Drawing	Writing	Theological society	—
1	Dinner	Dinner	Dinner	Dinner	Dinner	Dinner	Dinner
2	Classics	Classics	Classics	Classics	Classics	—	—
3	French	French	French	French	French	—	—
4	Do.	Do.	Do.	Do.	Do.	—	—
5	Anatomy of Chemistry	—	—	Anatomy of Chemistry	Hebrew	—	—
6	—	—	—	—	—	—	—
7	Composition society	Speaking club	Book club	Classical club	Divinity club	—	—
8	Supper	Supper	Supper	Supper	Supper	Supper	Supper
9	Prayers	Prayers	Prayers	Prayers	Prayers	Prayers	Prayers

Source: (from McLachlan, 1931: 227).

Notes
Evening prayers are now at 7. Several societies after supper.
a Wilson's *Memorials*, II, p. 39, at New College, Hampstead.

The similarity with a secondary school timetable today is remarkable. Time per day spent on studies may have been longer, but there is the same injection of knowledge in short bursts, with a shift to entirely different subject matter at the end of each period (see also Comenius, 1907, XXIX: 17). The Old Dissenters had their own rationale for this. It was partly about the least wasteful use of time (on Puritan time-valuation, see Thompson, 1982) and partly reflected the Ramist tradition of classifying knowledge and packaging it into easily learnable chunks (see also Young's reference to the modern version of 'bite-size chunks' in chapter 1).

Today's subject-based curriculum is one which makes a sharp distinction between mind and body, with physical education at its periphery. It is also centrally an *intellectual* curriculum, foregrounding subjects concerned with the pursuit of knowledge like mathematics, science, history and geography. Artistic subjects – literature, the visual arts and music – are mainly nineteenth-century additions to a narrowly intellectual core and still play second fiddle to the knowledge-seeking subjects. We may not see the imagination and the emotions as 'springs of false judgements' as the Old Dissenters did, but they are still given less priority than knowledge acquisition. Of the artistic subjects, English Literature tends to be taken more seriously than the other two. This may be partly because it is more easily assimilable to a knowledge-seeking subject. In secondary schools, to judge from examination and test items (e.g. questions on Shakespeare in the Key Stage 3 literacy test for 14-year-olds), the intensity and delicacy of pupils' aesthetic response to drama, fiction and poetry are often rated less highly than their competence in evidence-based critical assessment. (See also Moore's comments in Chapter 6.)

Like the dissenters' curriculum of the eighteenth century, ours is dominated by non-instrumental goals. This is not to deny that, science, for example, is often studied with extrinsic aims in view. An upper secondary student may have her mind on doing physics at university or on a job in pharmaceuticals. Something of the same outlook, *ceteris paribus*, must have been true of some lay students of Warrington Academy. But the *intended* goal of science teaching among the dissenters – intended, that is, by the establishment, not necessarily by each student – was to reveal the manifold glory of God's creation. In our own age, defenders of a traditional curriculum are often equally attached to non-utilitarian aims. They hold science, history and mathematics to be significant achievements of human culture in their own right. Schools should, as their primary purpose, inculcate a love of learning, rather than to be vehicles of career advancement, citizenship or self-exploration. (Sometimes, indeed, the term 'education' itself is defined in terms of intrinsic goods, with instrumental aims falling outside it, and belonging to 'training'.) Examples of this non-instrumental way of thinking are found in the works of educational philosophers like Richard Peters (1966), Paul Hirst, (1965; Hirst and Peters, 1970), and Michael Oakeshott (1971) as well as later writers like Anthony O'Hear (1991: 43–45), although the last two of these have been more traditionalist about the curriculum than Peters and Hirst, who saw themselves as basing a broad, discipline-focused, curriculum on rational principles rather than a respect for what has been. (On the indebtedness of 1960s philosophy of the curriculum to the dissenting tradition, see White, 2005.)

In one way, this position is more purely non-instrumentally orientated than that of the Dissenters. Behind the latter, after all, there was an extrinsic consideration of a sort, and one of great importance. Knowledge of God's world was crucial in the dissenting thought world as a necessary condition of personal salvation. This did not necessarily make salvation an acknowledged *aim* of education; indeed, to have done so would have been arrogant towards God himself, since salvation was in his gift alone. The more recent position lacks this ambiguous relationship to purposes, or considerations, which lie beyond this. The learning is unalloyedly non-instrumental.

There are two more features, however, which the modern subject-based curriculum shares with the Dissenters. First of these is the greater prestige given to more abstract subjects like mathematics and science. Logic was also prominent in the earlier curriculum, but its only counterpart today is in the 'thinking skills' which are now part of the official school curriculum in England and Wales. The second feature is the organization of the curriculum around discrete subjects. There is no reason why it *has* to be arranged in this way, however inconceivable any departure from this may seem to some. The subject-basedness of the dissenters' curriculum goes back to the Ramist project of dividing and subdividing areas of knowledge in neat, visually presentable, ways. Attempts during the late twentieth century to play up interrelationships between areas of knowledge and play down discreteness made little headway, finally foundering in Britain when the rigidly subject-based National Curriculum was made mandatory in 1988.

Conclusion

Although the role of the Dissenting Academies in originating the broad subject-based curriculum we have today may have been exaggerated, the broader thesis, that non-Anglican Protestant educational institutions – including those in Scotland as well as in England – play an important part in the story, is on stronger ground.

Two and a half centuries ago the academic subject-based curriculum had a clear rationale. A comprehensive understanding of the myriad features of God's created world, coherently marshalled under discrete, non-overlapping subjects was seen as a necessary condition for one's own salvation. This justi-fication has long since crumbled away and no compelling alternative has taken its place (White, 2004). The groundlessness of the curriculum *status quo* is now, in 2005, becoming more evident – not least to those responsible for school curricula in different parts of the United Kingdom. There are a number of official initiatives at work which, while not denying the contribu-tion that subject-teaching can make, begin their curriculum planning at a different point – with overall aims, not subjects. Northern Ireland and Scotland have already published schemes for aims-based curricula; and England is not far behind. It is not too optimistic, perhaps, to hope that sometime in the twenty-first century our eighteenth-century curriculum may no longer have a future.

4 The instrumentalization of the expressive in education

David Hartley

Sharing Young's concerns about the role of central government in curriculum policy in relation to incipient instrumentalism, David Hartley notes that there is currently a resurgence of matters emotional in education around the globe, citing the concept of 'emotional intelligence' as an example. Far from representing a turn away from the over-instrumentalization of education to serve specific social and economic ends, Hartley argues that this new interest in the emotional, the affective and the expressive is rooted in similar instrumental purposes. Some possible explanations of this emerging tendency are considered, including the possibility that, though presented within discourses of altruism and the development of the 'whole person', the increased curricular emphases on the emotions and creativity are more fundamentally concerned with meeting the changing demands of national and global 'high-tech' and 'high-touch' economies. Introducing a subsequent theme of the book concerning the ways in which school students are perceived and constructed through the curriculum experience, Hartley goes further to suggest that these curricular developments produce, in school students, particular identities as (would-be) consumers. Like White, Hartley seeks to locate current curriculum policy and design in wider socioeconomic contexts. Intriguingly, however, his analysis suggests that the largely static curriculum design described by White may be experiencing – albeit for the same instrumental reasons – something of a new development as the economic and social contexts of formal education evolve.

Introduction

Recent decades have witnessed a search for the effective school. Standards have been to the fore on policy. Notwithstanding the notion of the local management of schools, highly bureaucratic national structures have been established. To this bureaucratic repertoire is now being added that which speaks of emotion and creativity. Having been consigned to the margin, the creative and expressive dimensions of education are being revived. In a response to calls by business leaders, government is seeking to generate in the schools new kinds of emotional and creative capital. It is now becoming a question of learning to labour; but to do so emotionally, creatively. The expressive seems set to be instrumentalized.

The emerging new economy is said to require it, both to maximize production and consumption. Take production. Culture is becoming commodified. More occupations in the service industries require emotional labour. The pace of fast capitalism requires ever more innovations which can be patented and turned into products. This itself requires the creative talent to come up with new ideas. Leaders, too, are being called upon to be emotional as well as rational. As for consumption, the market spawns choice. It requires of consumers the capacity to create new 'makeover' identities. They must be 'in touch' with their emotions, and be reflexive, so that they can best choose those products which express themselves and give their lives meaning, however provisional. Indeed, how to think about one's emotions (emotional intelligence and emotional literacy) – how to 'manage' them – become central attributes of the sophisticated consumer and citizen. If it is agreed that the new economy is becoming more of a cultural economy (du Gay and Pryke, 2002) – that is, if culture itself is becoming commodified – then creativity is crucial for production. But it is equally important for consumption: within postmodern culture, with all of its contingencies, ambiguities, risks and uncertainties, the individual is prompted continually to create a makeover of the self. In the interface between the economy and the self is situated both the creative producer *and* the creative consumer. In order to be *e*ffective as a producer and a consumer, it is necessary to be *a*ffective.

This may have consequences for education. The creative or expressive arts have been in relative decline (Department of Media, Culture and Sport [DMCS], 1999: 65), regarded as frills – too much sentimental, too little instrumental. But in contemporary society, creativity is said to be at a premium: it is being 'universalized'. The reasons for the resurgence of creativity – it had loomed large in the 1960s – have been stated as 'creativity is good for the economy, good for society and good for education' (Jeffrey and Craft, 2001: 11). Scase (1999), for example, in his study *Britain Towards 2010: The Changing Business Environment*, suggests that nursery and primary education will need to provide for effective interpersonal skills and personal creativity so that corporate creativity and innovation can be developed. The emotions, too, seem set to be rationalized for performative purposes, even though, as recently as 1998, they were relatively neglected in schools in the UK (Best, 1998: 80). Now there is an emerging discourse on 'emotional intelligence' (Goleman *et al.*, 2002) and on 'emotional literacy'. All this is in addition to the traditional concern about the emotions on the part of behavioural psychologists and counsellors in education. At issue here is the central question: why, now, is there an 'affective' and 'creative' tendency in education? Of particular concern are the socioeconomic conditions which have allowed for a renewed interest in creativity. At issue here will not be the neurobiological aspects of emotional intelligence (Goleman *et al.*, 2002), nor the policy detail of this affective tendency; rather it is to point up the tendency itself, and some of the possible reasons for it.

The argument is in two parts. I consider the affective and creative turn in education at two levels: first, how it might relate to the needs of producers in different sectors of the economy; and second, how it is relevant to the needs of consumers within contemporary culture. For its part, government has attended mainly to the first level, ignoring the important implications of the second for the social cohesion of society.

Education, production and the instrumentalization of the expressive

The past two decades have seen a search for certainty and standards in education. But there now emerges a quest for creativity within both government and business. The impetus now is education *for* creativity. The creative impulse inserts into education some decidedly non-rational aspects which seem to sit uneasily with a discourse of efficiency, standardization and measurable outcomes. In its White Paper *Our Competitive Future: Building the Knowledge-Driven Economy* (Department for Trade and Industry, 1998), the government states that

> In the global marketplace, knowledge, skills and creativity are needed above all to give the UK a competitive edge. These are the distinctive assets of a knowledge driven economy. They are essential to creating high-value products and services and to improving business processes. They are as vital in traditional engineering industries and in services as in high-technology businesses.

Creativity and innovation now take on a greater poignancy within 'fast' capitalism (Seltzer and Bentley, 1999). In the Report of the National Advisory Committee on Creative and Cultural Education (DMCS, 1999), *All Our Futures: Creativity, Culture and Education*, similar sentiments are stated: 'The business community wants education to give a much higher priority to promoting young people's creative abilities; to developing teamwork, social skills and powers of communication' (Department of Media, Culture and Sport, 1999: 8) and 'Many businesses are paying for courses to promote creative abilities, to teach the skills and attitudes that are now essential for economic success but which our education system is not designed to promote' (Department of Media, Culture and Sport, 1999: 13).

In the government's response, published in January, 2000, the theme is repeated:

> We want to emphasise the impact the report has had on our thinking. The report has an excellent analysis of the role of creativity and culture in education – both for their own sake and in building the skills

that young people need to achieve their potential in the knowledge economy of the future. They are key in developing the capability of future generations.

(Department for Education and Employment [DfEE]/DMCS, 2000: para 3)

Of interest here is that although the response to the paper was from two ministries – the DfEE and the DMCS – the initiative came from the DMCS, not from the DfEE.

Turner, in a recent analysis of contemporary capitalism, regards it as both *high-touch* and *high-tech* (Turner, 2001: 51). He states further that, notwithstanding the influences of globalization, many commercial activities remain local, service-based endeavours: they are, in many instances, *high-touch* services (Turner, 2001: 57). They require emotional labour. Equally, knowledge-based, *high-tech* industries require creativity, as do the emerging so-called 'culture industries'; these latter requiring creativity of a more artistic kind. Before considering the high-touch and high-tech modes of economic activity, I consider a further current issue in education: that of leadership.

Re-enchanting school leadership

Within the economy, the commitment of workers to their organizations is in decline. They feel detached. They show little loyalty and commitment to their organizations (Gallie *et al.*, 1998). They feel themselves not to be trusted, not to be valued as persons. They are insecure, the result of what Beck (2000: 1) refers to as the 'Brazilianization' of the West. Rational management is now regarded by some as ineffective. Bureaucracy needs softening. Employers should appeal both to the heart and to the head. Emotion and reason need to combine into a productive relationship. Given this, management theorists now attempt to insert into their work the echoes of a pre-modern era: charisma, enchantment, delight, vision, mission, the spiritual, and passion. Goleman *et al.*'s (2002) 'primal leadership' is indicative. The management seminar now seeks to combine 'drill and, increasingly, religious revivalism' (Thrift, 1999: 148).

A few examples can be cited in more detail. Noting the diminishing commitment of workers to their organizations, Biggart (1989) concludes, 'Firms, I believe, have begun to reach the limits of rationality as a strategy for controlling workers. [. . .] Independent work that relies on solidarity, respect, or mutual trust, is poorly served by bureaucratic structures that create authority differences' (ibid.: 169–170). A recent elaboration on this is in the work of Thomson: for example, *Emotional Capital: Capturing Hearts and Minds to Create Lasting Business Success* (1998a) and *Passion at Work* (1998b). Emotional capital can be either *external* ('held in the hearts of the customer and the external stakeholder' – as in 'brand value') or *internal* (within the 'hearts of the people within the business') (Thomson, 1998a: 7).

Emotion, too, can be 'deadly' (as, for example, with fear, anger, apathy, envy, greed) or 'dynamic' (as with obsession, passion, delight, love, desire, trust) (Thomson, 1998a: 23–24). What is needed, so the argument runs, is a new 'emotional contract' (ibid.: 92). But this 'contract' requires more to be known and recorded about the emotions of those in organizations. It requires a data-base, kept up to date. This in turn requires '360-degree appraisal': that is, 'everyone is responsible for gathering feedback from everyone' (Thomson, 1998a: 205). Within education, there have been calls for 'rethinking educational change with heart and mind' (Hargreaves, 1997), for 'passionate management' (Brighouse, 2000), for 'balancing logic and artistry in leadership' (Deal and Peterson, 1994), all this constituting what Hartley (1999) refers to as the 're-enchantment' of school leadership.

The high-touch economy

Nearly fifty years ago, in his classic study *White Collar: The American Middle Class*, C. Wright Mills noted the pressures of emotional labour:

> They sell by the week or month their smiles and their kindly gestures, and they must practice the prompt repression of resentment and aggression. For these intimate traits are of commercial relevance and required for the more efficient and profitable distribution of goods and services.
> (Mills, 1951: xii)

Even more so today, in a reversal of Weberian disenchantment, the emotions are being rationalized so that workers will be 're-enchanted' (Ritzer, 2000). The heart is being managed (Hochschild, 1983). Mestrovic (1997), in his *Postemotional Society*, argues that society is becoming interminably 'nice'. Emotions are 'cognitively filtered', thereby rendered safe. From an historical standpoint, Elias (1994), in his two-volume *The Civilising Process*, sees all this as part of the process set in train in courtly society wherein the affects had to be suppressed and managed once the pacification of the realm no longer allowed the military power of the nobles to hold sway. As we have become more interdependent, this 'civility' has proceeded apace. The 'battlefield' is now 'within us'.

To return to the present: the formal recording of the workers' emotions in the sort of database recommended by Thomson would extend the range of the audit society (Power, 1997), portending an emotional audit. But this formal audit would at least be explicit. Bauman, however, suspects that deeper forces are at work: 'Seduction, as Pierre Bourdieu intimated, may now take the place of repression as the permanent vehicle of systemic control and social integration' (Bauman, 1988: 889). Bauman adds the caveat that this does not apply to those who cannot afford to consume: for them, more explicit modes of surveillance will be required. The emotions, therefore, are being appropriated for performative and instrumental purposes. Emotion and capital are now linked productively in a new configuration: emotional capital. Within education, notions such as emotional intelligence (Goleman *et al.*, 2002) and 'emotional literacy' are being given currency, especially in the United States. For the most part, emotional literacy courses are a form of behaviour modification, one resting on an interpretation of neurobiological research and on a presumed notion of what counts as the good citizen (Boler, 1999: 77). Reference to 'emotional intelligence' includes also its measurement, in the form of an emotion quotient (EQ), the counterpart to an IQ. As with the early history of the IQ-testing movement (Kamin, 1974), the current quest for an EQ implies some universalized fixed 'attribute' called emotional intelligence, one unrelated to gender, class or race.

The high-tech economy

Whereas, in the high-touch economy, the emotions are perhaps more to the fore, within the high-tech economy, the matter of creativity looms larger. This is not to say that in the emerging 'culture' industries creativity is not essential; on the contrary, in the emerging new knowledge economy, creativity becomes crucial. At present, the new economy is in the making (Leadbeater, 1999). That said, any putative new knowledge economy would, by implication, require a knowledge worker. The term 'knowledge worker' is itself problematic: workers have always required knowledge, even in highly Taylorized settings. A more appropriate term would be a 'learning worker' (Jacques, 1996: 143). That is to say, 'Increasingly, the problem of organizing has to do, not in the content of worker knowledge, but in the ability to revise this content as required' (Jacques, 1996: 144). Here Jacques' 'learning worker' comes close to Castells's (1998: 340) 'self-programmable' workers who can change themselves as the conditions of production require. This is distinct from 'generic' workers who simply apply knowledge and routines as directed. All this represents a shift in the worker's mode of consciousness. Formerly, it was 'mechanical' in its orientation. It emphasized 'instrumentality, emotionless, accumulation, skepticism, individual consciousness, standardization and objectification' (Jacques, 1996: 37). This mode of consciousness will not suffice in the knowledge economy, one wherein creativity produces innovation and new products. It requires not only a 'maximally creative' worker, but one who can also generate short-term returns (Thrift, 2002: 202–205). It is said to be in the performing arts that inspiration can be found (Thrift, 2002: 213). Thus the expressive or creative arts can provide a curricular route towards fostering creativity. But, perhaps more so, corresponding pedagogical changes, associated with, say, neo-Vygotskian approaches (which are not considered here), can also complement this curricular quest for creativity.

Thus far, the argument has considered the relationship between the affective aspects of education and economic production in both high-touch and high-tech sectors. There is, however, a further aspect to the economic relevance of the 'emotions' and creativity in education, and it has not been one to which official discourse has directed itself. That aspect is consumption, which for some is the defining aspect of contemporary postmodern culture.

Education, consumption and the instrumentalization of the expressive

Campbell (1989), in his *The Romantic Ethic and the Spirit of Modern Consumerism*, cites Lukacs: 'In the modern world the production of consumption becomes more important than the consumption of production' (Lukacs, quoted in Campbell, 1989: 36; see also, Bauman, 1988). Allen (2002: 41) argues how production and consumption combine: 'Overall, this symbolic activity adds up to an aestheticization of the economic, which takes place within the sphere of production as well as in the circuits of exchange and consumption.' Consumerism is becoming a way of life, at least for those who can afford it. This contrasts with a period of thirty years ago when our lives turned more on work. Now, there is the potential for consumerism to become the central purpose of life (Miles, 1998: 146). Bauman puts it well: 'In other words, what is needed are new conditions which would favour habits and attitudes diametrically opposed to those which the work ethic prophesied' (Bauman, 1998: 112).

Drawing here upon the work of Bauman (2000), Beck (1998, 2000), Giddens (1991) and Melucci (1989, 1996a,b), I suggest that contemporary postmodern culture – itself partly the result of consumer capitalism – places individuals in the position of having to re-produce creatively their own identities, using the goods and services which the economy sets before them. And this, for different reasons, leads to a celebration of difference. It can lead also, for those who lack the wherewithal to buy into this, to exclusion and despair, opening the way towards sources of identity associated with nationalism, religion and racism. In these conditions of fragmentation, cultural education becomes not the search for a shared way of seeing the world, but for recognizing and coping with its complexity and diversity (DMCS, 1999: 6). The government's call for creative education – that is, education for creativity – appears to turn upon creativity for production, not consumption.

In contemporary social theory, there is much made of uncertainty, risk provisionality and limitless possibility. But this uncertainty does not exist in the expectation of disaster; rather, it is part of the everyday flow of fast capitalism. And perhaps, too, the 'corrosion of character is an inevitable consequence' (Sennett, 1998: 31). These risks and uncertainties prevail at a number of levels. At a very general level, in our modernist quest to impose order and to ascertain cause and effect, more and more unintended consequences are revealed as the complexity of life increases: the 'uncontrollability of the consequences grows with the claims to control instrumental rationality' (Beck, 1998: 27). But insecurities beset us also as consumers: 'The common denominator is the dissolution of the self. And if the latter process differs according to the way in which the self is culturally constituted, it leads none the less to a universal core of narcissistic experience in which dependence on the defining gaze of the Other becomes the lifeline of personal survival' (Friedman, 1992: 358). Here is a culture of symbolic possibilities limited only by the power to pay for them. Identity is fleeting, but the search for it is not. And no longer do individuals live according to a fixed moral code (Giddens, 1991: 153). Indeed, the recent interest in value education is an attempt to reassert one.

We are witnessing 'the gradual collapse and swift decline of early modern illusion: of the belief that there is an end to the road along which we can proceed' (Bauman, 2000: 29). Given 'the unrelenting interrogation directed at the self: [the central question now is] "Who am I?" [. . .] What distinguishes contemporary society is its multiplication of memberships' (Melucci, 1996a: 123–124, brackets added). Melucci elaborates:

> Answering the basic question 'Who am I?' becomes progressively more difficult; we continue to need fixed anchor points in our lives but even our personal biographies begin to fail us as we hardly recognize ourselves in our memories. The search for a safe haven for the self becomes an increasingly critical undertaking, and the individual must build and continuously rebuild her/his 'home' in the face of the surging flux of events and relations. [. . .] A world that lives by complexity and difference cannot escape uncertainty, and it demands from individuals the capacity to *change form* (the literal meaning of 'metamorphosis') whilst still continuing to be the same person. The constitutive dimension of the self – time and space, health and sickness, sex and age, birth and death, reproduction and love – are no longer a datum but a problem.
>
> (Melucci, 1996b: 2; italics in original)

The constant re-creation of the self (Wexler (2000) calls it 're-selfing') implies that education for (re)creativity and reflexivity becomes important for dealing with the uncertainties of postmodernity. There is little formal education for this, but much informal, as Willis in his study of the symbolic creativity of youth in their everyday settings has reported (Willis, 1990: 207). But this trend towards greater individualization has a concomitant effect. It is the shift from the pursuit of a 'just society' to an emphasis on 'human rights' (Bauman, 2000: 29). Or, as Melucci has it: 'The right to *equality*, under whose banner all modern revolutions have been fought [. . .], is being replaced by the right to *difference*' (Melucci, 1989: 177; emphasis in original). This has consequences for citizenship, which, Bauman argues, is now subjected to 'corrosion and slow disintegration' (Bauman, 2000: 36). This is because it is *individuals* who 'fill the public space to the brim, claiming to be its only legitimate occupants, and [who] elbow out from public discourse everything else' (Bauman, 2000: 37). In short, consumerism can lead to *de*-socialization and to fragmentation. It is little wonder, therefore, that the school becomes yet another site wherein there are attempts to re-socialize individuals and to provide civics education.

Insofar as the economy is concerned, schools transmit messages which serve both production and consumption. The correspondence is by no means complete, and 'production' messages prevail. That said, notions such as having 'ownership' of one's learning, or of being 'reflective' of oneself, or of keeping up the good image of the school, all arguably resonate with consumption. Of necessity, these are mixed messages: 'the consumer self is diffused while the producer self is condensed' (Wexler, 1997: 44). Particularly within the service-based sector, the emotions of the worker must be managed for performative purposes. It is the safe 'emotions' which are required, not the 'deadly' ones; and it is these presumably 'desirable' emotions which are the object of emotional literacy programmes (Boler, 1999).

The requirements of the consumer self are altogether different. Consumers are encouraged to have it now, not later. Advertisers appeal to the emotions, either directly or subliminally. The emotional education of would-be producers emphasizes the management of emotions in relation to others – how to work in teams, how to relate to customers or parents, for example. The emotional education of would-be consumers requires a focus on the self, as a distinct identity. 'Divided, we shop' (Bauman, 2000). Whereas, for production, integrating rituals are needed; for consumption, disintegrating, self-centred, preening rituals are required. And paradoxically, the more the school contributes to the production of 'emotional' labourers and consumers, the more fragmented will the society become within a consumerist, postmodern culture. If capitalism is a cause of a fractured, consumer culture, and if schools are increasingly instrumental in the further-ance of capitalism, then an unintended consequence of a school system which is effective for the economy may be its contribution towards a de-socialized society (Wexler, 1992). There seems to be some recognition of this. Calls for value education and for cultural education may be attempts to reduce the centrifugal forces of consumer culture.

In passing, the issue of the 'co-existence' of a work ethic and a consumerist ethic can be addressed historically. Consumption is not new. On this, Campbell states: 'Perhaps there was a "Romantic ethic" working to promote the "spirit of consumerism," just as Weber had postulated that a "Puritan" ethic had promoted the spirit of capitalism' (Campbell, 1989: 6) and

> If, as I imagined, Romanticism served to facilitate the emergence of modern consumer behaviour in late eighteenth- early nineteenth-century England, to legitimise, in effect, a 'consumer ethic', then how could a diametrically opposed 'production ethic', that derived from Puritanism, have been operating in the same place at the same time? [. . .] Were there really two social ethics, opposed in form, existing side by side?

Campbell takes issue with the usual explanation of eighteenth-century consumerism, which is that the middle classes emulated the upper classes. The explanation, he argues, is not merely material. It is emotional. The site, so to say, of the emotions has been historically contingent. In pre-modern times, the emotions are seen as 'inherent in aspects of reality, from whence they exert their influence over humans. [. . .] They "filled" him [*sic*] with those distinctively aroused states called emotions' (Campbell, 1989: 72). During modernity, the emotions come to reside within individuals. Campbell speculates that 'there is a sense in which the disenchantment of the external world required as a parallel process some "enchantment" of the psychic inner world' (ibid.: 73). The Protestant work ethic suppressed the emotions, whose expression could only be imagined. The 'release' of emotions and the imagination is enabled by consumption. There has emerged an industry of therapists who facilitate the release of emotions in a world where 'cool' is necessary. This is an educated and controlled release of safe emotions, one required of both producers and of consumers. But, as Mestrovic (1997) notes, the body is now ever-more tightly self-regulated. Consumption does not release the emotions, which may explain why there is a new-found search for what Durkheim (2001(1912): 164) called 'collective effervescence', or what Wexler (1997: 121) refers to as the 'resacralization' of education. The emergence of emotional literacy and of emotional management imply a new formalization of education in the form of audits and outcomes. Hitherto, matters emotional had been regarded as implicit in the pedagogical process, especially of child-centred education. Now, they seem set to be 'lifted out' of the hidden curriculum, and to be made explicit, until such time as they become 'natural'.

Conclusion

Government is now beginning to attend to aspects of education which hitherto were part of the discourse of progressive education. Creativity and emotional literacy are being 'attached' to an educational practice which remains decidedly performance-driven, standardized and monitored. This creative impulse is said to derive from an increasing awareness that both a successful knowledge economy (one which includes the 'cultural economy') and a service-based economy cannot be constructed and sustained unless more of the creative and emotional self can be appropriated for instrumental purposes. It is not yet clear whether there will be a creative-and-emotional approach 'across the curriculum', or whether there will emerge a re-emphasis on the creative arts as a 'vehicle' for it; or both. But, in management – or, to be more precise, in leadership studies – there are already repeated suggestions for an appropriation of other 'intelligences', such as 'emotional intelligence', which can somehow combine seamlessly with bureaucratic rationality as a way of creating more successful schools and businesses. Self-managing, 'emotional' and creative pupils; creative and 'emotional' teachers; and creative and 'emotional' leaders could all come to share a common discourse. But this will, on present trends, be managed and monitored formally as sets of competences and outcomes. There will be a clear market opportunity for those who would offer both the emotional audit of educational organizations and the objective testing of the emotional intelligence of those within them. Perhaps, in England, the 'emotional hour' will come to complement the 'literacy hour'. Notwithstanding the appeals to a decidedly pre-modern, religious, awe-inspiring world, what will count as creativity and emotion in education seems set to be filtered through a modernist sieve, thereby producing (at least as policy) a pastoral or therapeutic bureaucracy (Wexler, 1997). If this were to be realized as practice, it would constitute a shift towards an instrumentalization and re-modernization of the expressive order of the school.

Part II

Values and learners

The issues raised in the Chapter 4 by David Hartley concerning the kinds of citizen that schools and school curricula, under the guidance of education policy, seek to produce are developed in different ways in Chapters 5, 6 and 7, each of which draws our attention to questions of curricular values and rationales, of issues of education and culture, and of the kinds of learner and citizen that may be perceived, promoted and constructed via the curriculum experience. As Hartley's chapter suggests, schools and teachers are not merely called upon to 'discover and respond' to different kinds of student (a notion embedded in discourses and initiatives of 'inclusion' and in pedagogical and curricular practices of 'differentiation'); they are also called upon to 'construct' different kinds of student through implementing the curriculum (a process often supported in the 'hidden' curriculum of pedagogies and expectations of student behaviour). While Hartley talks of the construction of consumers, students are also, it could be argued, constructed as girls and boys, black and white, middle class and working class, and so on. While such identification clearly has some basis in the socio-physical world (some students are boys and others are girls, some are white and some are black, some are working class and some are middle class), its purposes are often unclear, and it has a tendency to stereotype and 'label' in its sidelining of major differences within imposed categories (not all boys, for instance, conform to a stereotype of preferring information books to fiction, being naturally louder and more aggressive than girls, being less organized than girls, and so on).

As Hartley suggests, the construction of different but clearly definable categories of citizen/student serves very practical – if ethically unacceptable – socioeconomic ends, in the case of many countries inevitably inscribed within the needs of capital (in which, for example, it is essential that wealth and goods are distributed unequally). A function of modern education, according to this view, is not merely to produce consumers but to produce different kinds of consumer for different kinds of product (we cannot all, after all, given the workings of local and global marketplaces, all consume the same products and not consume others). It is equally important from this perspective that societies continue to produce – both traditional products and businesses and new ones. Commenting on Apple's conceptualization of the partially concealed rationales for state education, Ross (2000: 83) describes how

> a schooling system which credentializes a particular proportion of the population roughly equivalent to the needs of the division of labour (and de-credentializes the rest) is an almost natural way of maintaining the economic and cultural imbalance on which these societies are built.

To an extent, this need for different types of consumer gets merged with the production of different kinds of learner/citizen and with the stereotyping of identified student groups. With reference to the identification and differentiation of boys and girls, for example, Spender (1980, 1982) has described the ways in which, in the official language of education, girls are effectively rendered 'invisible' through practices such as repeatedly referring to students and teachers as 'he' (see also Weiner, 1985; Torbe, 1986; Paechter, 1998), as well as through male-oriented selections of knowledge and facts, over-referencing to male scientists and historical figures, and so forth – a situation which may be seen to have the effect of reducing or destroying the desire (and ultimately the capacity) of girls to take up professions in science and technology or to develop science – and technology-related interests outside of work. Other writers have commented on similar negative effects in relation to race (Connolly, 2000) and social class (Lucey and Reay, 2002), as well as in relation to the negative effects not just of curriculum but how 'achievement' is identified and assessed. Reay and Wiliam (1999), for instance, have described how assessment practices can lead some young students to construct negative identities which contribute to current underachievement and a degree of fatalism about future prospects.

Elsewhere, Michael Apple (1995) has been one of a number of commentators suggesting not simply that particular student identities are constructed through the curriculum experience but that, generally, curricula act conservatively not to liberate students or to produce a critical citizenry but rather to reproduce an essentially compliant, obedient, 'quiescent' workforce, generally accepting of their lot regardless of what it might be. Apple may be seen to be contributing to the development of earlier work by Bowles and Gintis (1972, 1976), in which schools were understood very much in terms of both mirroring and (partly through that mirroring) preparing young people for differing roles in the world of work. The school, they argued

> is a bureaucratic order, with hierarchical authority, rule orientation, stratification by 'ability' as well as by age, role differentiation by sex (physical education, home economics, etc), and a system of external incentives (marks, promises of promotion, and threat of failure) much like pay and status in the sphere of work.
>
> (Bowles and Gintis, 1972: 87)

Four years later, in an even more vigorous attack, they were to declare, 'Schools are *destined* to legitimate inequality, limit personal development to forms compatible with submission to arbitrary authority, and aid in the process whereby youth are resigned to their fate' (Bowles and Gintis, 1976: 266).

Many may find the analysis of Bowles and Gintis, with its strong emphasis on structures and on what might sometimes be seen now as an overly straightforward and one-directional account of the workings of power relations, somewhat over-deterministic in its conclusions. It might also seem disrespectful to teachers struggling in often very difficult circumstances to promote social justice as well as providing an interesting and relevant curriculum for their students. They raise serious issues, however, not just about the kind of learners and citizens we want our young people to become (and how this might be achieved through the curriculum) but also about what kind of society we want them to contribute to – and how. Do we, for example (as Apple seems to suggest is the norm) want to ensure that they work to preserve essentially an unchanged and unchanging society, including the preservation of existing power relations and wealth distribution? Or would we rather they grow up to be critically active citizens (of their own country, but also, perhaps, of the world) – contributing to an evolution of society which might, among other things, seek to change existing power relations and wealth distribution? I am reminded here of Ross's helpful summary of Ivan Illich's (1973) account of the form and functions of formal education (2000: 85):

> Far from having the function of developing a democratic and participatory society, Illich argued that the main tasks of the school were in reality four-fold: they provided custodial care for children, freeing parents' time; they effectively distributed pupils into occupational roles; they transmitted the dominant value system; and they taught pupils to acquire socially approved knowledge and skills.

In his own work, Apple (Apple, 1995; Apple and Beane, 1999; see also Hahn, 1998) takes rather more account of the power of individual agency than Illich or Bowles and Gintis, suggesting that schools and teachers can go against the tide and, rather than accepting the compliant orientation embedded in the wider system (including its curricula), promote active, critical citizenship in young people in the manner of transformative intellectuals operating within the discourse of critical pedagogy described by David Scott in Chapter 2 of this volume. This is achieved partly through attempts at the production of more democratic classrooms, on the basis that young people are unlikely to become active, critical citizens later in life if their habitual experience at school is of being on the wrong end of an autocracy, and it is premised on a view – amply illustrated in Audrey Osler's chapter on 'New directions in citizenship education' – that young people are engaged in active, relatively independent identifications of their own, irrespective of the plans the wider system might have for them.

In a model promoted by Apple and Beane (1999), which does not merely theorize or hypothesize about more democratic classrooms but, critically, provides examples of them in action, the development of the democratic involvement of students includes practices such as a negotiated curriculum, extensive community and student involvement, flexible forms of assessment, and a more equal and democratic student–teacher relationship – with an emphasis on experiencing and doing democracy, rather than just learning 'about' it. In line with what McFarlane will argue later on, the 'content' of such lessons (in terms of the texts used, the facts to be learned, and so on) may be seen as less important than the processes of the lesson and the skills which the students are developing: skills, essentially, not simply for certain kinds of work but for active and meaningful participation in society. Another way of putting this is that the processes and skills become the 'content' – so that an activity like group-work is not just a means to an end (the 'acquisition' of some particular 'item' of knowledge, perhaps) but (in that it improves and develops collaborative decision making or whatever) an end in itself.

Inevitably, we have returned once again to questions of knowledge – including, here, the issue of 'knowing how' versus 'knowing that'. In particular, the following questions refuse to leave center stage:

- Who decides what kind(s) and items of knowledge should be included in the curriculum?
- What ends do those kinds and items of knowledge serve – both for society and for the individuals of whom it consists?
- What sort(s) of people are being constructed via the curriculum, and what kind of society is envisioned in that construction?

These issues will be addressed in three different contexts and from three different perspectives in each of the three chapters that follow.

5 Gender, power and curriculum

An inevitable interconnection

Carrie Paechter

Developing the theme of the construction of subjects via the curriculum experience, and relating this to wider issues of power relations in society, Paechter highlights the continuing value of feminist theory in studying and making sense of the school curriculum along with an expose as to why such theory has failed to make a more practical and lasting impact. Adopting a Foucauldian perspective in which power and knowledge are seen as both gendered and mutually implicative, she offers a fresh take on curriculum analysis in indicating how the particular histories of Western educational systems may be understood as having led to a situation in which the school curriculum is inevitably gendered – an argument she supports with reference to how gender issues are actually played out in the school setting. Like White earlier, though from a rather different starting-point, Paechter traces current received practice historically, to the point at which Enlightenment thinking suggested a split between body and mind/reason that was paralleled by a reconceptualization of males and females as fundamentally different from one another. In describing the ways in which both girls and working-class students continue to be excluded from curricular experiences despite rhetorics of inclusivity, Paechter suggests that only through direct action in relation to compulsory curriculum content and wider social attitudes will a situation be changed in which girls are pressed into certain areas of study and forms of employment and boys into others.

Introduction

I have chosen my title quite deliberately. I do believe that there is an inevitable interconnection between gender, power and curriculum, and, furthermore, that this relationship has been widely neglected in the study of curriculum. Hence, much of the point of this chapter is to demonstrate that interconnection, and to urge that it be taken more seriously in future by curriculum theorists and practitioners. For it seems to me that unless we recognize the importance that gender and power play in the negotiation of curriculum, between policy makers, teachers and students in various combinations, then we will fail to understand what is happening when such negotiation takes place, and, in particular, when it goes awry.

Of course the relationship between power, knowledge and curriculum has been recognized for some time, and was brought to the fore in British sociology of education by the groundbreaking collection *Knowledge and Control* (Young, 1971) and subsequently taken up by other writers, particularly those working in curriculum history and the investigation of subject cultures (Ball and Lacey, 1980; Goodson, 1983; St John-Brooks, 1983). However, in most of this work the concept of power remained largely undertheorized, and the gender dimensions of curriculum negotiation were ignored. I am going to argue that if we conceive of knowledge as intimately entwined with power, as power/knowledge (Foucault, 1977, 1978, 1980) then, as knowledge is gendered, the power/knowledge relation is itself gendered. This has far-reaching consequences for curriculum.

I should make it clear that while I think the connection is inevitable, I do not consider it to be one of logical necessity. We can conceive of, and, indeed, might prefer, a world in which knowledge was not gendered, but we do not happen to live in one. In the West, in particular, our specific historical circumstances have made such a link unavoidable, as will become clear from my argument that follows. In particular, a series of linked dualisms that emerged during the Enlightenment period set masculinity against femininity and reason against emotion, valuing certain forms of knowledge while associating them firmly with the masculine. This means that while it is possible that gender and knowledge could be separated, in practice they cannot be. This is my argument in this chapter.

Gender, power and knowledge

My approach to power is basically Foucaultian, and thus treats power and knowledge as intertwined, as mutually implicative, within the combining formulation power/knowledge (Foucault, 1977: 27). This mutual implication of power and knowledge is underpinned by a capillary conception of power. Power is not a unified entity, located in a few, particular places; it is distributed throughout society. Consequently, Foucault argues, power operates and should be studied at the microlevel. We should therefore begin our analysis of power where power itself begins, in small interactions working outwards towards the global, in 'an ascending analysis of power' (Foucault, 1980: 99). For our present purposes, this means that in considering the operation of power in the negotiation of curriculum, we need to consider what happens in policy making meetings, in classrooms and in staffrooms, and not assume, for example, that what is sent down from government through policy documents is the only thing that matters in the study of curriculum.

Such a view of power is important for understanding the complexities of how curriculum is negotiated, enacted and resisted in schools. It allows us to consider the local and practical implications of curriculum development and reform, and to see how we can resist them if they are not in the best interests of our students. It allows us both to understand why change can be so slow to take place, and to find the tools to move things forward. Most important, focusing on micropowers enables us to see the corresponding microresistances of teachers and students and to explain how and why they come about.

Once we start to treat power as operating in everyday, microlevel situations, and as intimately entwined with knowledge, it becomes clear that gender must have a close relationship with this consequent power/knowledge relation. This is for two reasons. The first is that interpersonal power relations are themselves gendered at all levels. Despite more than a 100 years of active feminist activity, women still have less access to power than men, both in the workplace (Equal Opportunities Commission, 2003) and in the home (Dryden, 1999). Thus when considering power relations, it is essential always to take into account the gender dimensions of those relations; gender cannot simply be ignored. While this seems obvious once it has been pointed out, it is interesting to note that most texts on the negotiation of curriculum, particularly in the field of curriculum history, do ignore it. The gender of the protagonists, while usually clear (as male) from their names, is not remarked upon. It is only when gender becomes so salient that it cannot be overlooked, as when the headteachers of the British elite girls' schools collectively resisted the establishment of domestic science as a female science curriculum (Dyhouse, 1976), that it emerges as a factor in many accounts.

Despite considerable feminist attempts to bring gender to the fore in relation to the school curriculum, both generally and in respect of particular school subjects (Deem, 1978; Head, 1985; Purvis, 1985; Yates, 1985; Burton, 1986; Isaacson, 1986; Attar, 1990; Thomas, 1990; Burton and Weiner, 1990; Riddell, 1992; Weiner, 1993, 1994; Acker, 1994; Moss and Attar, 1999), thinking around gender has had little impact on curriculum theory more widely. Much work on gender and curriculum has been confined to the sidelines, associated with particular curriculum forms, rather than central to the curriculum field as a whole.

The gendering of knowledge originates in the Enlightenment period, when two major changes took place concerning how people thought about men and women. The first was the disappearance of the one-sex model of human beings (Laqueur, 1990). This model saw males and females as being essentially of the same physical form, with female genitals seen simply as male ones turned inside out and held inside the body (Laqueur, 1990). Men and women differed, on this model, in their roles, in their social positioning, but not in their essential makeup. Moving from this model to one of two, clearly physically differentiated, sexes, during the Enlightenment period, changed the focus to one which saw males and females as fundamentally different, rather than fundamentally the same, and grounded their previously accepted roles in underlying physical characteristics.

At the same time, Descartes (1637/1641/1968) was instigating a clear separation of mind as certain, body as contingent, locating personal identity in the mind. This location, however, was gendered, if not in Descartes's original formulation, then in its subsequent interpretation. In an understanding of the body dating back to Plato (Spelman, 1982) as inhibiting rational thought, men (or middle-class men, at least) were perceived as being able to transcend their bodies and focus on the life of the mind, while women were not. They were considered to be fundamentally tied to their bodies, through their wombs, now seen as having no male counterpart, and treated as the seat of hysteria and irrationality (Foucault, 1978; French, 1994). This allowed the appropriation of all forms of knowledge associated with reason and abstraction as masculine, along with a concomitant valorization of these forms as superior to and more powerful than others.

This appropriation of the rational is further complicated by the pleasurable side of what Foucault terms our 'will to knowledge' (Foucault, 1978: 55); the pleasure that comes from the illusory power of pure reason. Walkerdine (1988: 186) points out that power is pleasurable. It is the power of the triumph of reason over emotion, the fictional power over the practices of everyday life. Exclusion from the practices of reason brings a concomitant exclusion from the pleasures associated with it. Thus one result of the masculine appropriation of abstract knowledge is that it can be harder for girls and women to claim and enjoy the pleasure associated with success in these fields. There is considerable evidence, for example, that school-age girls are expected by their peers to downplay their academic success and instead focus on their failings; this also has implications for the ways in which women are able to take delight in higher academic study, particularly in more abstract or reason-based fields (Paechter, 2005).

The dominance of reason in post-Enlightenment thought has thus rendered power/knowledge fundamentally gendered. In excluding women from this dominant, rational knowledge, and from the empowerment that comes with it, Enlightenment traditions have simultaneously excluded women from power, and in particular from the pleasurable power of engagement with and mastery over the discourses of mathematics and pure science.

Power/knowledge and dominant curriculum forms

The contemporary school curriculum has its origins in both the theory and the practice of education for ruling-class boys and young men during the Enlightenment period. This is particularly true of curriculum form, which has remained relatively stable, for elite students at least, over the last 150 years. While the details have changed, particularly in the move from the nineteenth-century pre-eminence of the classics to the current situation in which mathematics and science are dominant (Delamont, 1994), the overall structure, and the emphasis on rationality and the abstract, have remained the same. Goodson *et al.* (1997: 181) point out, for example, that elite private schools in the United States have been able to introduce computers, the arts and international perspectives to their curriculum without compromising their underlying principles.

In effect, one can introduce innovations into the classical curriculum that appear technical, or even egalitarian, without in any way diffusing the super elaborated code in its abstractness and imperial suppositions. The apparent blurring of the classical curriculum by the introduction of innovation only serves to emphasize that the class relations inherent in differentiated curriculum forms may take a variety of disguises, but the reality is as unalterable as class relations. The contemporary curriculum, therefore, emphasizes and gives status to those subjects which are associated with reason and rationality, with abstractness, and, therefore, with masculinity.

This means that those students who are excluded from these subjects, or who choose to exclude themselves, are also excluded from power, both the power of the 'mastery of reason' (Walkerdine, 1988) and the power, that runs parallel to it, to operate within the world. Historically, moves on the part of elite male groups to exclude others from gaining access to dominant positions in gendered power/knowledge relations were quite blatant. Women were excluded by reference to their embodied states; it was argued that excessive learning, particularly higher level learning such as college education, was injurious to their health and fertility (Dyhouse, 1976). Associated with this, girls' future roles as wives and mothers dominated thinking about what would constitute a suitable education, from at least the time of Rousseau.

Because of this exclusion of women from dominant educational forms, when the elite girls' schools were set up in the mid-nineteenth century, it was clear to their founders that the education they provided should be the same as that supplied to boys of the same social class. This meant that a supposedly gender-neutral, but actually very masculine-marked, curriculum was established, by the end of the nineteenth century, in elite schools for both boys and girls. Although there was a long-running debate about the possibility of a female curriculum, and, in particular, about the importance of science and mathematics, prevailing power/knowledge relations meant that it was inevitable that ruling-class girls would be offered the same curriculum as their brothers. The heads of the elite girls' schools simply could not afford to do otherwise if their pupils were going to be able to compete with men in intellectual and professional spheres. Consequently, the dominance of the archetypal subjects of pure reason, mathematics and science, went unchallenged.

Embodiment and curriculum marginalization

I explained earlier how powerful masculine disembodied knowledges have become associated with reason, which, as a result, dominates the elite school curriculum. This has a concomitant effect on those subjects which have a direct relation to the body, such as physical education (PE), the many forms of design and technology (D&T), (a subject that in England and Wales encompasses food and textiles technology, work with resistant materials, and graphics) and related subjects such as mechanics, and to some extent music, drama and art. All of these have been marginalized in relation to school knowledge, with a variety of gendered effects.

First, these curricula, particularly D&T and PE, have a partially contradictory position in many schools. While they are not considered important in terms of their examination results, teacher status or curriculum time, they are often the most visible areas of the school, forming its public face. Entrance halls have prominent displays of art, design and craft work, and cups won by sports teams, and the school play or concert is considered an important aspect of the school's profile in the local area. In the United States, school sports fixtures and cheerleading teams (Adams and Bettis, 2003) are an important aspect of the life of some communities, and, while this is less the case in the United Kingdom, sports are a central part of the public profile of many schools, part of the business of demonstrating to parents and others that the school is a 'good' one.

The very direct relationship of PE and D&T to bodies and to working with the hands has given these subjects an image that, outside of the elite private school system (where sports are seen as having a role in forming the leaders of the future), relates closely to ruling-class ideas about working-class life and interests, and to class-based power/knowledge relations. Similarly, the forerunners of food and textiles technology, the domestic subjects, were seen at the start of the twentieth century as being essential aspects of girls' mass education, with housewifery becoming compulsory in English girls' secondary education from 1905, and it being permitted for girls to replace science with domestic science from 1907 (Hunt, 1987). At this time, a working-class girl might spend half of her time in the last year of (elementary) schooling on domestic subjects, doing needlework while her male peers were studying basic arithmetic (Turnbull, 1987; Attar, 1990). Even in the late 1980s some girls in England were able to spend more than a quarter of their time in their last two years of schooling studying domestic subjects (Attar, 1990). It is not hard to guess which girls these were.

Meanwhile, working-class and black teenage boys, particularly if they were considered to be disaffected, were encouraged to spend a considerable proportion of their curriculum time in the craft workshops. In these spaces, relationships were more informal and the need for good discipline, because of the nature of the machinery, was more obvious and less likely to be seen as arbitrarily imposed by the school. Consequently, as noted by Penfold (1988: 20), craft teachers were and are likely to be seen as overalled equivalents of the community policeman, especially in our more robust schools. The workshop was the one area of the school where disciplinary problems receded and the air hummed with purposeful activity.

Subjects associated with the body, then, are also associated in school with working-class, 'less able' and disaffected students, performing an essential service (from the school's point of view) in keeping these students from inhibiting or interfering with the smooth running of more academic areas. Their low status and their origins in working-class education fit them perfectly for this role. Success for working-class students in these subjects does not affect prevailing power/knowledge relations and leaves the elite curriculum more or less intact; more able and middle-class students do not usually study them for very long.

A further, and extremely important feature of these marginal and body-related subjects, however, is that they are often gendered. This gendering ranges in intensity from a situation in which a subject is marked as masculine or feminine, with a correspondingly gendered take-up (an example of this from the United Kingdom is drama, studied by female and male 16-year-olds at a ratio of approximately 2:1 (Department for Education and Skills, 2004b), to one in which fully developed separate forms have arisen and been perpetuated despite equal opportunities legislation and widespread co-education (in the United Kingdom; PE being a clear example of this). Even in music, where take-up is more evenly balanced, there are important differences in the responses to the subject shown by boys and girls. Green (1997) notes that the two genders align themselves with very different musical practices within school, favouring different instruments, using different musical styles and being seen by teachers as having talents in different areas. For example, girls tend to play plucked and bowed stringed instruments, and overwhelmingly dominate singing groups, while boys focus on improvised electronic music and drumming. As a result, teachers see boys as more successful and adventurous than girls, particularly in composition, which is strongly marked as masculine. This can mean that young men's and women's experiences of music, both within and out of school, can be very different.

Gendered traditions in embodied marginal subjects

The D&T/workshop subjects and PE, being even more closely associated with the body, have correspondingly more extreme gendering. Physical Education at examination level is marked as masculine, with, in England, almost twice as many young men as young women taking it as part of national examinations at age sixteen (*The Guardian* newspaper, 2003), and research from both the United Kingdom and the United States suggesting that teenage girls are reluctant to take part in co-educational PE classes (O'Sullivan *et al.*, 2002). The gendered nature of this subject, however, is much more clearly marked when we consider how it is taught, in the United Kingdom and some other Western countries, throughout compulsory schooling. Physical Education has clearly differentiated male and female forms, with radically different emphases and traditions, and even international moves towards co-education (Skelton, 2001; O'Sullivan *et al.*, 2002) and, in England and Wales, a nationally prescribed curriculum, have done little to change this.

The consequence of this is that, in the United Kingdom, prospective PE teachers arrive at their now co-educational training colleges with very different backgrounds in and attitudes towards the subject, which are perpetuated through their training. Male students in mixed PE colleges have, for example, been found systematically to exclude females from full participation in mixed games and actively to distance themselves from the feminine by avoiding or messing about in dance classes (Flintoff, 1993). When they join schools as teachers they are likely to find themselves teaching one gender only, and giving that gender a very particular diet. Girls and boys play different sports, with those offered to girls (such as netball or touch rugby) generally being reduced, 'feminised' versions of those played by boys. As they get older, partly because of teachers' perceptions of what girls want to do in PE lessons, the curriculum diverges further, so that by the age of sixteen many girls are being offered a degraded, 'fitness-based' curriculum rather than a full physical education (Harris and Penney, 2002). Attempts to develop co-educational PE in the United Kingdom have largely been unsuccessful, and, as is also the case in the United States and in the Netherlands, where mixed PE is more widespread, have usually resulted in the female tradition being completely swamped by the male as both genders do what has traditionally been part of the male curriculum (O'Sullivan *et al.*, 2002; van Essen, 2003). Sports, in particular, are so masculine-marked that boys and young men use them to display masculine dominance by excluding girls and young women (Flintoff, 1993; Scraton, 1993), who in any case are likely to arrive at the lesson with fewer skills because of their lower prior experience of male-dominated sports such as football.

Design and technology, similarly, has a strongly gendered heritage, and, indeed, it is arguable that it retains several distinct and gendered forms. In England and Wales, the extremely feminized former domestic subjects of home economics (HE) and textiles were renamed as food and textile technology and brought under the supposedly gender-neutral D&T umbrella with the introduction of the national curriculum in 1990 (Paechter, 2000). They were joined by the masculine-marked former craft-based subject of craft, design and technology (CDT) in a government-led attempt to develop an integrated curriculum organized around a common cycle of designing, making and evaluating (National Curriculum Council, 1990). This attempt was largely unsuccessful, so that in most schools there is now a *de facto* separation of the different areas, with students studying D&T in completely independent food, textiles and resistant materials lessons, and, in many cases, with the former CDT departments having taken over the D&T title. Thus the clearly distinct traditions of these two highly gendered areas have been resistant to attempts to change them and render them more gender-neutral, while the masculine-marked form focusing on resistant materials has become dominant, both in policy documents (Department for Education and Employment, 1999) and in school practice.

In the United States, where gendered technical subjects have remained separate, gender segregation at high-school level is widespread and pervasive. For example, in a study of students in vocational programmes in thirteen states, the National Women's Law Center found that

> Female students make up 96% of the students enrolled in Cosmetology, 87% of the students enrolled in Child Care courses, and 86% of the students enrolled in courses that prepare them to be Health Assistants in every region in the country. Male students, on the other hand, comprise 94% of the student body in training programs for plumbers and electricians, 93% of the students studying to be welders or carpenters, and 92% of those studying automotive technologies.
>
> (National Women's Law Center, 2002: 4)

Similar levels of gender segregation are to be found in vocational courses in the United Kingdom (Equal Opportunities Commission, 1999, 2001).

The freedom that lower status subjects have had to retain strongly gendered forms is related directly to their position within power/knowledge relations. The dominance of the mental in our conception of education and the concomitant sidelining of physical aspects of learning and knowledge (Paechter, 2004) have meant that, to put it bluntly, we do not care whether children and young people have an equitable education in these subjects. Middle-class students do not study them anyway, once they are no longer compulsory, and they are of no importance for entry to the more elite forms of higher education. These are working-class subjects for working class students, areas with so little leverage in power/knowledge terms that they have been left to carry on with a gender-divided curriculum which would be considered anathema in a higher-status area. They suffer the same fate as the vocational subjects, which, even as they spread downwards into compulsory secondary education, offer a gendered diet which is taken up by young people in an overwhelmingly differentiated manner (National Women's Law Center, 2002), 'with teenage girls largely training to be hairdressers and boys to be car mechanics and computer specialists' (Equal Opportunities Commission, 2001: 2).

Meanwhile, powerful knowledges have retained their masculine marking. Mathematics and science, though successfully studied by girls throughout compulsory education, are overwhelmingly rejected by them as soon as they are able to choose. The result of this is that, in England in 2004, only 39 per cent of those taking university entrance level mathematics and 22 per cent of those taking equivalent examinations in physics were female, compared to 70 per cent of those taking English. This has a seriously limiting effect on what is open to them in terms of future study and career options. It is notable, however, that takeup of higher level high school mathematics courses in the United States is more equal, presumably because of the importance of mathematics in the Students' Aptitude Tests (SAT) for university entrance.

Gendered power/knowledge relations in the staffroom

Gendered power/knowledge relations between subjects also have an effect on the balance of power between faculty members. Although within any particular school other factors of course play a part, masculine-labelled subjects such as mathematics and science are usually able to use their pre-eminence in negotiations over curriculum time, precedence on the timetable, and promoted posts. Teachers of these subjects, recognized as compulsory at the national level and required for university entrance in some countries, can not only ensure that their content is prioritized (e.g. in the National Literacy and Numeracy Strategies in the United Kingdom) but that their approaches win out in battles over approaches to teaching and learning (Paechter, 2003b).

Teachers of marginal, body-related subjects can, conversely, find staffroom life much more difficult. Sparkes *et al.* (1990) note that PE teachers tend to operate as restricted professionals early in their careers, not taking a full part in school micropolitics, and that those who want promotion leave the subject at a relatively early stage. They also point out that, in common with teachers of other practical subjects such as art, CDT, HE and music, PE teachers are statistically less likely to gain promotion and so have restricted career development generally. Teachers of practical and body-related subjects are also less likely to be taken seriously in curriculum debate (Sparkes *et al.*, 1990). Sikes (1988: 26) found that male PE teachers in particular are seen by their colleagues as ' "Thick Jocks" with brawn but little in the way of brains'. Home economics departments in some schools are still seen as providing a catering service for school functions alongside their role as part of the core curriculum (Paechter, 1993). In one school in my own research, HE was referred to by senior managers as 'the buns department', and an HE teacher in another school complained that 'People come down with their repairs or if they wet themselves, or God knows what . . . It's all these little things that you get, tears in the pockets or buttons come off, go and see home economics' (Florence Telemann, HE teacher, Knype School).

Given this attitude on the part of senior colleagues to them and their subjects, it is unsurprising that teachers of practical, body-related subjects find it hard to resist the dominance of those working in the realms of pure reason.

Is it possible to have an ungendered curriculum?

Clearly if there is no logical connection between gender, power/knowledge and curriculum, it is possible to have a curriculum that is free from gender. In practice, however, and in the current social formation, it is not possible.

We cannot have a society without power relations (Foucault, 1982), and, while we continue to see the differences between men's and women's bodies as having consequences for who we are (Paechter, 2003a), then these power relations will remain gendered. Because of the intimate connection between power and knowledge, power/knowledge is thus gendered, with concomitant gendered effects on what knowledge, and how, becomes part of the curriculum.

Consequently, if we want to give young men and women a more balanced education than they get at the moment, we need to try alternative approaches. Presenting curriculum subjects as ungendered, when the underlying assumptions of the society in which we live suggest that they are not, is hardly likely to have an effect on children and adolescents at points in their lives in which gender is particularly salient (Lloyd and Duveen, 1992; Head, 1997). We need instead to say to young people that despite their gendered distaste for certain subjects, we think that it is important that they study them. However we feel about the origins of the dominance of masculine-labelled, reason-based subjects, it remains the case that studying these successfully has a strong impact on future life chances, so if girls are currently giving them up at sixteen, then maybe we need to lengthen the period for which they are compulsory. This might not be popular, particularly with young women, but the evidence is that, when forced to take mathematics and sciences, girls are largely successful, so it could be a particularly powerful intervention. Alternatively, while not compelling girls to study these subjects, we might want at least to pursue the route taken (to some extent by default) in the United States, of making them an important aspect of university entrance. While this would not ensure that all girls studied mathematics and sciences for longer, it would encourage those with academic ambitions to do so. While this might be seen as a surrender to reason, the power of reason and reason-based knowledge in adult life is such that it remains, for the moment at least, a necessary element of the wider feminist project of reducing social inequality. At the same time, we need to work with girls and young women to help them to acknowledge and enjoy the power of the knowledge that comes with success in reason-based subjects.

We also might want to examine which aspects of the high-status curriculum are emphasized by schools. Jones and Kirk (1990), while finding differences in the aspects of school physics preferred by boys and girls, discovered that neither had any interest in ' "school physics" type activities' (p. 312), particularly when divorced from human applications of these ideas. This suggests that many school students are unimpressed by the purely rational and abstract, whatever its currency in the adult world. Attempts to raise the status of practical subjects have, however, in the United Kingdom at least, largely failed, with the inclusion of D&T as part of the core curriculum (DES/Welsh Office, 1990) being a particularly clear example (Paechter, 1993, 2000).

In addressing these issues we need to be clear that legislation alone is not enough to bring about change. For example, while Title IX in the

United States has been of enormous importance in changing patterns of sporting provision for boys and girls, this has not meant that participation has become equal, particularly in the teenage years. Curriculum is negotiated through gendered power/knowledge relations at every level, and policy does not become practice in any straightforward manner.

Finally, we might want to continue to work with students to encourage them to challenge stereotyping around school subjects. Although there was a considerable amount of work done in this area in the 1980s and in the early 1990s (Kenway *et al.*, 1998), in recent years this has been eclipsed by concerns regarding boys', and particularly working-class boys', comparatively poor achievement during compulsory education. Moves to deal with this, especially the introduction, in England and Wales, of vocational education as an option before age sixteen, are likely to exacerbate gender divisions within the curriculum (Equal Opportunities Commission, 1999), unless considerable work is done with students to help them to think about non-traditional options and support them in taking them. This will require thorough education of counselling and guidance staff, so that they do not, wittingly or unwittingly, steer students into particular, gendered options (National Women's Law Center, 2002). We also need to raise awareness of the long-term effects of selective takeup of a gendered curriculum: those subjects preferred by girls, particularly in the vocational arena, tend to lead to occupations with lower opportunities for development and promotion and lower lifetime earnings than those preferred by boys (Equal Opportunities Commission, 2001; National Women's Law Center, 2002). Long-term social equity therefore depends on us struggling with the gendered power/knowledge relations that underpin the school curriculum.

Power, gender, and curriculum are, I have argued, inevitably, and at all levels, interconnected. We need to be fully aware of this when we discuss the curriculum. Curriculum form, content, inclusion and exclusion are all saturated with gendered power/knowledge relations that we ignore at our peril. Curriculum Studies as a discipline needs to take this fully on board if we are to have a clear picture of the implications of curriculum change, and if we are to work towards providing a better, more equal education for both boys and girls.

6 Curriculum as culture

Entitlement, bias and the Bourdieusean arbitrary

Alex Moore

Developing some of the ideas introduced by Hartley in relation to the 'hidden' rationales and values of school curricula, by Young in relation to issues of knowledge and of curriculum selections of knowledge, and by Paechter concerning the existence and nature of power relations embedded in the school curriculum and the curriculum experience, this chapter introduces the value and relevance of Cultural Studies in curriculum analysis. It is argued that, though school curricula are often presented and understood in terms of selections from the knowledge and culture of a nation, what is typically selected continues to draw almost exclusively on the cultural skills and preferences of already privileged social groups. With reference to the ways in which the school curriculum 'responds' to the school-work of many students, it is suggested that, far from adopting an inclusive, pluralistic turn, the school curriculum – at least in England and Wales – may be seen as continuing to act as a culturally conservative force that encourages and promotes success for some at the cost of failure for others. Claims that the curriculum has become more 'multicultural' are interrogated with reference to Bourdieu's notion of curriculum arbitrariness.

Introduction: English teaching and assessment in the 1980s

In the often-demonized 1980s, when I was Head of English at a multi-ethnic, inner-London secondary school, it was not uncommon for schools to be allowed to design, subject to an examining board's approval, examination papers in some subject areas leading to nationally recognized qualifications at 16 plus. Such examinations – and, where relevant, their marking by the schoolteachers who had designed them – were, of course, subject to careful monitoring and standardization processes in order to ensure equity and fairness; however, they offered English teachers genuine opportunities to put into practice locally some of the lessons about learning, teaching and cultural bias in the curriculum that had begun to alter the curricular and pedagogic assumptions of many schools and teachers since the late 1970s.

For English Departments such as mine, whose teachers were committed both to a comprehensive education for all and to the recognition and celebration of student diversity within that education, these locally designed syllabuses achieved two things:

- First, they provided modes of public assessment that, while conforming to national expectations and standards of comprehension and performance, enabled school departments to take full and appropriate account of the specific interests, backgrounds and strengths of their particular students in designing curricula for students at 14 plus.
- Second, they enabled and supported the school-based development of lower-school curricula that gave English departments further opportunities to develop those interests, backgrounds and strengths alongside the more general skills and competences that their students would need (e.g. the development of expertise in standard English) in order to be able to make the most of their lives both at school and in adulthood.

Pluralism and inclusion: Errol's literature exam

In collaboration with my department and our partner examining board, I had helped develop two examinations for our 16-year-old students, one for GCSE Ordinary level English Language and one for GCSE Ordinary level English Literature. The Literature examination was in two parts. Fifty per cent was covered by coursework, whose central component was an extended essay on a negotiated subject of each student's choice. This was marked by the teachers and moderated by the Board. The other 50 per cent comprised an examination on (at the Board's insistence) one Shakespeare play. This was marked exclusively by the Board's own examiners and students had to score at least 40 per cent on this paper to pass the examination overall even if they scored very highly on the coursework component.

In my own Literature class, which, like all others, was both mixed-ability and open to all students, there was a young man, Errol, who had started off at school nearly five years earlier in what was then called the remedial class for children deemed to be academically 'backward'. This student had not been born in England but in the Caribbean, and tended not only to speak in a Caribbean dialect of English but also to include strong traces of that dialect in his written work. He was one of many students at the school for whom the mode of public examining for English at 16 plus was particularly helpful. This was a bright, interested young man with a great deal of imagination and plenty of critical ideas who, however, in most school subjects had clearly struggled to achieve to his potential. Our view as his English teachers was that this apparent failure on his part had been brought about at least partly by the fact that he was continually being assessed not just through but in his use of standard English, rather than in his cognitive-affective knowledge and skills: that is to say, one perceived weakness (a linguistic one) was not allowing his very many strengths (both cognitive and expressive) to be recognized and validated within the system.

I had negotiated with this particular student that his extended piece of writing would be on the life and work of one of his favourite Caribbean poets. When he first showed me a draft of the work, it was clear that, far from seeking to 'standardize' his language, as I had half expected him to do, he had, on the contrary, exaggerated its non-standardness on (so he told me) the grounds that he felt that this was an appropriate language to use in writing about a poet whose work was written in the same dialect. Fearing the worst, I felt that I should run this proposal past the examining board. To my surprise, they were not only accommodating in their response to the idea but expressed pleasure at the student's approach, telling us that this was just the sort of creative response to the coursework element of the examination that they had been hoping for. There might be issues in relation to marking the work, they said – that is to say, in making sure that the examiner was able to understand what the student was saying – but they felt that this was something they would simply have to deal with.

In the event, Errol passed his examination comfortably, obtaining the second-highest pass grade at the time, a grade B. I had been curious, however, as to how the coursework assignment had been assessed, and equally, if not more so, in relation to the marking of his set Shakespeare paper (*Julius Caesar*), on which I had feared he might fall down even though the Board's regulations only allowed examiners to dock a maximum of two marks out of a hundred for what they saw as technical inaccuracies.

We used to attend the Board's headquarters in those days for annual meetings between their nominated examiners and all the heads of English of schools operating this particular scheme. Because of this, I was able to discuss my student's work with one of the Board's examiners, who kindly shared with me the examiners' reports both on his coursework and on his unseen paper. To paraphrase these reports, I learned that, in respect of the coursework, expert advice had been sought and a special examiner had been brought in to evaluate the assignment. This had not been possible with the Shakespeare paper; however all examiners had been reminded about the 2 per cent rule for perceived technical inaccuracies, including deviations from standard English written expression. This second examiner's report was paraphrased for me by the examiner to whom I was speaking as follows:

> The examiner encountered some difficulty in reading these essays, since they had been written in a particular dialect of English with which she was not familiar. There was evidence, however, of the candidate's having a sound knowledge of the text and of using quotation and paraphrase to support points. Each essay was also characterized by an all-too-rare willingness on the candidate's part to be critical of those aspects of the play with which he was less than happy. He offered a particularly memorable critique, for example, of Shakespeare's representation of

ordinary working people, comparing this to some of the prejudices that exist in modern-day society toward certain ethnic minority groups.

Bernstein's codes: from 'collection' to 'integrated'

Errol's experience is not, I hasten to add, offered as typical: in another school, whose English Department had opted for standard 'off the peg' examination syllabuses, for example, I have little doubt that this student's ongoing difficulties with standard English would have resulted in his failing the Literature exam. It is, however, indicative of a certain possibility that existed at that time, itself linked to a more pluralistic approach both to curriculum and to assessment. At this point in curriculum history in the United Kingdom, when schools and education authorities were beginning to recognize and do something about racism in curriculum, pedagogy and assessment (there was a plethora, for example, of professional development 'racism awareness' programmes for teachers), here was a major examining board not only encouraging a student to base half his literature work around the study of a little known (outside the Caribbean) poet writing in a non-standard dialect of English, but clearly prioritizing what the student had to say about this and more 'canonical' work – that is, his own creative, critical response to the works – above his grasp of a particular, standardized form in which to say it.

I can remember calling to mind at the time Basil Bernstein's conceptualization of curriculum and pedagogy, made ten years earlier, in terms of two different and oppositional 'codes' (Bernstein, 1971a,b). The first of these codes, the 'collection code', described an approach to and style of curriculum and pedagogy that separated learning and teaching into distinct subjects areas (what Bernstein referred to as 'strong classification') and suggested grouping pupils according to notions of ability, giving very limited choice to pupils over lesson content, relying on single-mode (typically by written, end-of-course/year examination) assessment, and traditional, front-of-class teaching (pedagogies described by Bernstein in the expression 'strong framing'). The second of Bernstein's proposed codes, the 'integrated code', promoted cross-curricular organization ('weak classification'), enquiry-based learning, mixed ability grouping, a wider choice for pupils, multiple mode assessment (including coursework/teacher assessment) and a more interpersonal mode of teacher control of pupils (in Bernstein's terminology, 'weak framing').

In the case of Errol, we appeared to have a situation of weak framing (enquiry-based learning, mixed ability grouping, a wider choice for pupils, multiple mode assessment) within a prevailing curriculum organization of strong classification (in the sense of identifying and organizing learning into separate subjects, and in the insistence of including a Shakespeare play for close study) but also – across the school, where ability grouping and front-of-class teaching still predominated – within a prevailing pedagogic model of strong framing. In other words, we were seeing the insertion, within one subject area, of aspects of an 'integrated code' into a still-dominant but apparently threatened 'collection code'. It seemed for many English teachers at the time (and not just English teachers) that an important shift had begun which, sooner rather than later, would take us out of the traditional collection code model of operating altogether into the (for us) infinitely more appealing integrated model.

Pluralism and exclusion: the National Curriculum

How wrong we were! It is probably something of an understatement to say that the pluralistic stance adopted by the examining board in Errol's case would, post the introduction of the first National Curriculum for England and Wales, be neither expected nor, I suspect, 'allowed' in this country. This is not to say that public examinations or the National Curriculum have entirely abandoned the embracing of pluralism, much of the rhetoric of which remains in the official documentation. It has become a very watered-down version, however, that is rather stronger in words than in practice, and that is characterized, as it becomes absorbed into dominant discourses of 'standards' and 'basics', by what Ken Jones (1992: 17–18) has called a 'tactic of half-recognition': that is to say, an approach in which 'within the shell of the new discourse ... restorationist meanings are accommodated' (ibid.).

A simple illustration of what is meant by this, and of what it might entail in terms of English Literature teaching, is provided by the original National Curriculum English Order of 1995 (see also Moore, 1998). Having first listed a number of 'great' works and authors deemed worthy of the name Literature, this document offered the following advice to teachers:

> Pupils should be encouraged to appreciate the distinctive qualities of [identified 'major', 'high quality'] works through activities that empha-sise the interest and pleasure of reading them.
> [. . .]
> Pupils should read texts from other cultures and traditions that repre-sent their distinctive voices and forms and offer varied perspectives and subject matter.
>
> (DFE, 1995: 20)

On the face of it, this curriculum directive suggests what to many might seem an appropriate level of cultural inclusion: the English Order states, for example, not that children 'might' but that they 'should' read 'texts from other cultures' in addition to those of the traditional English canon. On closer consideration, however, difficulties reveal themselves, as the produc-tion of 'otherness' marks its presence. In relation to appropriate Literature study, for example, some works are immediately othered through their being referred to as works from 'other cultures' (inevitably prompting the question, 'Other than what?'). These works are further marginalized through being presented as literature to be aware of – to have a passing knowledge of – rather than as items worthy of serious study or indeed capable of offering real enjoyment. The wording of the Order is highly significant here. In relation to the 'major' works of 'high literary quality', pupils are to be encouraged to 'appreciate' their 'distinctive qualities' through 'activities that emphasize the interest and pleasure in reading them'. In relation to the 'other' texts, 'read' replaces 'appreciate'; 'distinctive voices' replaces 'distinctive qualities'; no activities are referred to; and there is no mention of either interest or pleasure. The clear message is that while some texts have intrinsic qualities (for which, read 'quality') that are, as it were, to be 'discovered' and discussed by the student, others merely possess curiosity value. 'Quality' itself, meanwhile, is presented in the Order not as a judgement or an opinion, but as an indisputable, culture-free fact of life.

It would be nice to be able to say that since the Order of 1995 – which may in part be seen as a reaction against what some saw as the 'excesses' of the 1980s – the curricular pendulum had swung back towards pluralism, particularly in light of the revised National Curriculum's repeated emphasis on 'inclusion' (see, for example, DEE/QCA, 1999; DfES, 2000). Unfortunately, however, the wording of the English order in relation to Literature study has not changed significantly in the intervening period. In the current KS3 National Curriculum requirements (DEE/QCA, 1999), for example, not only is English Literature still identified as a separate subject from English, but there is also the identification of, effectively, two subjects within that subject, through an insistence that students must study works (1) from what the Curriculum requirement calls the 'English Literary Heritage' and (2) 'Texts from Different Cultures and Traditions'. The word 'different' may have crept in to replace 'other', but an essentialist view of Literature still prevails whereby some is identified as more intrinsically worthwhile than some other: a canon of texts that are both 'appealing' and 'important' versus 'different' texts whose study is primarily of interest value. This Anglo-centric othering of 'different' literature, meanwhile, is further promoted through the examples given of 'important' and 'significant' texts and by the suggested readings under 'literary heritage' and 'different cultures and traditions'. Examples of important texts – curiously, perhaps, for a multicultural and largely secular society – are given as the Greek Myths, the Arthurian Legends and the Authorized Version of the Bible. Under 'major' playwrights, poets and writers from the English Literary Heritage, a lengthy list of Anglo-Saxon authors is given, while the much shorter recommended list under 'examples of drama, fiction and poetry by major writers from different cultures and traditions' includes, among the twenty two suggestions over a third – Arthur Miller, Tennessee Williams, Ernest Hemingway, Doris Lessing, John Steinbeck, Emily Dickinson, Robert Frost, Robert Lowell – who might seem equally at home in the longer 'canonical' list.

This is, I would suggest, a worrying trend, comprising an increasing cultural 'Puritanism' (the re-assertion of a dominant white, middle-class canon) that deliberately marginalizes just about all and any literature written in non-standard dialects and genres of English including a great deal of important poetry, drama and fiction, and that finds its parallel in the introduction of a 'National Literacy Strategy' that, in its espoused aim of developing standard English skills, does little or nothing about recognizing, valuing and promoting non-standard forms and skills. In his book *Cultural Imperialism* (1991) John Tomlinson, with a nod to Herbert Schiller, writes: ' "Cultural imperialism" is a critical discourse which operates by representing the cultures whose autonomy it defends in its own (dominant) Western cultural terms' (1991: 2).

Such imperialism, I would suggest, is not only present in the naturalized selection of 'great', 'important', 'significant' writers in the English 'canon' (and indeed in the identification of a canon at all) but in the way in which – and the agency through which – 'major writers' from 'different' cultures and traditions are selected. In this connection, it is important to note that each of the terms 'major', 'cultures' and 'traditions' is itself defined within an Anglo-Saxon canonical discourse by people in positions of authority, and that anything not included in the lists of suggested readings is clearly intended to be seen as falling outside those definitions.

Inclusivity and selection: difficulties with the common curriculum

This last point raises several important and abiding issues for teachers, for policy makers and for curriculum theorists regarding (1) tensions between curricular inclusivity and selection; (2) conceptualizations and understandings of knowledge (epistemological issues); (3) cultural inclusion and cultural reproduction.

It may seem ironic that the pluralist practices that were possible in the pre-National Curriculum 1980s, when it was often argued, not without some justification, that the curriculum offer for any given student depended too heavily on the school they happened (often for purely geographical reasons) to attend, have been so greatly reduced following the introduction of a National 'Curriculum for all' aimed in no small part at overcoming such inequalities. Certainly, one of the central rationales for the development of a national curricula – be they in the United Kingdom or elsewhere – concerns fairness and equity. One of the earliest and strongest voices for the development of such a curriculum in England and Wales, Denis Lawton, argued very persuasively (Lawton, 1968, 1975) that the development of comprehensive schools to which all children, regardless of their background and achievements to date, would go for their secondary education, made little sense if they continued to follow separate curricula within those schools. Indeed, a fundamental underpinning of his argument for the comprehensivization of schools was his argument for a comprehensivization of the school curriculum: an entitlement, common, or core curriculum for all students. This curriculum, Lawton argued (interestingly and importantly in light of what I have already said), should be based on the identification of a 'common culture' (Lawton, 1975: 114).

The belief in a 'sufficient' common culture (sufficient, that is, to provide the basis of a core – though not, we are intended to think, a completely common – curriculum) which we find again in the more recent Crick Report on Education for Citizenship and Democracy (QCA, 1998), is, I believe, a problematic one for all its good intentions. It is, furthermore, as I shall argue below, one that becomes increasingly problematic the more detailed and prescriptive the common curriculum becomes and indeed the more culturally heterogeneous a society becomes. It also raises important questions as to how much knowledge – and what kind(s) of knowledge – can ever really be 'culture free' or indeed, as Lawton suggested, 'classless' (Lawton, 1975: 51; see also Cairns, Gardner and Lawton, 2000). We might, I suppose, agree that (for example) five fours are twenty, or that the Battle of Hastings took place in 1066. Once knowledge begins to move beyond such basics, however, it inevitably becomes more interpretive as well as more selective. Students may be able to cite, in examination, the causes of the First World War – but what they are actually citing might be what Apple (1993) calls 'legitimate' causes rather than 'unlegitimated' ones. Similarly, students might become very adept at explaining what it is that makes Shakespeare's plays 'great' without ever really believing that they are great or truly benefiting from the plays themselves (a kind of knowledge akin to the 'ritualistic' knowledge described by Edwards and Mercer (1987) and to the generic skills described by Kress (1982) whereby the tokenistic 'display' of knowledge takes on greater importance than its internalization or retention). In other words, what counts as 'knowledge' on these occasions is inextricably interwoven with what most of us would recognize as opinion – although the interweaving may remain disguised as the curriculum is presented to and experienced by the student.

An additional difficulty arises in the selections of curriculum items in the first place. Just as the ways in which knowledge is presented cannot be culture free, neither can the selections of knowledge that find their way on to the curriculum. Sticking with History, it is not unreasonable for us to ask why we should be studying the Battle of Hastings in the first place. Is this a fundamentalist, self-validating choice based on an unelaborated argument in favour of the need to know about our national history simply because it is our national history? Or are there any enduring benefits to accrue from the study of this particular curriculum item that could not be as readily obtained from the study of some other? I am often asked in relation to my objections to the standard inclusion of Shakespeare in the English Literature curriculum if I think that it would be equally justifiable for students to study a children's comic like the *Beano* – presumably by way of obtaining an admission that for all my objections, some works of literature really are intrinsically superior to and therefore more worthy of curricular inclusion than others. My response to this is that, depending on the manner of teaching and the curriculum objectives, huge numbers of young students might, indeed, gain more plea-sure, more instruction and more enduring knowledge and understanding from studying contemporary comic books than from studying Shakespeare's plays, regardless of what I might think of the relative merits of the two sets of work: in other words, our view of what should be included in the curriculum might need to begin with what we hope students will learn and how best they might learn it than from the imposition of a curriculum item on the grounds that we ourselves may have drawn some lasting benefit from it – a selective act born not so much of wisdom as an inability to decentre.

Culture and knowledge

As I have argued elsewhere (Moore, 2005) Lawton was absolutely right to remind us that knowledge is not – and should not be – the preserve of the middle class: that a classless system of schooling needs to be accompanied by, in a sense, a classless curriculum. The problem arises, however, when the science, history, art, philosophy, moral education and so forth that finds its way on to the common curriculum is only – or practically only – the science, history, art, philosophy and morality of the dominant social classes: a problem that is exacerbated when attempts are made to squeeze rather too much curriculum into rather too narrow a timetable. Unfortunately, this is exactly what has happened with the curriculum for English Literature and Language in England. This curriculum has not only resided over a steady erosion of 'non-dominant', 'non-standard' forms of expression but, in so doing, has produced a far less pluralistic and indeed a far more sterile curriculum for all our young people, whatever their home backgrounds.

All of this suggests a particular set of questions which never quite goes away from curriculum theorizing but which is more likely to be overlooked, ignored or denied by governments locked into more pragmatic orientations to curriculum means and ends (in this regard, see Young's chapter). That is to say:

> If we feel that a core or common curriculum is the only way of ensuring equity and social justice for our young people, how detailed should – or indeed can – that common curriculum be? Should it, for instance, account for the *entirety* of the curriculum or for only a part of it? Should it be *primarily* knowledge-based or skills based? And in what ways might a higher degree of specificity work for or against the interests of a curriculum that is both fair *and* pluralist (i.e. that is genuinely 'socially just')?

What I am suggesting – and of course I am by no means the first or only commentator to do so – is that there are at least two unresolved crises at the heart of the so-called entitlement curriculum. First is the question of who decides what the entitlement should be – and what desires those choosers bring to their choices. (The choices are not made, for example, through what we recognize as normal democratic processes.) Second, the notion of entitlement assumes a certain commonality of desires, needs, requirements that is not necessarily reflected in society. Some desires in this entitlement, then, will be repressed or marginalized, while others will be celebrated and prioritized. Indeed, it is not difficult to see how entitlement for one student may be perceived and experienced as imposition by another.

In addressing these questions and issues, it seems very important that we think carefully about what we mean by culture and what we mean by knowledge – and the extent to which the two can be treated as separate entities. There is, I think, something of an abiding confusion here which may well encourage us to see all knowledge as culturally produced and embedded, but which may differentiate between subjects and topics in terms of the relative strengths of their claims (however spurious in reality) to some kind of objective truth. With reference to what I have already said about knowledge's increasing incapacity to be class and culture free the more complex it gets, this becomes a particular problem when we look at a subject like Mother Tongue (in the case of England, the subject we call English). Here, it is not only the curriculum selection that is problematic (in the English curriculum relating to Literature, for example, a preponderance of white, dead, male authors writing in 'standard' English) but the fact that, in their own assessed writing, young people are required specifically to replicate certain expressive genres (Kress, 1982; Britzman, 1989) and are judged on their capacity to do so, rather, often, than what they actually have to say. What (English teachers and their students might, not unreasonably, ask) is the Shakespeare play as a curriculum 'object'? Is it knowledge that we are acquiring through its study? Is it cultural experience? Or can it be both? And what is a 'good' short story? Is this, likewise, a question of knowledge embedded in some kind of eternal, unquestionable criteria, or is it more about the acquisition and display of certain cultural norms?

The possibility that we may need to identify and to understand different kinds of knowledge differently is not a new one. The relation of these different forms to culture, however, continues to demand a great deal of thought. It may appear to make sense and be socially just that we all have access to the same knowledge if that knowledge really is of any value ('intrinsic' or contrived) – any value, that is, that can be distilled from its social and cultural contexts, questionable though such a possibility is. But if, as I am suggesting, there is culture-embedded knowledge (of science, maths, technology, and so forth) and knowledge 'of or in' culture (for example, Art, literature and music), it may well be the case that different, if related, purposes are served in the selection processes for either domain. I am thinking, for example (although Hartley's argument, in Chapter 4, renders the discussion rather more complicated), of the possibility, given obvious overlaps and exceptions, that selections in relation to subjects such as maths, science and technology may be more directly referenced to the requirements of the workplace, while selections regarding literature, music and art may have (or traditionally have had) rather more to do with reproducing dominant cultures and thereby producing a docile and compliant workforce (Apple, 1979). If we consider the various attempts to identify the different underpinning values inherent in school curricula (Walsh, 1993; Moore, 2000; Chitty, 2002), the curriculum selection of Shakespeare's plays, for example, is clearly not made to satisfy a sudden demand for Shakespearian actors or critics; nor, bearing in mind the negative responses to 'the Bard' of the vast majority of young people, is the argument very convincing that it is there to delight them or to improve the quality of their lives.

'Getting away with it': meconnaissance and the Bourdieusean arbitrary

I referred in the Introduction to this book to the fact that in one of our leading retailers of books about education works on Curriculum Studies, which seek to critique and offer better understandings of the origins, the role and the nature of school curricula, had become marginalized in favour of a plethora of practical guides for teachers and practice workbooks for students and their parents. That is to say, major discussions about the nature and form of the school curriculum appear to have become sidelined, in England at least, to the margins by concerns about implementing an implicitly unquestioned and 'naturalized' National Curriculum.

This is an important point, because at the moment both politicians and dominant sociocultural groups in British society (and arguably very many other societies) are continuing to get away with things that work against the best interests of the intended beneficiaries of the common curriculum, the 'curriculum for all': that is to say, those students who were most discriminated against in pre-comprehensive, pre-National curriculum days. What politicians are getting away with is the avoidance of debating key issues in education and curriculum in the same way that they are being addressed in some other countries. They are doing this by cramming the curriculum with knowledge content and then focusing the debate on issues of how best to 'deliver' that content. What the bearers and perpetuators of dominant ideologies are getting away with is the selling of a curriculum as intrinsically 'right' and 'neutral' that continues, in fact, to be biased and marginalizing. This is achieved through the naturalization of what Bourdieu calls an 'arbitrary' curriculum and its acceptance and perpetuation by those whose interests it works against via processes of misrecognition or 'meconnaissance'. For all the talk of change, and the recent introduction of more and more 'specialist schools' in the United Kingdom, the truth is that, as

John White reminds us elsewhere in this book, the curriculum followed by today's young people in England and Wales – in terms of both shape and overall subject content, anyway – is very little different from that followed by young people 100 years ago, and (I would add) no more adept or intentioned in overcoming cultural bias.

Bourdieu's conceptualization of curriculum and culture (e.g. Bourdieu and Passeron, 1977) is worth dwelling on here – indeed worth dwelling on by students of curriculum generally – since, for all the accusations that it gives insufficient weight to human agency in its focus on social structures, it still provides one of the most helpful frameworks for understanding and critiquing not only curriculum selections but their general and often surprising acceptance. Of particular interest for advocates of Bourdieu's analysis is the issue of the assessment criteria against which school students are deemed to be 'good' or 'bad', 'able' or 'less able' intellectually and academically. As with the curriculum, these criteria are generally presented (if not always experienced) as fair, in that they are universally applied and in that they claim to give everyone an equal chance to show their worth against the same measures of achievement. If we accept this 'fairness', then we may draw the conclusion that when working-class children (for example) do less well than middle-class children, it is either because they are less intelligent, or because their schools and their teachers have somehow failed them: perhaps, indeed, that it is their schools and teachers who are prejudiced and unjust, rather than the curriculum, the criteria or the education system in general.

In reality, of course, the assessment criteria, like the curricular items they promote and underpin, are, to use Bourdieu's term, 'arbitrary'. This does not imply that they are 'chance' or haphazard or provisional: far from it. When Bourdieu talks of the 'arbitrary' selections of curriculum knowledge and assessment criteria, that arbitrariness lies in the fact that the selections are not universal, 'natural' or 'God-given' (as they are typically presented), but that they are culturally, historically and socially produced. As Ross (2000: 10) reminds us:

> a national curriculum requires someone, somehow, to rule that certain cultural artefacts (selected, by very definition, from particular cultures) should be elevated to be passed on to all children, and that other cultural manifestations be excluded from formal education, even though they will probably be the principal cultural determinants of many children in the system.
>
> (See also Apple, 1993, 1997;
> Geyer, 1993; Goldberg, 1994)

Related to this notion of arbitrariness – very importantly if we are to take account of human agency as well as of social structures – is the concept of misrecognition or 'meconnaissance'. Meconnaissance refers to a certain self-deception on the part of the learner experiencing, for example, the curriculum encounter, that goes hand in hand with and reinforces the rather more deliberate deceptions of those by whom and on whose behalf the curriculum itself is constructed. According to this part of Bourdieu's theory, the dominated individual's lack of choice and opportunity – caused by the conditions that prevail in the very real social circumstances, infused with power relations, into which that individual is born and lives – is either not seen at all by the individual or else is misrecognized in terms of their own deficiency. That is to say 'power relations are perceived not for what they are but in a form that renders them legitimate in the eyes of the beholder' – (Bourdieu and Passeron, 1977: xiii) the beholder here being both the curriculum designer/imposer and the curriculum consumer.

This notion of meconnaissance (see also Bourdieu's conceptualizations of habitus and field (1971, 1977)) provides a part answer to the question as to why more of us do not question more often than we do the biased systems within which we operate and which clearly work against many of our best interests. Bourdieu's suggestion seems to be that this is partly because the social fields in which we operate and gain our experience of social life are so tightly structured and controlled that resistance is at best very piecemeal. Equally importantly, however, is the suggestion that the dominated, excluded, marginalized members of society do not necessarily '*know*' that they are actively dominated, excluded or marginalized in the particular, often carefully disguised or hidden ways that they are – or, if they do recognize it, that they may themselves be inclined to impute social inequalities and their own underachievement to the natural order of things.

If we focus our attention on the school setting, this particular configuration suggests that marginalized students from working-class or ethnic-minority backgrounds do not necessarily view (to take one example) the selection of literary texts on an English Literature syllabus as being based on cultural preference (the cultural preference, that is, of the English middle class), but rather on matters of intrinsic quality. It would not be surprising if they then, as a corollary, view 'other' literary texts, favoured by and within their own 'home cultures', as inferior and not worthy of wider study. To return to the two examples elaborated earlier of Errol and the National Curriculum Order for English, while Errol's choice of literature for academic study was validated by a wider curricular and assessment system which, for all its lack of consistency across schools enabled, in this particular case, a non-standard work to achieve the same status as – say – a Shakespeare play, the subsequent 'inclusive' National Curriculum, in the very act of providing greater levels of consistency of curriculum offer across State schools, achieves the very reverse through over-detailing what that inclusive curriculum should comprise. In the process, it reinforces the ex-clusive view that there is culture.

7 New directions in citizenship education

Re-conceptualizing the curriculum in the context of globalization

Audrey Osler

In this chapter, Audrey Osler argues the need for a curriculum that does not prioritize the preservation and reproduction of dominant cultural forms and preferences but that seeks to incorporate interculturalist perspectives into a curriculum aimed at preparing diverse but cohabiting students for life in a diverse but increasingly connected (and rapidly evolving) world: that is to say, for 'cosmopolitan citizenship'. The curriculum implied in her analysis is not, therefore, a retrospective one, nor one aimed primarily at promoting social stability through social stagnation or through over-reliance of disciplinary knowledge. Rather, it is future-oriented, with a central goal of promoting responsible, critical citizenship that will enable the evolution of societies and encourage the development of and respect for universal human rights. At the heart of such curriculum work is the need for young people to address and discuss matters of culture in ways in which different cultural perspectives can be freely and sensibly considered without fear of rancour: not to accept that any one culture is wholly good or wholly bad, but that there are many different cultures to be respected, understood and indeed questioned in relation to those elements that we may personally find unacceptable. Not surprisingly, skills and attitudes – centrally, social, collaborative skills and pluralistic attitudes – are at the heart of this curriculum endeavour, alongside socially relevant knowledge. As Osler indicates, the concept of community is itself expanding as the social world shrinks to include, inter alia, virtual communities. Curriculum, Osler indicates in her closing paragraph, can contribute to social stability – but only through encouraging young people to accept and adopt dynamism and difference, and specifically to embrace and to work for change. Among other things, Osler's chapter raises interesting questions as to what we feel constitutes 'relevant knowledge' and the grounds on which we might justify the inclusion of any item or area of knowledge in the curriculum.

Introduction

Across the globe, at both national and international levels, there is a renewed interest in education for democratic citizenship (EDC). In established democracies, such as those of Western Europe and North America, in newly established democratic states, such as those of Eastern and Central Europe and Latin America and, indeed, in countries taking steps towards democracy, there is a recognition that democracy is essentially fragile and that it depends on the active engagement of citizens, not just in voting, but in developing and participating in sustainable and cohesive communities. Programmes of citizenship education and awareness-raising are promoted by policy makers as a means of strengthening or revitalizing citizen engagement.

In this chapter, I explore the reasoning behind this renewed emphasis on citizenship education, as articulated by policy-makers and scholars, examining it in the context of globalization. I argue that the considerable growth of interest in citizenship education as a feature of the school curriculum needs to be understood in terms of the impact of globalization on local and national communities. Drawing on theoretical work and empirical research undertaken with colleagues (Osler and Vincent, 2002; Osler and Starkey, 2003, 2005a), I argue for a re-conceptualization of EDC, to promote new forms of cosmopolitan citizenship for the twenty-first century.

The chapter begins by reflecting on the need for the school curriculum to respond to the processes of globalization. I examine recent debates about the purposes of citizenship education and the ways in which these debates are themselves a response to the processes of globalization and related socio-economic and political change. In the second part of the chapter I discuss the concept of cosmopolitan citizenship, presenting on the one hand some theoretical debates related to cosmopolitan democracy, and on the other, research into youth identities and young people's experiences and understandings of community, and the implications for citizenship education. Drawing on this research, I argue that a new form of education for cosmopolitan citizenship is required which acknowledges the impact of globalization on local and national communities as well as the global community; addresses human rights, democracy and development; and equips young people to make a difference at all levels from the local to the global.

A global vision and intercultural evaluation

An international and interdisciplinary seminar held at Harvard University in 2002 set out to consider the challenges which schooling will need to address if it is to respond to the needs of young people living in the globalized world of the twenty-first century. The seminar noted that 'the lives and experiences of youth growing up today will be linked to economic realities, social processes, technological and media innovations, and cultural flows that traverse national boundaries with ever greater momentum' (Suárez-Orozco and Qin-Hilliard, 2004: 2).

While our lives are increasingly influenced by global networks and global social, economic and political developments, our everyday experiences as citizens are shaped in local contexts; the communities in which we live, work and learn are those within which we enact our citizenship. It is within these communities that we usually first practise our citizenship and campaign for our rights and/or those of others, learning directly from these citizenship activities. Nevertheless, in acting at the local level we are still drawing on internationally recognized and legitimized rights. All members of the local community, and indeed the school community, are guaranteed human rights, whether or not they hold national citizenship. So, for example, within the United Kingdom, everyone is covered by the European Convention on Human Rights (ECHR), which guarantees protection regardless of citizenship status. All are covered by the ECHR whether or not they hold British citizenship or have other legal citizenship rights, such as European citizenship; whether they are citizens of other states, or are asylum-seekers or stateless persons.

A global vision for the school curriculum needs to incorporate an inclusive approach to citizenship education. Not all members of the school community will necessarily have national citizenship, but all are holders of human rights. It is critical that all know about internationally guaranteed rights and the relevance of these rights to living in a community:

> While international legal instruments provide a framework for understanding human rights, and teaching about human rights arguably should have international agreements and covenants as a point of reference (Council of Europe, 1985), it is of course within local contexts that individuals struggle to claim these rights and develop a deeper understanding of what it means to be a citizen.
>
> (Osler, 1994: 73)

Since the local and the global are inexorably linked in our daily lives, the school curriculum needs to make these links explicit. Within increasingly diverse local communities (communities which are also increasingly recognized as diverse) we need some common agreed principles for living together. We also need to develop education systems and approaches to schooling which respond to the changing global context and enable young people to develop skills to participate as citizens within this changing context. Those present at the Harvard seminar recognized that

> These global transformations...will require youth to develop new skills that are far ahead of what most educational systems can now deliver. New and broader global visions are needed to prepare children and youth to be informed, engaged, and critical citizens in the new millennium.
>
> (Suárez-Orozco and Qin-Hilliard, 2004: 2–3)

As Suárez-Orozco and Qin-Hilliard (2004) acknowledge, young people growing up in communities characterized by diversity are more likely than any previous generation to require skills which enable them to live and work alongside other people from different national, linguistic, religious and racial backgrounds. These skills are not automatically acquired in diverse communities. Schools, regardless of the degree of diversity within their populations, do not necessarily have a curriculum which supports the development of these skills. Rather, schools in this new global context need to adapt their curricula to support the development of multiple perspectives: 'When distinct cultural models and social practices are deployed to address a common set of problems, youth gain the cognitive and metacognitive advantages inherent in examining and working on a problem from many angles' (Suárez-Orozco and Qin-Hilliard, 2004: 5).

To support the process of examining issues from a range of perspectives students need to develop skills of intercultural communication, enabling them to engage in dialogue and understand that belief systems are socially constructed. These skills will support their understanding of the bigger picture, whether the issue under consideration is a local or an international question (Banks *et al.*, 2005). Students who are engaged in intercultural learning need to venture beyond knowledge of other cultures and a simple comparison of other cultures with their own.

It is sometimes asserted that, in a multicultural society, we need to be tolerant, implying that we should accept all aspects of other cultures. Multiculturalism is often characterized as relativist, but recognition of diversity does not necessarily imply a relativist position. Indeed, a relativist position is not sustainable in practice. Whether or not they are encouraged to do so, students will be making judgements about other cultures. It is not helpful to promote uncritical acceptance of other cultures, or indeed of one's own culture. The recognition of multiple perspectives does not imply relativism. As Figueroa (2000: 55) has observed: 'Pluralism does not mean a radical relativism.... One must stand somewhere. It is not possible to stand nowhere. But neither is an attempt to stand everywhere tenable.'

Students need to develop skills of intercultural evaluation (Hall, 2000; Parekh, 2000). Intercultural evaluation implies critical examination of various cultural perspectives, including one's own, against agreed common principles. Human rights provide us with a set of universally agreed principles from which we can begin to engage in this process of intercultural evaluation (Osler, 2005; Osler and Starkey, 2005a). Students who acquire skills of intercultural evaluation will be able to examine critically different cultural perspectives, including their own, and will recognize that all cultures, including their own, have their strong points and weak points. They will learn to recognize that culture itself is not static. The processes of intercultural evaluation require all of us to engage in recognizing both difference and similarity. They also imply recognition and analysis of power. Communities are composed of different individuals, groups and interests.

There may be tensions and conflicts between and within particular groups. The processes of intercultural evaluation involve critical analysis in which we make provisional assessments which are subject to further processes of enquiry. In the processes of intercultural evaluation our assessments, and those of our students, will always be open to revision: 'A provisional affirmation [is] subject to further comparison, a questioning of views, a shifting of focus, a self-correcting and mutually correcting process of enquiry' (Figueroa, 2000: 55).

Education for citizenship: a response to globalization?

From the early 1990s, we have seen a renewed and increasing interest in citizenship education as an aspect of the school curriculum. In each of the justifications for citizenship education examined subsequently, proponents of curriculum change are identifying challenges facing local communities, the national community and/or the global community, which are linked, directly or indirectly, to the processes of globalization or to perceived problems arising from these processes.

Addressing global inequalities

Citizenship education programmes are justified and promoted by international organizations, notably UNESCO, as a means of addressing global injustice and inequalities. For example, UNESCO's International Bureau of Education has emphasized the need of 'education for active and responsible citizenship – the willingness and the capacity to live together and to build peace in a world characterized by inter-state and internal armed conflicts and by the emergence of all forms of violence and war' (IBE, 2004). This perspective has been strengthened since 11 September 2001 because of a growing awareness of the links between poverty, injustice and inequality in the world and terrorist movements. These links strengthen the political will to address poverty and injustice through international co-operation.

Democratization and human rights

Processes of democratization have contributed to the renewed focus on education for citizenship in regions such as Eastern and Central Europe and Latin America. Between 1980 and 2001, 81 countries took significant steps towards democracy, with 33 military regimes replaced by civilian governments. The number of States holding multiparty elections more than doubled over the period. The number of countries ratifying human rights conventions and covenants has risen dramatically since 1990: numbers ratifying the International Covenant on Economic Social and Cultural Rights (ICESCR) and the International Covenant on Civil and Political

Rights (ICCPR) grew from 90 to nearly 150 (UNDP, 2002). These initiatives have taken place alongside parallel ones to increase awareness about democracy and human rights. Projects which promote education for human rights and democratic citizenship in schools and in communities have been given particular emphasis and support by the Council of Europe since the 1980s.

Migration and xenophobia

The increasing international interest in education for citizenship has developed alongside a growing political and media focus on questions of citizenship and rights of residence, as global pressures for migration have grown and the numbers of refugees and asylum seekers rise. Castles and Davidson (2000) assert that international migration and ethnic minorities have always been viewed as problematic by nation-states since they undermine ideologies of cultural homogeneity. We might therefore expect, at a time of increased international migration, for there to be a renewed interest in citizenship education as a means of reasserting a myth of a strong and homogeneous national cultural identity within nation-states which are countries of immigration.

At the European level, official interest in education for European citizenship has paralleled political developments. In the European Union (EU), the Single European Act 1992 led to the relaxation of internal border controls and greater freedom of movement between member-states. Since the early 1990s, with the opening up of internal borders there has been a popular demand for the creation of a Fortress Europe, articulated by former British Prime Minister John Major at the Luxembourg Summit 1991 as 'a strong, tight perimeter fence around Europe'. He argued that: 'We must not be wide open to all comers simply because Paris, Rome and London seem more attractive than Algiers and Bombay' (quoted in Osler, 1994: 43). Although, since September 2001, some internal border controls have been reintroduced, European Community (EC) citizens continue to enjoy freedom of movement and opportunities to study and work in other EC member-states. By contrast, some non-EC nationals resident in Europe (known as third country nationals) have increasingly been viewed as outsiders and have more recently been perceived as a terrorist threat.

Throughout the period since the early 1990s, the European Commission (EC) has funded a number of projects supporting the development of a common European heritage and shared identity (Osler *et al.*, 1996; Osler and Starkey, 1999). Such projects have generally placed considerable emphasis on universal human rights as a feature of this common heritage and some have been explicitly antiracist in focus. Yet, by focusing on a common European heritage and a shared sense of belonging, European citizenship (like national citizenship) can be conceived in an exclusive way. In identifying a common citizenship we also identify those who do not belong and who are not citizens (Osler and Starkey, 2002). Ill-conceived projects on education for European citizenship may also, inadvertently, promote a sense of European superiority in relation to other regions and cultures. An emphasis on intercultural education and intercultural understanding within EC-funded citizenship education projects (Osler and Starkey, 1999) has addressed these tensions to a degree. Nevertheless, some forms of intercultural education which promote tolerance and acceptance of different (mainstream) European identities may promote understanding between European nations while failing to address racism within these nations.

The potential for the far-right to play on xenophobic fears has grown since the terrorist attacks of 2001. Popular xenophobia is promoted and exploited by unscrupulous politicians and media, with both Muslim and Roma communities being particularly vulnerable targets. For example, the accession of new EU member-states in June 2004; discussion of Turkey's possible future entry into the EU; and the 2005 British General Election (when immigration policy was a central campaign issue for both the Conservative party and some far-right parties) were all occasions when both sections of the media and particular politicians seeking short-term political gains fuelled xenophobia. On these occasions the anxiety engendered is not that migrants may target European cities because they are seen as more attractive than Algiers or Mumbai, but that these groups place the very survival of European ways of life under threat. One fear engendered is that terrorists from Algiers and other countries with Muslim populations may target Europe in order to undermine its culture and civilization; another is that Roma from Eastern and Central Europe may seek to undermine the welfare system or health and education services by making fraudulent or unreasonable claims upon them.

In this kind of political climate, where barriers are erected to prevent the full and equal participation of particular communities on the basis of ethnic, cultural or religious characteristics, democracy itself is undermined. The re-assertion of democracy implies an antiracist position. Education for democratic citizenship must necessarily be antiracist, since racism serves to undermine democracy and prevents the full participation of citizens from specific communities (Osler and Starkey, 2002; Banks *et al.*, 2005).

There are concerns, particularly among policy makers at a European level, about the growth of anti-democratic and racist movements which serve to undermine democracy. Citizenship education is seen as a means of strengthening democracy by challenging such anti-democratic movements and attitudes and promoting antiracism. This perspective reflects, in part, a historical consciousness of the legacy of fascism. The Council of Europe is particularly mindful of its responsibilities to prevent, through the democratic means at its disposal, a resurgence of racist ideologies. Working with the European Commission, the Council of Europe convened a number of preparatory meetings before the 2001 UN World Conference Against Racism. The governments of Council of Europe member-states made a formal declaration at the European conference *All Different All Equal: from Principle to Practice* held in Strasbourg in October 2000. Governments committed themselves 'to give particular attention to education and awareness-raising in all sectors of society to promote a climate of tolerance, respect for human rights and cultural diversity, including introducing and strengthening such measures among young people' (Council of Europe, 2000).

Unity and diversity

As discussed earlier, there is increasing diversity and increasing recognition of diversity in industrialized countries across the globe. The development of multicultural nation-states has led policy makers to advocate citizenship education as one means of addressing the tensions which exist between unity (or social cohesion) and diversity. This argument for citizenship education is proposed as a means of addressing these tensions and accommodating and indeed, supporting a diverse range of cultural communities within nation-states characterized by diversity (Taylor, 1994). This argument demands a re-conceptualization of the aims and processes of citizenship education in schools. The new form of citizenship education is concerned less with the old myth of a homogeneous national cultural identity and more with creating a more complex new myth which continues to promote shared values and ideals while at the same time incorporating diversity:

> Increased diversity and increased recognition of diversity require a vigorous re-examination of the ends and means of citizenship education. Multicultural societies are faced with the problem of creating nation-states that recognize and incorporate the diversity of their citizens *and* embrace an overarching set of shared values, ideals, and goals to which all citizens are committed. Only when a nation-state is unified around a set of democratic values such as human rights, justice, and equality can it secure the liberties of cultural, ethnic, language, and religious groups and enable them to experience freedom, justice and peace. Citizens who understand this unity–diversity tension and act accordingly do not materialize from thin air; they are educated for it.
>
> (Banks *et al.*, 2005: 7)

Education ministers from the Organisation for Economic Co-operation and Development (OECD) member countries, meeting to discuss the subject of 'Raising the Quality of Education for All', noted the need not only for skills directly relevant to the workplace, but also skills which would support democracy and social cohesion. They addressed the tensions between diversity and unity (nation-building), and the importance of citizenship education which addressed both these dimensions:

> [T]he issue for education is how to develop not only successful individuals with good workplace skills, but also 'democratic citizenship' – an outcome both linked to, and supportive of, social cohesion. Defining the

qualities we might wish to see in citizens of democratic societies remains a political and context-dependent task. It might include qualities such as fairness, tolerance and a co-operative approach, recognition of the value of social norms, and a civic spirit. While education and informal learning, in isolation, cannot create model citizens, they can, alongside other factors, make a constructive contribution.

Devising a policy response will require clear objectives, keeping a balance between the 'nation-building' role of civic education and its role in valuing and recognising social diversity. At the same time, choice and diversity in educational provision may have to be increased to meet individual needs.

(OECD, 2004 www.oecd.org/edumin2004)

Perceived youth deficit

The emphasis on citizenship education is also closely linked to a tendency, in many countries, to blame youth for the problems and challenges facing society as a whole (Griffin, 1993; Osler and Vincent, 2003). Citizenship education is often seen as a means of addressing a perceived deficit among the young (Osler, 2000), whether this relates to low levels of voting (inevitably interpreted as political apathy), violence or antisocial behaviour. In France, for example, the government has placed a renewed emphasis on citizenship education in response to public concerns about antisocial behaviour and violence in schools (Debarbieux, 1999; Osler and Starkey, 2001, 2005b).

In England, the government-commissioned Crick report to support the introduction of citizenship education into schools in England expressed concerns about 'worryingly low levels of apathy, ignorance and cynicism about public life' which unless addressed, threatened the security of British democracy. One of the proposed solutions, in addition to providing space in the formal school curriculum for citizenship education, was to 'extend radically to young people the best in existing traditions of community involvement and pubic service, and to make them individually confident in finding new forms of involvement and action among themselves' (QCA, 1998: 7–8).

Cosmopolitan democracy and cosmopolitan citizenship

David Held (1995, 1996) is among a number of political theorists who have argued that we need to re-think democracy in the context of our increasingly interdependent and globalized world. He proposes a model of 'cosmopolitan democracy', challenging the notion that the nation-state is the only locus for democracy and that the state alone has the power to guarantee the rights of its citizens. Today, no one, wherever they live in the world, can remain completely isolated within a single nation. As I have already discussed, one of the most striking features of globalization is that local communities become more diverse. If democracy is now conceptualized as cosmopolitan, citizens within the democracy are, by extension, cosmopolitan citizens. Citizens now find themselves belonging to what Held (2001) calls 'overlapping communities of fate': local, regional, national, international and, increasingly, virtual. Although citizens may have very different cultures and beliefs, they have a number of shared interests. Some shared interests may result from living in a community, for example the national community, and may be expressed through processes of democracy within the nation-state. Other shared interests can be found at a local level, because a group of people live in a particular neighbourhood. Not all shared interests arise from a particular location or a community whose members live in proximity; some are supranational and arise, for example, out of membership of a diasporic group or a common faith or political agenda.

These changes provide opportunities for the development of new forms of inclusive democracy and democratic decision-making. Held argues for the building of human rights into the constitution of states and for the democratization of international and global institutions. The introduction of the Human Rights Act 1998, which incorporates the European Convention on Human Rights into UK law, is an example of the ways in which national institutions are voluntarily subjecting themselves to international standards. The setting up of an International Criminal Court shows how new supranational institutions are being created in the image of those operating at the national level. As Habermas (1996: 515) notes: 'Even if we have a long way to go before fully achieving it, the cosmopolitan condition is no longer merely a mirage. State citizenship and world citizenship form a continuum whose contours, at least, are already becoming visible.'

While there is on-going debate about the degree to which these developments constitute a processes of democratization (Miller, 1999; Kymlicka, 2001), the concept of cosmopolitan democracy is nonetheless helpful insofar as it recognizes the existence of transnational communities composed of individuals entitled to and aware of their human rights (Gilroy, 1997). With Hugh Starkey, I have attempted to define what education for cosmopolitan citizenship should look like (Osler and Starkey, 2003, 2005a). Our work seeks to promote a form of education which goes beyond the traditional education for national citizenship, which continues to dominate the agenda of much of current discussion about this area of the curriculum.

We might expect that an educated cosmopolitan citizen will be confident in his or her own identities and will work to achieve peace, human rights and democracy within the local community and at a global level, by:

- developing skills to cope with change and uncertainty
- accepting personal responsibility and recognizing the importance of civic commitment

- working collaboratively to solve problems and achieve a just, peaceful and democratic community
- respecting diversity between people, according to gender, ethnicity and culture
- recognizing that their own worldview is shaped by personal and societal history and by cultural tradition
- recognizing that no individual or group holds the only answer to problems
- understanding that there may be a range of solutions to problems
- respecting and negotiating with others on the basis of equality
- showing solidarity with and compassion for others
- resolving conflict in a nonviolent way
- making informed choices and judgements
- having a vision of a preferred future
- respecting the cultural heritage (both national and global)
- protecting the environment
- adopting methods of production and consumption which lead to sustainable development
- working to achieve harmony between immediate basic needs and long-term interests
- promoting solidarity and equity at national and international levels

(adapted from UNESCO *Integrated Framework of
Action on Education for Peace, Human
Rights and Democracy*, 1995)

Youth identities, globalization and citizenship

Education for citizenship can be conceived as addressing structural and political issues on the one hand, and cultural and personal issues on the other (Osler and Starkey, 1996, 2005a). Another way of expressing this is recognize that citizenship education (of any kind, whether it be education for national citizenship or education for a new cosmopolitan citizenship) needs to build upon and extend young people's existing identities. In order to apply our model of citizenship education, we set out to explore with young people in a cosmopolitan city in England their feelings about community and belonging and how they negotiate their multiple identities and sense of belonging within multi-localities. We were particularly interested in how, in practice, young people felt themselves to be engaged in different communities, whether these were local, linked to religious or political identities, or diasporic communities. Our research with young people was designed to inform citizenship education programmes in schools. We were interested in the degree to which young people are already acting and identifying as cosmopolitan citizens through their activities and interests beyond school (Osler and Starkey, 2003). In discussions and workshop activities our research participants highlighted important sites of learning for citizenship beyond the classroom.

The findings of this research are intended to inform citizenship learning in schools by making links with learning experiences from the home and the community. In this way it should be possible to propose a comprehensive and sustainable programme of education for citizenship that recognizes a cosmopolitan dimension and builds on the citizenship experiences and understanding of the learners. We recognize that 'people learn to be responsible citizens not only in schools, but in the family, neighbourhood, churches and many other groups and forums in civil society' (Kymlicka, 2001: 293).

Young people's identities and community

Young people in our study regularly identified strongly with a multiplicity of places, including Leicester, the city in which they were living. They often had a sense of family history, which linked them to other parts of the world. Many of the young people had strong affective ties with other countries and places. Some, like Abdul, who had recently fled with his family from Malawi, were recent migrants, others, like Asha, had lived all their lives in Britain:

> I am from Malawi and I was born in Leicester in the General Hospital. My father and mother are from Malawi and my grandmother is from India. We left Malawi because almost every day people were getting shot in their houses and one of them was my neighbour – Abdul.

> I was born in Manchester and [lived there] until I was six months old. I moved from Manchester because my mum and dad had a divorce. My mum, dad and granddad are from Africa and my grandma is from India – Asha.

The ability to identify with a range of places, beyond the city in which they lived and beyond the United Kingdom, gives these young people the potential to see themselves and to develop as cosmopolitan citizens.

Self-definitions

The students were invited to write about how they defined themselves. Most considered ethnicity, culture, colour or race. A number also stressed their bilingualism. Many chose to explain their values, sometimes drawing on religious beliefs:

> I believe in God. I am a Hindu, my language is Gujarati and I like my religion. I HATE people who are RACIST! I don't have a problem with people who have a different culture than me, I mix with other religions. I am a very strong believer in God – Nadeera.

> I am Methodist. Don't really believe in God – Ayleen.

> My parents and my grandparents are both from Bangladesh. And we speak Bengali. I have been to Bangladesh and it is a nice place with a beautiful countryside – Rehana.

Concepts of community

In workshops, students were invited to create an exhibition of photographs illustrating themselves in their communities and to write descriptive captions. Their pictures were largely of friends, family, home and their neighbour-hood. Although many lived within a few minutes' walk of the city centre, only a few students chose to take photos there. The captions reveal much about their sense of community and belonging.

Rehana, for instance, views community in terms of what she sees from her house and in her street. This includes the local park and two places of worship. This is a community in which she feels at ease; she judges people to be friendly and she gets a sense of occasion from crowds attending religious services:

> I quite like my community where I live because I get a good view of everything. I have very good neighbours – they are very friendly. At the bottom of my street I have a small park and pond. Old people go there for a walk, it's a small pond. In the summer little kids go there to play.
>
> This is St Peter's Church. I see lots of people go. I see weddings, funerals.
>
> This is the big mosque in St Peter's. Lots of people go there every Friday to pray. The mosque is just behind my house. When it's a big day, I always go up in the attic to see people and I get a very good view.

Morgan, too, feels at ease in the cosmopolitan neighbourhood where he lives, which he contrasts with the more homogeneous neighbourhood in which he grew up in Zimbabwe. He is proud of the cultural diversity he experiences, and identifies with his place of worship and the community centre where he spends his leisure time:

> My church is a very important place for me. I am not very religious but I love going to pray every Sunday. It's a really old building and on its other side there is our community centre. At my community centre is where people go and relax and chill. At the same centre there are clubs, karate, drama etc. I do karate at this centre and it is good fun.
>
> My street is called G. It's in Highfields, there are many people living there, people of many cultures, religion and race. I like my street people and these many cultures which are fascinating and you can learn more in life with many cultures surrounding you.

Many of the young people had been involved in a campaign to save a local school and had been engaged in fundraising efforts for earthquake victims in Gujarat. They were clear about how they would improve their city: in general they were concerned about other neighbourhoods which were perceived to be dangerous because of 'bullies' and 'racists'. They wanted more cinemas, fewer racists and fewer gangsters, who led, they explained, ruined their own neighbourhoods, smoking drugs and hanging about in groups, extorting money and ruining parks. In general the students were sensitive to injustice, although they were more likely to understand how to respond politically to local issues than to injustices or inequalities in other parts of the world. The major response to this was to give charitably.

Cosmopolitan citizens?

Cosmopolitan citizenship does not mean asking individuals to reject their national citizenship or to accord it a lower status. Education for cosmopolitan citizenship is about enabling learners to make connections between their immediate contexts and the global context. It is not an add-on but rather it encompasses citizenship learning as a whole (Osler and Starkey, 2003). It implies a broader understanding of national identity. It also requires recognition that British identity, for example, may be experienced differently by different people. Cosmopolitan citizenship implies recognition of our common humanity and a sense of solidarity with others. It is insufficient, however, to feel and express a sense of solidarity with others elsewhere, if we cannot establish a sense of solidarity with others in our own communities, especially those others who we perceive to be different from ourselves.

A forward-looking and cosmopolitan citizenship education

The young people in our research demonstrated multiple and dynamic identities, embracing local, national and international perspectives. An education for national citizenship is unlikely to provide a sufficiently comprehensive context for them to integrate their own experiences and identities. As this chapter has argued, and as our emprircal research (Osler and Starkey, 2003) suggests, citizenship education requires reconceptualizing in the context of globalization. It is true that not all young people may be as experienced in or already engaged as cosmopolitan citizens as those in our sample. Nevertheless, the social, cultural and political processes of globalization suggest that there is a growing need for education for democratic citizenship which is cosmopolitan in nature. All young people have an entitlement to an education which will enable them to see themselves as citizens with rights and responsibilities and with the skills and understanding to influence what is happening both in their immediate communities and in the wider global community. It is not a process that can be realized exclusively at school. Learning is taking place beyond the school and the school needs to build on this learning and to encourage learners to make connections between their experiences and learning in the school and in the community.

Education for cosmopolitan citizenship, must of necessity address peace, human rights, democracy and development. It is about equipping young people with the knowledge, skills and attitudes to enable them to make a difference. It must be orientated towards the future, preparing young citizens to play an active role in shaping the world, at all levels, from the local to the global. The forces of globalization make this a pressing task.

Part III

School curricula in the digital age

In the *Preface* to their edited book *Computers into Classrooms: More Questions Than Answers* (1993), Beynon and Mackay answered their own question 'Of what should technological literacy consist?' as follows: 'Our view of technological literacy is very different from a narrow, skills-based, technical perspective. We see the cultural and social as central to the technological curriculum, not marginal' (vii).

In exploring how such an approach might be framed and articulated, they went on to acknowledge their debt to the work of Michael Young, referring to the following quotation:

> What will be needed [with reference to embedding IT related activity into the curriculum] will be knowledge about how technological choices are enmeshed in organizational, economic and political choices...what is needed is a concept of technology as a social phenomenon...[W]e have to find ways of making explicit how different purposes are involved in its design, its implementation and its use, and how at each stage there are potential choices and decisions to be made. This means a technologically literate population and an increasingly wide debate about the content and meaning of technological literacy.
>
> (Young, 1991)

In the same volume (Beyon and Mackay, 1993), I commented on some of the more extravagant claims then being made about the effects of Information Technology (IT) use (principally in school settings, since relatively few at that time had substantial access to computers at home) on young people's social and cognitive development (this was, remember twelve years ago, before any of us had experienced the introduction and rapid development of email and the World Wide Web):

> Burke *et al.* (1988: 16–17) maintain...that the introduction of the computer into the classroom can have a positive anti-sexist effect, while in the area of cognitive development Papert (1980: 995), supported by Noss (1988: 75), has claimed that if properly introduced to [the maths

program] LOGO at an early stage children can develop computational concepts 'even earlier than the numerical', thereby 'reversing what has appeared to be a universal of cognitive development'. Clark, meanwhile, (1985: 19), taking a stage further Papert's view that the regular availability of computers at home could result in children learning to write almost as soon as they learn to talk, suggests the exciting possibility of some kind of computer-inspired socio-literacy revolution, in which children become 'no longer passive consumers of the written word' but... 'producers' who 'make books'.

(Moore, 1993: 26)

Later on in this same chapter I referred to some of the practical difficulties faced by teachers and students in making use of the new technologies that came even close to achieving the results predicted by some of these commentators. Computers were in short supply and often located in specialist rooms, away from the daily flow of lessons, frequently staffed by librarians or technicians with little understanding or training in learning and teaching; teachers themselves were often very nervous about the technology, preferring to rely on more traditional educational aids that were less likely to go wrong on them; activities themselves were often decontextualized from the students' other learning, in many cases embedded in behaviourist models of learning; and in the course of the activities, too often the computer merely acted as a surrogate, traditionalist teacher, requiring not originality, creativity and exploration as much as arriving at the answer deemed by the programmer to be correct. (As Dillon (1985: 92) had said some years previously: 'It is the student who must fit in with the program's structure, to respond to the machine's initiative, to be evaluated by the machine.')

I refer to all this because despite some astonishing and unexpected developments in digital technologies since then, including a great proliferation of personal computers in homes and the access of millions of young people to mobile phones (and thence to textmessaging and, often, the World Wide Web), in terms of computer use in schools it might be argued that not a very great deal seems to have changed. A recent research study carried out at the Institute of Education, University of London into the impact of curriculum reforms on primary, middle and secondary schools in England, for example, which employed questionnaires with three hundred teachers in ten schools and in-depth case studies at those ten schools, found that computer use was highly variable across schools and typically dependent on levels of resourcing, often themselves linked to Local Authority support (Moore *et al.*, 2003: 32–33). The report concluded, in relation to Information and Communication Technology (ICT) use:

> Our... research revealed considerable variation in ICT resourcing across the sample, highlighting the significance of local variations concerning numbers and kinds of computers/computer networks and the quality of

teacher expertise, confidence and related INSET. We also found more common issues relating to the spatial and curricular location of ICT teaching and ICT facilities. While most teachers and schools, for example, seemed in favour of cross-curricular delivery of ICT and convinced of the value of 'computer rich' classrooms, there was evidence that they were being constrained into a continuation of – or reversion to – the discrete teaching of ICT away from mainstream curriculum delivery. In some of the case study interviews, this was implicitly and explicitly related to issues of the central function(s) and purpose(s) of ICT in the school curriculum: specifically, whether it was to be perceived and treated as both a useful tool/set of skills in itself *and* as a stimulus to/support for the development of pupils' general cognitive development, or whether it is identified primarily as the acquisition and development of a specific set of *technical* skills and expertise which may or may not have implications for learning across the curriculum.

The confusion discovered in this research study highlights two very important issues in relation to ICT use in school settings, both of which are further developed in the following chapters by Bridget Somekh and Angela McFarlane. The first of these concerns the functions of ICT use in the school curriculum – an issue which continues to cause heated discussion not only in relation to ICT in the curriculum but also to other 'cross curricular' skills such as literacy and numeracy. Questions here include: Should ICT skills be taught in a 'decontextualised' way for their own value – because of perceived personal and economic needs in being ICT literate? Should ICT, rather, be seen as a support or context or vehicle for learning across the curriculum? Should it seek to do both (in which case, how might the two functions articulate with one another?)? Or should ICT be seen as something rather different again (in a way, that is, which circumvents such polarities)? According to the research study by Moore *et al.* (2003), this set of confusions appears (at least in the opinions of many teachers and school principals) to exist not only in schools and classrooms but at the level of policy making and curriculum design. Some teachers and principals in that study, for example, spoke of a tension between the National Curriculum's encouragement to approach ICT in a cross-curricular way and the competing demands of a 'Key Stage Strategy' (for students aged eleven to fourteen), that seemed to be promoting a return to the discrete teaching of ICT skills. To quote one high school principal interviewed in the study:

> ICT should be an obvious cross curricular thing as far as I'm concerned, and we tried to do it that way, but what our ICT teacher says is that it's very difficult to convince the head of Maths, the head of Science and the head of English to deliver their little part in that cross curriculum approach because they're so busy trying to meet the requirements of their own subject area rather then seeing what's outside the box.

And...the Key Stage 3 Strategy is now recognising that, and is saying to us 'You will teach a separate hour a week of ICT' – and we're timetabling that from September.

The second issue takes us back to questions about definitions of knowledge, to the (re-) identification of 'useful knowledge', and to understandings of the nature of learning. As Somekh and McFarlane both argue, ICTs not only have the capacity to support learning and knowledge acquisition: they also suggest radically different conceptualizations of learning, teaching and curriculum than those embedded in most current school curricula, including:

- abandoning the persistent non-negotiability of a fragmented, discipline-based curriculum;
- placing greater responsibility for the content and direction of learning in the hands of students;
- reconceptualizing the teacher's role away from gatekeeper/bearer/transmitter of skills and knowledge to co-constructor of knowledge;
- and emphasizing learning – that is to say, learning skills and orientations – as opposed to knowledge 'acquisition'.

8 New ways of teaching and learning in the digital age
Implications for curriculum studies

Bridget Somekh

In this chapter, Bridget Somekh returns us to some of the tensions identified in Michael Young's chapter and elsewhere in the book, including the tension between a perceived need for education to be about active learning but at the same time for it to be about acquiring useful, important, pre-identified knowledge. Placing a Vygotskyan emphasis on the importance of the teacher–pupil relationship, Somekh focuses on what happens when ICT is introduced into the teaching–learning situation, suggesting that this inevitably changes the pedagogic relationship by introducing (so to speak) a third party into the teaching–learning relationship in a way in which textbooks do not. Somekh suggests that these changes open up possibilities for quite radical changes in the ways in which teaching, learning, schooling and curriculum are understood and designed. That such changes have not taken place cannot, she suggests, be blamed on schools and teachers, since 'teachers alone cannot bring about fundamental curriculum change' – although they can (in an expression that anticipates David Halpin's argument in our penultimate chapter) 'begin the process of transformation'. Drawing on the ideas of Turkle, McLuhan and Wertsch, and on her own experience and research in the field, Somekh argues that current curriculum and pedagogic practices in schools (a curriculum fixed by adults, comprising learning episodes in short bursts, with a body of knowledge to be covered), while they may have been appropriate in the past, work counter to the modes of learning promoted by and appropriate to ICT and currently followed by many young people in their out-of-school learning. This is not, Somekh argues, an argument for schools becoming redundant, but for different forms of curriculum and pedagogy, in which the role of the teacher changes 'from that of manager and controller to that of co-learner' in a more flexible curriculum allowing for genuinely constructive learning.

Introduction

This chapter presents a theory of curriculum with ICT as the basis for developing a vision of transformed schooling. It draws upon empirical work carried out at the Centre for ICT, Pedagogy and Learning at Manchester

Metropolitan University UK over the last five years as well as my own involvement in the field of Curriculum Studies over two decades.

Curriculum is initially defined, building upon the work of Stenhouse (1975), as the learning, both planned and unplanned, which results from interactions between teachers and learners within an educational setting. This definition is significantly different from the assumptions about curriculum embedded in many of the current educational systems developed by national governments. Instead of curriculum being defined in terms of goals, targets and syllabus specifications, it is located in the interactive process between learner and teacher: the underpinning assumption is that learning will not take place without the active inspiration of the learner, through drawing in and constructing new ways of configuring, shaping and understanding what was known, in the light of what is new. This definition of curriculum assumes a constructivist theory of learning in which interaction with the teacher is an essential component. It does not, however, remove from schools and teachers the responsibility for selecting and presenting knowledge and activities designed to educate learners. Perhaps we can say that this approach to curriculum necessarily incorporates a tension: on the one hand, learning is understood to be a natural process that is situated in human engagement with experiences and relationships, a normal – indeed a necessary – component of human activity (Lave, 1993); while on the other hand, education involves collaboration between one generation and the next, not merely a 'drawing out' (Latin: *educare*) of innate capacities, but an induction into the specialist knowledge and cultural tools that previous generations have worked hard to develop. As Newton said, great discoveries occur when we 'stand on the shoulders of giants', and curriculum is essential in enabling all learners to be raised to new insights and understandings that are both personally empowering and make a contribution to our social formations and culture.

The impact of ICT on teacher–pupil interactions

The introduction of ICT into schools has an immediate impact on the interactions between teachers and learners. Thereby, it necessarily changes the curriculum. This impact is most obvious – and for many teachers most unsettling – because it draws the focus of attention away from the teacher to the computer screen. This can be observed to occur with different degrees of 'distancing' from the teacher. At one end of the continuum the teacher may be using an interactive whiteboard or data projector and remains very much in control, although the learners' eyes are focused on the large display screen rather than on the teacher's face. This is already different from the learner's experience when the teacher uses a traditional board and writes on it by hand because the teacher's embodied presence is withdrawn from the line of vision for much of the time. At the other end of the continuum learners are working with interactive computer-based materials, such as the internet, autonomously from the teacher, singly, in pairs or in small groups. Once again the teacher's embodied presence is withdrawn from the learners' line of vision, but now for a much larger proportion of the time. In this chapter I do not deal directly with e-learning of the kind where the teacher's embodied presence is withdrawn altogether and the learner works physically alone supported by an online teacher and peer group. However, the ideas developed here have implications for this scenario and may help to explain why it is often so difficult to motivate learners to participate fully in online environments, let alone to develop anything resembling the vision of an online community of practice.

In this chapter I am concerned with understanding the radical changes to curriculum practice – that is, to the educational experience of learners – that *could* occur as a result of the intervention of ICT in teacher–learner interactions. From my early work with Richard Davies and other colleagues at the University of East Anglia, it became clear that when technology is introduced into classrooms it becomes a 'third partner' and transforms the pedagogic process into a 3-way interaction (Somekh and Davies, 1991). The result is a considerable increase in the potential for autonomy in learning, although the teacher's role remains a crucial factor in whether or not this potential is realized. Nevertheless, fifteen years later, there is plenty of evidence that in English schools (and in most other countries too) learners' experiences of curriculum are often little changed because of the introduction of ICT. In this chapter I want to suggest that not only the teacher's role, but the wider structures of schools and the cultural tools of education systems, are crucial in realizing the potential of ICT to transform schooling. There is an urgent need for radical, systemic change. Teachers alone cannot bring about fundamental curriculum change, although they can begin the process of transformation. I will end by extending and refining the theory of curriculum presented at the opening of this chapter, to build a scenario for new social practices and institutional structures in which learning with ICT would be able to realize the aspirations for transformed schooling.

Learners' current experiences of using ICT at home and at school

If we look at learners' experiences of using ICT at the beginning of the twenty-first century, in the United Kingdom, the most startling fact to emerge is the difference between those experiences at home and the ones at school. Many young people have access to state-of-the-art computers and broadband connectivity at home, as well as peripherals such as speakers, camcorders and digital cameras; their access to ICT, including the internet, is often unrestricted both in terms of time and screening filters (Somekh, Lewin *et al.*, 2002; Facer *et al.*, 2003).

Unrestricted use of ICT provides young people with access to a very wide range of resources and information which were out of reach of their parents' generation. The power of technology to transform the nature and procedures of almost all human activities is evident in the spectacular changes that have taken place in most of our social practices, from stock control in supermarkets, to personal online banking from home, and databases that enable companies to call up full details of any customer from a postcode and house number. Its transformative power is equally evident in access to information and the construction, production and publication of knowledge, for example using the internet, *google.com* and web-publishing. Young people are using these technologies to engage in a wide range of activities, such as: surfing the web to find information; sending emails; downloading music – or composing their own music; creating their own websites or 'blogs' where they construct and represent their identity through personal writing, images of favourite celebrities, their own digital photos and clips of video; 'meeting' new people – who may go on to become online friends – in chat rooms, where there is the fun of creating fictitious identities and experiencing the adventure of playing a role; visiting the websites of their favourite football club or pop star where they can find out more about them and engage in activities, enter competitions, perhaps make purchases; downloading games; or playing interactive online games in which 'playing' involves creating a personal/virtual identity and exploring a virtual terrain, acquiring special possessions, overcoming obstacles and interacting with other personal/virtual identities. Some of these activities are purely for fun but nevertheless involve learning, including the acquisition of ICT skills; others are focused more obviously on learning and may be directly related to school work. And almost always young people engage in these activities not one-at-a-time but through multitasking, with several 'windows' open at the same time: either arranged alongside each other so that one is visually there at the side or in a corner of the screen while another is the focus of attention; or one behind another so that a flick of the fingers on ALT+TAB calls a new one to the front; or 'minimized' and waiting at the bottom of the screen to be called up with a mouse-click. Almost always one of the windows will be for the music which is playing, and another for a messaging service, so that quick breaks can be taken from school work or a game to have a conversation with a friend, and the webcam perched on top of the monitor sends a picture to the friend along with the written message. These activities are supplemented, of course, by text-messaging with mobile phones, and the discourses are permeable, so that a message like 'y r u 18?' might be sent on either medium.

Sometimes adults express concern about the amount of time that young people spend on the computer at home, but nearly always they are not fully aware of the range and complexity of these activities. The culture shift for an adult to this new, virtual world is huge. In a very real sense the online world has empowered young people, bringing youth culture into the home and making their friends much more accessible, so that the cocoon-like formation of the home is invaded. (For those whose home lives may not be as idyllic as adults like to think, this may be a lifeline of support.) There are websites that cater especially for young people, but the real empowerment is that they can access a very wide range of information without it being pre-selected or controlled by parents or teachers. Adults fear the dangers of the internet for young people, and seek to control it, partly because newspapers have sensationalized a small number of cases where it has played a part in bringing children into danger, but probably more because the adult instinct is to control and constrain young people. We often do not accord them rights and responsibilities, but treat them as children from birth to adolescence – to their age-old infuriation.

In developing a new theory of curriculum I am particularly interested in the learning that results from these home-based ICT activities. Can these kinds of experiences be used as models for new ways of working with ICT at school? To explore these questions we wanted to understand the nature of young people's experience when working with ICT at home. Our starting point was the notion that people are likely to be highly motivated when they are engaged in play, but while it is certain that young people experience a lot of their ICT activities as fun, only a small number of them are specifically focused on games. To supplement the notion of play we, therefore, turned to Csikszentmihalyi's (1996) concept of 'flow'. From a large number of interviews with highly creative and successful people, ranging from musicians to internationally known scientists, Csikszentmihalyi found that their engagement in activities was characterized by a state of heightened consciousness, which often involved loss of awareness of other factors such as physical location or the passing of time. He called this state of heightened consciousness 'flow'. To find out whether 'flow' is characteristic of some ICT activities, we have developed a method of interviewing which involves asking the question, 'Have you ever found that while you were using ICT you forgot the time or forgot where you were?' In almost every case young people have known immediately what we meant and were able to provide good descriptions of the exact activity they were engaged in when they experienced 'flow'. Children as young as eight were able to give us examples of 'flow' drawn from their use of ICT both at home and at school, and analysis of their accounts clearly showed that these were linked most strongly to either 'gaming' activities where they were working 'against the clock', and perhaps striving to complete a task and 'go up to the next level', or to creative activities such as building their own website (Csikszentmihalyi, 1996; Somekh *et al.*, 2003).

Yet, very few young people in the United Kingdom are experiencing this kind of transformation in the activities they are involved in at school. Their experiences of using ICT at school are less frequent, restricted in terms of both time and filtering software, and characterized by 'broken flow'. Broken flow is the term we use when the story of the ICT activity which triggered flow ends with having to stop because time had run out, or the teacher interrupted to start a new activity, or access to a website was blocked by the school's filtering software. Elsewhere, I have written about the institutional constraints of schooling which perpetuate traditional structures of time-tables, divisions into 'subjects' and prescribed tasks (Somekh, 2004). The traditional formation of the school is focused on control as much as on teaching and learning. When curriculum is pre-specified nationally as a body of information and concepts to be transferred (apparently unproblematically) from teacher to students, and pupils are subsequently tested to measure the effectiveness of the transfer, knowledge itself is tightly controlled. The English national curriculum, with its levels and targets of attainment, and regime of national tests, closely fits this model. In defining curriculum in this way, much of the opportunity for constructivist learning is lost. Teaching becomes a technical process of transferring information rather than the kind of inspirational mentorship that Polanyi refers to when he defines learning alongside an expert adult in terms of 'indispensable intellectual powers and their passionate participation in the act of knowing' (Polanyi, 1958: 17). What is taught and the subject divisions into which knowledge is organized, how it is taught in terms of locations (movement between rooms), time-frames (periods) and pedagogic methods (whole class teaching, numeracy and literacy hours) create a matrix of traditional practices which act as constraints on the use of ICT tools. In Bernstein's terms knowledge, within the current education system in the United Kingdom, is both strongly classified and strongly framed (Bernstein, 1971b). Working under pressure, senior managers/administrators keep tight control of the overall structures of schooling and teachers keep tight control of classroom practices within the parameters set by managers and inspectors. When individuals or groups at any level try to institute change they meet with resistance from either peers or those at other levels. The result is that the school operates as a steady state system which is remarkably resistant to change (Bidwell, 2001).

There is an urgent need to transform schooling but the task is a complex one requiring commitment to a shared vision of radical curriculum change from teachers, pupils, parents, school managers/administrators and policy makers. Despite the almost ideal conditions for engagement in computer-based activities that many young people experience at home, the answer is not, in my view, to abandon school and expect children to learn at home without the assistance of the teacher. We know that use of computers at home is strongly differentiated in terms of the existing cultural capital in the home (Somekh, Mavers and Lewin, 2002). The conditions for engagement may be ideal, but the choice of the focus of engagement is haphazard and unlikely to maximize learning opportunities for young people without some external intervention. Teachers have an important role to play in making specific links between learning at school and at home, encouraging young people to use ICT at home to explore and investigate – as a means of extending the curriculum; and as role models of learners themselves – a role which they could fulfil much more easily with ICT tools to assist them, through their capacity to draw the focus of young people's attention to the screen, allowing teachers to shift their role away from that of manager and controller to that of co-learner. At its best, education systems should provide the essential structure for learning, selecting from the accumulated knowledge of generations what the next generation needs to know to play a full part in society's activities. However, rather than tightly specifying what students will learn, the curriculum framework should be flexible and locally negotiated by schools, to take account of parents' and communities' interests and leave room for students to follow their own paths of investigation. The curriculum as experienced by students would then be mediated by interactions with teachers and a range of tools – including ICTs – within the learning process, and strike a balance between suiting the needs of individual students and the needs of society as a whole.

Re-defining curriculum with ICT: some key theories

There are three theorists I want to refer to – Turkle, McLuhan and Wertsch – whose work extends our understanding of the reasons why ICT can transform human activities. Together they provide the basis for a new theory of curriculum grounded in interactions between pupils, teachers and a range of technology tools.

Turkle's work focuses on the way in which humans build intimate relationships with technology tools, categorizing the computer's role vis-à-vis humans in three ways: 'as tool, as mirror, and as gateway to a world through the looking glass of the screen' (Turkle, 1995: 267). Her early studies (Turkle, 1984) showed that humans enjoyed the fantasy of endowing computers with life, regarding them as objects of emotion rather than being wholly inanimate and mechanistic. When playing electronic games like 'tic-tac-toe' (noughts and crosses), young children were strongly engaged and animated and appeared to feel that they were competing against some tangible being – much in the same way that a chess player engages strongly with the challenge of 'beating the computer'. Graduate students, too, displayed high levels of engagement with technology, and spoke of their work in terms of emotional satisfaction. Perhaps there is an innate awareness of the software developer's skill and knowledge embodied in the tool, or perhaps it is merely that we are encultured, from a very early age, to enjoy turn-taking and engaging in making meaning out of all our experiences. Turkle's later work (1995) uncovered the exploratory world of fantasy identities and virtual relationships which her teenage and adult interviewees were experiencing as participants in internet chat rooms. They invented new personalities, played with changing their gender and age, and in some cases formed more intimate and satisfying relationships through 'virtual' meetings in cyberspace than they had so far been able to form through 'physical' meetings. Turkle's work has fascinating implications in terms of the role that embodiment plays in enhancing – or in some cases inhibiting – relationships. While it seems certain that it is mainly those with a particular social need who invest their main emotional energy in online relationships, Turkle's research indicates the power and intimacy of our engagement with technology tools. For those of us who use computers regularly, they become an integral part of our activity system, radically changing the way that we engage with tasks.

It is not so much the affordances of any particular technology as the revolutionary impact of technologies as a class of tools which makes their power to change human activity so significant. This is what McLuhan meant by 'the medium is the message': it is not their content or specific uses which constitute the significant change but the new way of working that they demand of those who use them fully. Writing more than forty years ago, McLuhan saw the telegraph and other 'electric technologies' as extensions of the body which necessitate radical changes in human systems in order to 'maintain equilibrium' (McLuhan, 1964: 273). This notion of technologies as extensions of the body is similar to Turkle's notion of their personal and intimate construction by their users. But McLuhan's understanding went further in seeing that they also acted to destabilize the processes of mechanization and the hierarchies of management in organizations, opening up the possibilities of much greater flexibilities of role:

> There is a collapse of delegated authority and a dissolution of the pyramid and management structures made familiar in the organization chart. The separation of function and the division of stages, spaces, and tasks are characteristic of literate and visual society and of the Western world. These divisions tend to dissolve through the action of the instant and organic interrelations of electricity.
>
> (1964: 268)

McLuhan writes specifically about 'electricity' but his focus in particular was on the telegraph and the kinds of radical changes in political practices, journalism and crime-detection (viz the arrest of Crippin mid-Atlantic in 1910) that its invention had brought about. The quotation can be applied with uncanny accuracy to the internet, particularly, perhaps, in relation to the impact on human activity of combining broadband access to the internet with the affordances of *google.com*. The controls over access to information have been fundamentally changed. Teachers, lawyers, medical practitioners, research scientists and indeed all experts are no longer able to act as gate-keepers to knowledge; instead, they find themselves engaging in new kinds of conversations with clients and patients who have been highly motivated to find the knowledge relevant to their case before the consultation with an expert. Yet traditional schooling, even in schools which are well endowed with equipment, often creates the conditions of poor access which reinstate controls over knowledge and emasculate the power of technology to transform the curriculum. For example, the assumptions, values and practices embedded in the discourse of 'lessons', teaching 'periods' (perhaps as short as forty minutes), 'subjects' (all taught separately despite clear overlaps of knowledge) and 'tests' (to check up on what has been memorized [?]) provide a hidden curriculum of top-down, external power over knowledge. Tight specification of the 'content' to be learnt is a significant additional feature, and the messages are further reinforced by extending the traditional discourse of schooling to emphasize the importance of 'training' and 'curriculum delivery'. The power of technology tools is further diminished by filtering software which is currently often set up in English schools to block internet sites indiscriminately. (We have come across many examples, including, for instance, cases where the NASA and BBC sites were blocked.) In some schools, the need to prepare pupils for tests and examinations has also meant an emphasis on using ICT for low-level tasks such as completing structured worksheets and preparing for tests through self-testing on 'revision' websites.

Both Turkle and McLuhan show how technologies have a radical impact on individuals and social formations when they become socioculturally embedded in human activities. Wertsch (1998), drawing on the work of Vygotsky and others, provides an explanation of this process in terms of the central role of mediating tools in all human activity. Human action is not the result of human agency alone, but of the combination of human agency with skilled tool use – whether the tool be language itself, the printing press, the telegraph or ICTs. The example he uses is of the pole vaulter who cannot perform the vault without the pole; he could as well have used the example of the high jumper who cannot jump as high without the Fosbury flop or the academic researcher who could not write so quickly and creatively without access to online journals. All new tools have the potential to transform human activity but they need to be used skilfully and the user (agent) needs to engage creatively in their use, with a vision of new possibilities to inspire a transformation of practices. Wartofsky's work (1979) unpacks the complexity of learning to use new tools through the development of mental models – or 'secondary representations' – of them, which, together with their exploratory and frequent use, enable us to use them creatively to transform previous working practices and develop 'tertiary representations' (in which yet more radical ways of using them are imagined).

A new theory of curriculum as the basis for transforming schooling

These theories shed new light on the definition of curriculum which I set out at the beginning of this chapter. There remains the tension of holding a balance between learner-led exploration, on the one hand, and induction of learners into the shared inheritance of our culture, on the other. My original definition of curriculum, building on the work of Stenhouse, is now refined and extended to become: the learning, both planned and unplanned, that results from interactions between teachers, learners and tools within an educational setting capable of maximizing their transformative potential.

The nature of technologies – their function in becoming extensions of the self and reconstructing identities, and their capacity to change the nature of human activity when they are in the hands of skilful users with strong mental models of their possibilities – impels us to rethink how we select and organize curriculum content. How that selection is made is always contested in a democracy, since governments have a responsibility to provide the best possible education for citizens while ensuring the continuing supply of educated adults to carry our society forward. But when new tools are designed for exploratory use, and offer a very wide range of possibilities, including extraordinary new opportunities for creativity and communication, a tightly specified curriculum with fixed learning outcomes, must necessarily inhibit development. We need a curriculum that uses both traditional technology tools (e.g. books) and new technology tools (e.g. the internet, digital imaging, dynamic modelling) to give school pupils opportunities for transformative learning. Our preliminary, operational model is of a curriculum which enables pupils: to learn creatively; to learn as active citizens (taking responsibility and making choices); to become intellectually engaged in learning and fascinated by new knowledge; and to engage in metacognition, reflecting on their learning and 'learning how to learn'.

The constructivist theories of learning, deriving from the work of Vygotsky (1978) and Bruner (1960) need to be supplemented by theories of situated learning (Brown *et al.*, 1989) and communities of practice (Lave and Wenger, 1991; Nardi, 1997), to underpin this new, extended definition of curriculum. A curriculum appropriate for the twenty-first century cannot be understood as an offering for individual learners, decontexutalized and isolated from human interaction. It needs to be reformulated as an open knowledge framework for collaborative learning, enacted by the interactions of teachers, pupils and a wide range of tools, in an environment which is inherently supportive of the kind of transformative learning that ICT makes possible. This was always the kind of learning perceived to be ideal, but previously the available tools – for example, school libraries, exercise books, text books and work sheets – did not support it well.

Curriculum, when defined in terms of the learning that results from teacher–pupil–ICT interactions, requires a commitment to an open, exploratory pedagogy, and the radical restructuring of schools to allow learners to take the kind of control of their own learning that ICT enables and invites. Pedagogy cannot but be constraining if it remains the same as it was twenty (fifty, one hundred) years ago. Children's ways of working in school should change as radically as adults' ways of working have changed in employment. If we want young people to grow up ready to work independently and take responsibility, if we want the curriculum to place creativity and critical thinking at its core, we need a theory of curriculum capable of inspiring the transformation of schools as organizations through radical changes in roles, relationships and structures. This newly defined curriculum should be the core focus of education: schools should be structured with the prime aim of supporting the interactions of pupils, teachers and technologies – of all kinds, including books – which are at its heart. The intimacy of human-computer relationships which Turkle uncovers points to the need for learners to have ownership of ICTs and constant access to their use. McLuhan points to the need to unpack the mechanistic structures or schooling that were set up to enable teachers to function with now outdated technologies (including, for example, blackboards, exercise books, worksheets produced by the teacher, and poorly-resourced school libraries), and provide much more open access to knowledge, flatter structures in which teachers' and learners' roles are interchangeable, and pedagogical practices in which learners play an active part in structuring their own curriculum. Wertsch illustrates the affordances of tools to transform human activity provided they are not forced to conform with inappropriate – because outdated – patterns of activity. Taken together, these three visionary thinkers provide evidence of the need to transform curriculum – and schooling itself – to overcome what McLuhan calls 'culture lag' in trying to carry out human activity – in this case learning – within an outdated infrastructure.

This theory of curriculum with ICT incorporates the learning, both planned and unplanned, that results from interactions between teachers and learners, within an educational setting where learners are always accompanied by personal learning technologies (with connectivity and unfiltered access to the internet and powerful tools such as *google.com*), and teachers provide role models as co-learners, specifying broad learning goals for their students and then supporting them in planning how to work to achieve them. Schools and education systems need to be radically reformed to allow this reorientation of roles and relationships and use the power of ICT to reinstate the pursuit of knowledge and the love of learning as the main aims of schooling. It may be necessary to employ others, alongside teachers, to assist with supervision of students working alone or in groups, but this would add greatly to the effectiveness and efficiency of schools which currently are hampered by society's expectation that they will shoulder all responsibility for controlling the nation's young people during school hours. The power of ICT to motivate students and support their learning makes this possible and affordable as it could not have been before.

9 ICT and the curriculum canon

Responding to and exploring 'alternative knowledge'

Angela McFarlane

In the second of these chapters focusing on ICT and education, Angela McFarlane begins by returning us to the questions of knowledge introduced by Michael Young in Chapter 1. After Bereiter, McFarlane describes knowledge as 'something to be worked on and with, not an entity to be passively consumed or even individually constructed': that is to say, an understanding of knowledge that stands in opposition to knowledge that is reified – whether 'received' or 'produced'. Such an understanding questions the very function(s) of knowledge, suggesting an understanding of knowledge not so much as an end in itself, nor as a means to some often tenuously connected end, but rather as a way of supporting and promoting the creative-cognitive development of the learner. With specific reference to developments in ICT, McFarlane indicates how new technologies in the classroom provide a fresh site for old, still unresolved debates concerning knowledge, including what the curriculum balance should be between different kinds of knowledge – her implication being that an underlying conservatism tends to pull even pedagogies and curriculum related to the new technologies in the direction of the 'declarative' and thence to performativity. Among the key issues raised in the chapter are the need for Curriculum Studies to give more attention to understanding the curriculum-as-experienced; the need to revisit forms and purposes of assessment in view of the developing use of the new technologies in schools; and the need to ask ourselves again 'What is the curriculum for? Have its purposes and imperatives changed?' In her promotion of a revised curriculum which has 'content' but in which 'the precise topic is not relevant', McFarlane cites Ridgway and McCusker (2003) in arguing for a curriculum reform that includes emphases on developing capabilities 'in finding rules and relationships and handling complex data, as well as [helping students in] developing meta-knowledge of their own problem solving'.

The nature of knowledge

> An idea can turn to dust or magic, depending on the spirit that rubs against it.
>
> Matsuo Basho (1644–1694)

There are those who argue that the advent of information technologies has changed the nature of knowledge, and of knowing (Lyotard, 1984; Lankshear *et al.*, 2000). Indeed there are those who believe that the way the mind works when using such technologies is different. A key premise for this difference is the identification of the technology- and information-rich era in which we live as the 'knowledge age', where knowledge creation is or is predicted to be the basis of wealth and economic growth in developed nations for the first half of the twenty-first century. As a result of this there are widespread calls for the education system to change in order to prepare learners to take their place in a knowledge economy. Bereiter (2002) argues convincingly that the theories of knowledge, and mind, that we need to understand and operate within the knowledge age have in fact been with us for some time, but are not used to inform modern theories of mind or pedagogy. Drawing on Popper (1972), he points out that we have had theories that go beyond the mind-as-container for some time, but that models of education still use that metaphor, which is partly why we have a situation in which we never manage to teach more than about 80 per cent of children to read fluently (Bereiter, 2002). Certainly policy discourse that speaks of 'delivering learning' resonates with the mind-as-container model of learning, seeing the learner as recipient of content – albeit content structured so that it can be assimilated easily into the learner's mind.

Bereiter argues for an extension of the range of types of knowledge beyond the declarative (i.e. what you know) and procedural (i.e. what you can do) dichotomy (although these are very like his own 'statable' and 'skills' knowledge), and offers four more types of knowledge needed to engage in true knowledge creation. These comprise implicit, episodic, impressionistic and regulative knowledge (the latter of which has some connections to the notion of metacognition in that it informs the learner of their own learning processes). Again building on Popper, Bereiter offers the notion of concep-tual artefacts to suggest an alternative way to think of both the mind and the way we think of knowledge. This idea draws on a connectionist model of the mind, where knowledge is no longer conceptualized as chunks of content in an individual's head but as a series of connections made between different ideas, some strong and some weak. Conceptual artefacts (Bereiter, 2002: 58) are 'human constructions like other artefacts, except that they are immate-rial...they serve purposes such as explaining and predicting. These concep-tual artefacts...become part of the vast array of things we can become knowledgeable about.' They include 'theories, factual assertions, problem statements, histories, interpretations and many other products of human thought' (ibid.: 236).

Bereiter uses the example of a recipe – which is neither the act of cooking nor the skills needed to do this but rather a blueprint that essentializes the process – as a conceptual artefact. 'The recipe...is an abstract object of which there may be various representations. When people criticize, argue about, or try to improve upon the recipe it is this abstract object they are attempting to deal with, not its representation' (2002: 73). Here the representation is the text, or presumably the finished dish. It is not just that children should work with such conceptual artefacts that is important, but that they should know they are doing so otherwise, they cannot be consciously knowledge-building. Moreover they should be aware that this is an important and useful thing to do, an objective to be achieved largely by encouraging children to work with ideas and content that interest them and making the elements of the knowledge-building process, in particular the relevant conceptual artefacts, explicit. In the model Bereiter offers of education, the production of new conceptual artefacts may be rare but the process of education involves working with conceptual artefacts to understand their nature, argue about and criticize them, and improve them. This echoes the work of Bereiter's collaborator, Scardamalia, who argues: 'To work creatively students must become constructivists, and understand that knowledge is created and continually improved upon by people and that this is something they can do' (Scardamalia, 2000).

The key to this idea may be the use of the term 'creatively'. Indeed, this may be the bridge between the curricula that have dominated Western school systems in the late twentieth century and those that are struggling to emerge in the twenty-first. Arguably, the test driven systems prevalent particularly in the United States and in the United Kingdom are beginning to break down. Levels of achievement have stagnated, following early apparent rises, and standards of pupil behaviour deteriorate year on year, according to annual reports from the UK Chief Inspector of Schools published by Ofsted over the last ten years. This latter decline clearly has causes beyond the school system, but a curriculum that offers little authenticity to learners does not help. As a response to the lack of creativity in the UK curriculum the National Advisory Committee on Creative and Cultural Education (NACCCE) has offered a definition of the essential elements involved in a creative process. These are:

- a fashioning process
- using imagination
- pursuing purpose
- being original
- judging value

(NACCCE: *All Our Futures: Creativity, Culture and Education*, 1999)

The Qualifications and Curriculum Agency (QCA) in England, drawing on a range of sources including the NACCE report, has subsequently offered a view of the kinds of pupil thinking and behaviour that would be involved in creative learning. These comprise:

- questioning and challenging
- making connections and seeing relationships

- envisaging what might be
- playing with ideas
- representing ideas
- evaluating the effects of ideas

(Taken from *QCA Creativity Pack Information Sheet 3* (September 2002): see http://www.ncaction.org.uk/creativity/index.htm)

It is very significant that these behaviours are clearly not unique to the traditionally creative elements of the curriculum, those that deal with the arts and crafts for example. Indeed this approach to learning could be easily applied irrespective of the subject area under study and clearly echoes Scardamalia's notion of working with and improving ideas. Moreover it goes beyond the notion of procedural knowledge, and what is usually called constructivism in the classroom with its emphasis on problem solving and project work. Here knowledge is something to be worked on and with, not an entity to be passively consumed or even individually constructed. Perhaps this is the most important aspect of the nature of knowledge we need to grasp in order to inform a curriculum that is both relevant and engaging for learners growing up in the knowledge age.

Moreover this way of working with ideas is inherently social, involving as it does discussion and argument, justification and exploration. This makes school an ideal site for such learning, which is much harder to do in isolation. Indeed research into attempts to foster such learning online in adults, using computer-based communication technologies, have not been entirely successful and face-to-face sessions remain a vital part of many courses. Bereiter suggests that this opportunity for social learning, along with child-care, may be the most powerful reason to retain schools as sites of learning in an information-rich age. Where Bereiter and Scardamalia make their most significant contribution is perhaps in the linking of theories of knowledge to models of education, moreover models of education that do not preclude a role for defined content, or the absence of a range of existing forms of teaching such as direct instruction, but rather weave these into a fabric that builds on what is good in the current system and takes it forward. For without coherent, scalable models of what it is to teach and learn using meaningful knowledge practices, no matter how convincing the theoretical arguments, they are unlikely to influence policy or practice.

Digital technologies in the school

After thirty years of computers in the classroom we are no nearer to the educational Utopia envisioned by early advocates of digital technologies, where these have replaced books and altered schools beyond recognition. Bork's prediction in 1980 that '[b]y the year 2000, the major way of learning at all levels, and in almost all subject areas, will be through interactive use of computers' (Bork, 1980: 53) has clearly failed to materialize, and in 2004 the UK project to create an eUniversity where students learn entirely online was prematurely curtailed having been widely viewed as a costly failure (e.g. Garrett, 2004).

The idea that the use of digital technologies improves learning persists, however, in a range of policy and research discourses on learning, either implicitly or explicitly. Often, these claims have been strongly made, and backed by significant levels of investment as in the *National Grid for Learning* initiative in England and Wales that attracted over £2 billion of funding. At the launch of this programme, at a primary school in his constituency, the British Prime Minister Tony Blair asserted that:

> This National Archives site from the Public Records Office shows how content providers can develop good learning resources for the Grid, which will stimulate children's interest. Today for example, children at Trimdon Junior school are able to get access to information and histor-ical documents relating to the Trimdon mining disaster in 1882, and its impact on the community.
>
> Before this development, unique and important documents could be read only by visiting the PRO in person, but now they can be delivered directly to classrooms homes and libraries throughout the UK via the Internet. That is the kind of learning revolution that will now become possible for every child in every school in the country.
>
> (Tony Blair, in DfEE press release, 6 November 1998)

Quite how this improved access to digital content would revolutionize learning was never articulated; neither were the presumed changes in pedagogy, or the skills needed to make sense of these new information sources. The ideal balance between content and skills in the curriculum remains contested ground, and is inseparable from the declarative and proce-dural knowledge dichotomy of cognitive science (Bereiter, 2002). It is possible to find a recorded view anywhere on the spectrum from content-defined to content-free as being the model for the school curriculum. It should come as no surprise then that advocates of technology-use also fall along this spec-trum from the digital content supporters to the 'computer as mediating tool' school (the most famous of whom is almost certainly Seymour Papert). National policies, where they exist, tend to the digital content end of the spectrum, where the focus is on the provision of information in a digital form. This model tends to best match the policy models of school-based learning. Perhaps the most eloquent example of this is the commitment of some £350 million for the purchase of digital content – not tools – by schools in England under the DfES *Curriculum Online* policy in 2003–5. It is also not surprising that the defined content view of curriculum accompa-nies the test-oriented model of accountability, where the success or failure of the school system, and even individual schools and teachers, is measured through the scores achieved by pupils in high stakes national tests, based largely on the test takers' facility with declarative knowledge. In this way, an interdependent set of links can be made between the view of what counts as success in the school system – test scores – to a defined curriculum that can be tested, and the role of digital technologies to provide access to that defined content for the teacher and learner.

Largescale assessment systems struggle with approaches to testing that do not rely heavily on the reproduction of declarative knowledge. There is some credit given for aspects of procedural knowledge, but as to the other forms of knowledge identified by Bereiter and Scardamalia and others, such as impressionistic, episodic or metacognitive knowledge, they are simply not on the testing agenda. Indeed opportunities to work with ideas is not part of the assessment framework even where it is promoted in the curriculum, as in the Design Technology Curriculum in England (e.g. see http://www.ncaction. org.uk/creativity/index.htm). And yet there is good evidence that this is vital to creative learning (NACCCE, 1999), and that the digital mutability afforded by computer-based technologies is ideally placed to support such learning (McFarlane, 2003).

One of the most powerful, and often overlooked, affordances of digital technology is the ability to edit data sets, from a word processed document to a digital video, with an ease that is unmatched in the equivalent non-digital media. The ability to work with ideas, evolving and honing one's expression or interpretation of them, until a personal understanding and accurate articulation of that understanding have been achieved is at the heart of the constructivist view of learning. It is also the mechanism underpinning the creative process (NACCCE, 1999) and has proved to be a vital element in the knowledge-building programmes of Bereiter and Scardamalia. Given that working iteratively in this way, individually or collaboratively, with review and comment from peers or experts, is at the heart of the process of formative assessment – which has proven power in the improvement of learning (Assessment Reform Group, 1999), it is perhaps surprising that this use of digital technology (to support learners' production of content) is given less prominence in policy models of pedagogies with ICT than an alternative that sees the learner as consumer of content. This content is, itself, conceptualized as vast, 'individualized', 'curriculum-relevant' and supplied online (e.g. the *Curriculum Online* consultation paper from April 2001: http://www.dfes.gov.uk/curriculumonline/genin.shtml and DfES, 2002). Perhaps the reasons for this are essentially pragmatic: the routine use of digital devices to generate personal content requires a level of access to computers in schools which is far in excess of that currently available; consequently, computing devices would need to be as readily available on demand as paper and pen. Realistically, this level of provision from central funds is unlikely, and such routine use will have to wait until the majority of learners do carry with them some kind of personal device, most likely a consumer product which is the descendent of today's handheld computer and phone combined. An alternative, and more worrying possibility is that policy will remain predominantly informed by a view of learning that sees the learner as a consumer of knowledge rather than a builder, and a belief that learning can be 'delivered' to learners as if it is a commodity. Woolgar (2002) points to the discourse that equates learning to activities such as shopping within the literature surrounding e-learning, which suggests that such a view of learning is widely held.

Alone together: the learner in formal education

Testing cultures tend to focus on the level of the individual – not the group. And like the notion of delivered learning discussed earlier, this has profound implications for the model of the learner, who is treated as a lone consumer of content to be re-produced on demand in the context of the test. This view has serious implications for learners' beliefs about themselves as learners, the nature of meaningful learning, and the role an individual needs to play in order to be successful within formal education. The game is to pass tests; what counts as useful knowledge is only that which contributes to test passing, and the trick is to learn only what you need to pass the tests. The notion of education as personal enrichment is entirely lacking in this conceptualization; learning serves an external purpose and the outcome is a certificate that entitles the holder to move to the next level. Learners who have experienced this model of education at school are likely to carry it with them into further and higher education, and even at postgraduate level will often focus only on that which is assessed. If the only purpose of formal learning is to pass externally set tests, the learner has no responsibility for or ownership of their learning for its own sake.

This can be contrasted with a view of the curriculum that focuses not on familiarity with pre-defined content, but on the ability to find, analyse and appraise relevant content, and construct coherent, justified views that could be construed as personal knowledge. Here the precise topic is not relevant. Some content clearly remains vital; however, the internal coherence and validity of the produced text and conceptual artefacts are what are paramount. It is easy to see that in this model access to content remains important, but delivery' of precise content is not. The tools and skills to locate, analyse, compare, critique and construct are what are needed here. One justification of this model of the curriculum is that this approach to personal knowledge building is the one that is relevant to those who live in the age of the Internet, and the necessary knowledge practices are those that will best prepare learners to take an active part in modern economic and social practices. In addition, these skill sets are best honed in a social context, working with others to explore, test and refine ideas. In this model knowledge is socially constructed.

In this kind of learning environment, as Goodyear (2001) has pointed out the roles of the teacher and student change. The teacher is no longer the main source of unchallenged declarative knowledge; rather, she becomes a consultant, guide, and resource provider. Her expertise is in asking good questions rather than providing all of the answers, and she is predominantly a designer of student learning experiences rather than a provider of content. In this changed environment, the learner must take some responsibility for their own, and others' learning. They must see themselves not as passive receptacles for hand-me-down knowledge but as constructors of their own knowledge, who refine their own questions and search for their own answers. Students need to work as group members on more collaborative/cooperative assignments; and as a result group interaction is significantly increased.

There has been much popular comment on the difficulty for teachers of this change in role, and the need for training to develop new pedagogical models: indeed, the need for professional development is a recurring theme in national policies. Some commentators seem to assume that the transition is easy, or at least easier, for the students, who are after all the children of the information age, used to high levels of access to information and communications technologies (ICTs). However, this change of roles is not easy for the student as research has shown, and seems to require far more than facility with the technology itself (e.g. Walker, 2004; Cox *et al.*, 2004; Soller, 2004). A sociocultural model of learning has informed much early practice with online technologies to support learners in higher education. The SOLE (Students' Online Experiences) project at Bristol, for example, reveals that a view of learning as some kind of collaborative act is far from embedded in student views of themselves as learners. Many students still saw themselves as primarily working alone: 'Well I would say I was more of a researcher...We all have to learn how to research and manage our time and how to learn on our own' (Student – Case Study 8 – Economics).

As Woolgar's (2002) first rule of virtuality states: 'The uptake and use of new technologies depend crucially on local social contexts.' And as Crook and Light's (2002) study from the same programme, on 'Virtual Society and the Cultural Practice of Study' illustrates, students' study habits have changed as they use computers and other digital devices simultaneously to access a range of resources and applications, not all of which are related directly to study. Despite this, they see themselves primarily as learning alone when they are not in class. To assume that the use of Internet technologies to chat with friends, listen to music, search for resources and check the precise assignment brief on the course's virtual learning environment while simultaneously working on the assignment on a word processor, may indeed represent a change in knowledge-building practice; however, it has not necessarily changed the learners' perception of themselves as lone learners or of learning as an essentially solitary practice. Moreover, when students do choose to collaborate using electronic communications they will tend to eschew the tools offered to them such as discussion boards in online learning environments, and stick to good old email and Internet relay chat. This model of themselves as working ultimately alone to build personal knowledge is of course the model that informs the assessment process: ultimately, high stake awards are made to individuals, not groups. Indeed, at the school level there is a thin line between working collaboratively and cheating. Given this, it is not surprising, perhaps, that students struggle to find new ways of working collaboratively simply because they are using a computer-mediated communication environment. Even making a posting to the discussion board, an assessment requirement is not enough (e.g. Cox *et al.*, 2004). There is a clear tension between the ways of working and the manifestations of knowledge that are credited and those that are required in a collaborative learning environment on or off line. Although students may be invited to discuss, debate, offer views and support arguments, they remain reluctant to do so online (e.g. Walker, 2004) perhaps in part because they see themselves ultimately as judged individually.

Recognizing value

Perhaps the most obvious gap to be bridged between the models of knowledge-based education and national policy models of curriculum concerns assessment. It is widely recognized that assessment drives teaching and learning (e.g. Clarke and Peter, 1993). Arguably, high stakes testing has changed the face of the school curriculum more than any other single factor; however, the precise role of digital technologies in this test driven system remains uncertain. There are three common perspectives on the complex relationship web that links digital technologies, assessment and learning (McFarlane, 2001): Are we interested in testing competence with the technology? Are we interested in using the technology to teach and possibly test a largely unchanged curriculum? Or are we looking for an element of revolution brought about by new knowledge practices and new ways of knowing and being seen to know?

To refer to the first of these perspectives, skills and competence with the technologies themselves have enjoyed an unsettled place in the curriculum since at least the mid-1980s. For example, the first version of the National Curriculum for England and Wales included Information Technology (IT) as a strand within the Design Technology subject area. It seemed that IT here was being understood as a craft, with associated craft knowledge and skill to be acquired. Fashions have changed repeatedly, as IT – and now ICT – has been recognized as an independent subject, albeit one that can be taught either separately or as an integrated part of the curriculum. When ICT skills in early secondary schooling in England and Wales (Key Stage 3, ages 11–14) were seen to be at least a grade behind other subjects at the same point, this was attributed to the teaching of these skills entirely within the context of other curriculum subjects. In an attempt to redress this imbalance the *Key Stage 3 ICT Strategy* was launched, focusing on the teaching of ICT skills explicitly. The results of this are still awaited at the time of writing.

The remaining two perspectives concern the use of digital technologies to teach and learn subjects other than the technology itself. The first of these focuses on using the technologies to support, or even 'deliver', a curriculum that is broadly unchanged. Digital technologies offer ways of teaching and testing what we have always taught and tested, but hopefully with some gains in efficiency and effectiveness. Indeed this is the model that has underpinned most research, policy and practice to date (McFarlane, 2001). The quest for evidence of an impact of this model has so far been frustrated. The most notable recent attempts include the Impact 2 study commissioned by and for the Department for Education and Skills in England and Wales (Harrison *et al.*, 2002) and the Burns and Ungerleider (2002) review. The overwhelming conclusion from these studies is that at best the impact of digital technologies on learning as measured through high stakes tests is neutral or very mildly positive.

Interpreting this outcome is problematic, given that overall levels of usage remain very low. Is it, for example, that there just is not enough time spent using the technology for there to be any overall, measurable effect on learning outcomes? Moreover, a vast range of practices from using the Internet as a source of information to using a word processor to make a good copy of a composition, via a drill and practice spelling programme, are all lumped together as using ICT. This could help explain why the effects at the school level, or at the individual research project level in a metanalysis, are entirely inconsistent. On the other hand, it could be that the kinds of learning supported by the use of digital technologies are simply not credited through traditional tests.

This last point brings me to the third perspective, on the interplay between digital technologies and learning, which is that this supports and indeed requires a very different set of achievements: skills, understanding, 'digital literacy' – or, as Bereiter (2002) argues, a different vision of knowledge based on a different theory of mind.

Current evidence suggests that the dilemma of whether technology supports a new curriculum or the old one is a false premise. We still do not know confidently whether or not well-designed digital experiences do in fact support learning in the traditional model, because frankly we have not seen enough of this to know. The gap between the theoretically possible with digital technology and the actually implemented remains a yawning one. Much digital content is poorly conceived, limited in scope and uses poor pedagogic models to inform its structure. The idea that such resources could offer a range of approaches to materials, favouring a range of preferred learning styles, is almost never realized in the end product (McFarlane *et al.*, 2003). The technology used to access this material in schools, moreover, remains unstable, slow, unreliable and largely available in configurations that do not blend easily with normal teaching and reduce flexibility (Somekh, Woodrow *et al.*, 2002).

For all this, we have machines in schools that are powerful devices for realizing and working with ideas, in the form of a wide range of digital texts that can be used, made, edited, changed and developed at will. From the simple word processor to the graphical geometry package, via a range of moving and still image media, schools are packed with machines that are used not to explore and work with ideas but to 'deliver learning'. It seems that this is an entirely ideological divide and largely persists due to a failure of imagination at the policy level as much as anything else. It is a divide that rests in no small measure on (how we respond to) a large question: If we move away from a curriculum that rests on facility with declarative knowledge, how can we ensure that 'standards' will not suffer?

What do you test? how do you test it?

There is widespread recognition that school curricula need to address issues such as problem solving and communication if they are to support a society composed of informed citizens capable of sustaining a growing economy. However, as Ridgway and McCusker (2003) point out:

> Change in educational practice is often found to be difficult (Fullan, 1991). The sorts of changes necessitated by the new political agenda for education are particularly difficult to bring about for two distinct reasons. First is the problem of communicating the new vision to be attained; second is the inherent stability of educational systems, in the form of elements which lock them in place, such as rigid assessment systems, or inflexible programmes for professional development.

Ridgway and McCusker argue that such new practices can only be communicated through exemplification, which their work then goes on to offer. They have developed and trialed computer-based assessment tasks that model complex processes and problems, using new representations and symbol systems that support constrained decision making. As a result of working with these tasks students show capabilities in finding rules and relationships and handling complex data, as well as developing metaknowledge of their own problem solving. All of these are skills that Ridgway and McCusker (2003) argue are now centrally important in the knowledge age, and certainly the last – knowledge of one's own problem solving – echoes the call for knowledge building of Bereiter and Scardamalia. Research in Brazil by Nunes *et al.* (2003) goes further and has developed computer-based tasks that seem to map levels of metacogniton directly. As Baker (2003) points out, such research is still in its early stages, however, and is a long way from offering an alternative to current high stakes testing.

If we are to move to a curriculum that values and supports knowledge building and working with conceptual artefacts, we will require a framework that recognizes competence with these phenomena, and in which all the stakeholders have confidence. This means an assessment system that has – and is believed to have -reliability and validity, capable of producing credible and relevant results for policy makers, learners, parents and employers as a starting point. Recent attempts to reform assessment systems through the Tomlinson Report (DfES, 2004) show what a sensitive and problematic process this is. In the longer term if we do move to a curriculum that is more oriented to knowledge building, and working with conceptual artefacts, it is likely that the assessment of the related practices will not be through computer controlled assessment tasks, but through teacher assessment of the student and her work over an extended period of time. This will require a fundamental change in the level of trust currently given to teachers to be fair and effective assessors of students' work. And yet this was a common practice in high stakes assessment until the advent of GCSE in 1988. Before that, syllabuses that used a significant component of school-based assessment were common. Indeed, the Hertfordshire Integrated Science Project, examined by the Cambridge Examinations Board, used 75 per cent school-based assessment in the ordinary ('O') level examination, and this was not unique. As a result it was possible to include a component that gave credit for the ability to carry out practical laboratory work as part of a team. Looking back, this now seems revolutionary, as the current view of the assessment of collaborative working at this level is seen as problematic. (Of course, if you rely primarily on individual test scores as the main data source, collaboration is indeed a problematic element to assess.)

Conclusion

It seems that the decisions to be made concerning the response to calls for a new curriculum for the knowledge age are ultimately ones of policy, and to some extent ideology. Are we to expand the curriculum to include, recognize and give credit for knowledge building, including an awareness of what this is and how it is being done? Or are we to stick with a highly content-defined curriculum with frequent high stakes tests that focus largely on facility with declarative knowledge? The former may be seen as a high-risk choice, involving as it does a move away from much though not all that has been held as sacred in the measurement of educational standards for the last decade or more. However, given the state of the school system as recorded in repeated annual reports from the chief government inspector for schools, with a failure to see any real improvement in test scores after initial rises and a steady decline in pupils behaviour, perhaps staying as we are presents, in fact, the greater risk.

Part IV

Foundations and futures

Exploring the possible

> Once a policy-maker grasps that the act of defining the curriculum is a conscious selection of which culture shall be transmitted to the next genera-tion, then it becomes possible to reverse the process: to decide what form of culture (or society) will be desirable in future, and to ensure that it is this which is included in the curriculum.
>
> (Ross, 2000: 11)

Earlier, I quoted Bowles and Gintis in connection with what may have seemed a somewhat deterministic representation of schools as the repro-ducers of dominant cultures and a hierarchical workforce. Later, however, these same commentators were to offer a more hopeful and perhaps more nuanced account of the operations and possible purposes of public schooling, drawing attention to a 'contradictory position of education' in which it had a 'dual progressive/reproductive role' – the former character-ized by 'promoting equality, democracy, toleration, rationality, inalienable rights', the latter (simultaneously) 'legitimating inequality, authoritarianism, fragmentation, prejudice and submission' (Bowles and Gintis, 1981: 57). This contradictory position, they suggest, 'is, in part, a reflection of the stress in liberal discourse on procedure over substance'. However 'it provides as well the tools by means of which it can be transformed into an instru-ment in the transition to socialism' (ibid.). Establishing a possible project for educational reform that appears to offer a genuine challenge to the dominant educational purposes of various kinds of social reproduction, they suggest:

> [T]he goal of progressive educational reform must be framed in the structural boundaries of liberal discourse, and can be simply expressed as the full democratisation of education. These goals can be divided into two complementary projects: the democratisation of the social relations of education and the reformulation of the issue of democracy in the curriculum.

This note of hope, this suggestion that there are possibilities for genuine transformation which might contribute to more just and equitable societies, this argument for greater democracy in classrooms and curriculum, underpin the penultimate chapter of our collection, 'Curriculum as Utopian Text' by David Halpin, while the concluding chapter, by Gunther Kress, takes a slightly different twist, in recasting the tensions suggested by Bowles and Gintis in terms of schools and markets and of individual, 'transformative' learning and collective understandings and endeavour.

In his chapter, Halpin indicates, like Ross (earlier on), that in order for genuine curriculum reform to take place we require theories and projections that will, as it were, stand curriculum policy on its head: that is to say, to envision the kind of society, the kind of 'culture', we would wish for our future citizens, and to return to first principles in order to fashion a curriculum and a pedagogy that will stand a good chance of realizing our vision.

In adopting such a stance, Halpin does not presume to provide specific answers or models to right current curriculum ills. Rather, he promotes a particular stance towards both curriculum and Curriculum Studies: a stance that combines the two imperatives of, first, adopting Pinar *et al.*'s (2004) suggestion of looking at curriculum as 'text' and, second, of rendering that process 'Utopian' – that is, of exploring how exercises of the Utopian imagination can facilitate fresh thinking about the form and content of the school curriculum as we move into the twenty-first century.

The suggestion that we look at curriculum as text is an important and powerful one, suggesting that our 'reading' of curriculum will, simultaneously, offer a reading of the wider social arrangements in which curriculum and schooling are located and which they reflect. It is the stance of the constructive curriculum critic, and one that has been adopted by all contributors to this volume. The suggestion that we take a 'Utopian' stance is also reflected in this contribution, although – as Halpin points out – we need to be clear about what we mean by 'Utopian' and in particular to avoid some popular (mis)understandings of the term as originally intended. In this regard, it is important to stress the importance of the Utopian imagination. Imagination is at the heart of the Utopian tradition, and it is this, more than anything, that sets it apart from the bad press it has often received from both conservative and progressive critics, for whom the Utopian approach is often configured as the province of idle dreamers. (For Freud, for example, Utopias were merely 'lullabies from heaven' – ways of putting off the confronting of social problems, whether individually or collectively experienced – rather than meeting them head on.) The Utopian imagination is forward-looking in its desire to envision better worlds, but it is at the same time keen to delve beneath the surfaces of current social arrangements, to imagine different worlds with different assumptions and to ask 'How different might our world look if those assumptions prevailed instead of the ones that do?' As the American Utopian scholar Brooks Spencer has argued in relation to Utopian Literature:

> At heart utopian literature is social commentary: social criticism of
> what is and social suggestion of what could be. Its means are social
> rearrangement. . . . Utopian literature . . . is more revolutionary than
> evolutionary and more revolutionary than reformist. . . . The very nature
> of utopias invites us, suggests for us, to question the very assumptions –
> and that is what they are – of our own society.
>
> (Spencer, 1997: 2–3)

Spencer's words – like Halpin's chapter – take us back to our abiding questions about curriculum, policy and the role of the academy. That role is, we are suggesting, both to explain, describe and account for curriculum, but also to offer constructive criticisms of it – a task that inevitably involves asking awkward questions concerning its historical, social, cultural and political origins. Students of curricula may not necessarily come up with 'alternative' curricula; however, their constructive critiques of existing curricula – of their overt and covert purposes, their measurable and non-measurable effects on a wide range of students, their internal tensions and inconsistencies – can and should support policy makers in imaginative, creative and, if necessary, wide-ranging and revolutionary curriculum revisions. Their studies can also throw light on the ways in which the wider society operates – and might better operate – in relation to authentic approaches to equity, to social justice and to genuine empowerment.

In the final chapter of this collection, Gunther Kress provides an embodiment of Halpin's appeal to the critical imagination, in his assessment of the difficulties and challenges currently facing public education. At the same time, he returns us to the issues the state–market–school relationship and of learning – what 'counts' as learning, how we assess it, where and how it takes place, its role in relation to 'knowledge' – raised by other contributors.

Kress is particularly keen to explore – and to encourage us to explore – what he sees as a global shift of emphasis from teaching to learning, and the impact this has (or might have or perhaps should have) on school curricula. Against a background of the 'marketisation' of the state, of an emphasis on reproducing consumers rather than producers, of a shrinking world, and of dramatic changes, through the development of the Internet and the World Wide Web, both in the speed and in the manner of communication, Kress argues that, in the world experienced outside the school, learners engage with new forms of text in new, more selective, more dialogic ways than before. Such engagements speak of a shift in authority and power in relation to texts and to knowledge, that is not yet, perhaps, reflected in school curricula and classrooms themselves. Proposing the adoption of a view of learning as 'the transformative engagement by the learner with an aspect of the world on the basis of principles brought by them to that engagement, leading to a change in the learner's conceptual resources', Kress effectively challenges the static, knowledge-based curricula still so prevalent in schools around the world. Far from arguing a case for the redundancy or irrelevance of schools, however, or indeed of curricular frameworks, Kress focuses on the central challenge to 're-make and re-think the school as a relevant, significant site of learning, alert and responsive to the shape, environments and demands of the contemporary world'. Such a project involves the embracing of the new kinds of learning experienced by students outside the school setting – including, centrally, allowing greater autonomy or 'agency' in the learning process – while at the same time holding on to and developing in organized sites of learning important collaborative, socializing processes and activities, and ensuring that common values and important knowledge are shared. In relation to this last point, the issue for curriculum subject areas is not so much whether or not to continue to exist, as to critically and creatively revisit the question: 'What is this subject *for*?' – part of that somewhat wider question, invited by implication in the previous chapter, 'What is the *curriculum* for?' In exploring this question, Kress leads us into preliminary considerations of the nature and role of ethics and aesthetics in society and in public schooling, through the example of English (and its counterparts elsewhere in the world) as a key curriculum subject.

10 Understanding curriculum as Utopian text

David Halpin

In this chapter, David Halpin reminds us of the responsibility of Curriculum Studies in offering constructive critiques of current curriculum arrangements, which all too readily become fixed in the needs and mores of a previous era. His argument for a prospective, progressive curriculum draws on Pinar *et al.*'s exhortation to stand back from curricula in order to read them as texts, and on the utopian approach of Thomas More and others which adopts a critical stance towards the current state of affairs through envisioning alternative realities and imagining a present based on different assumptions from those which currently prevail. In suggesting a new starting point for curriculum conceptualization and design, Halpin invokes Malcolm Skilbeck's three-dimensional heuristic for curriculum development and design: that is to say, the identification of 'areas of [worthwhile] knowledge and experience'; a set of 'learning processes' to help interrelate them; and a selection of 'learning environments' within which desirable teaching will be provided and effective learning promoted. Working with such a heuristic, teachers would (if so permitted) be better able to develop a core curriculum that reconstructs rather than reproduces experience and culture, in ways that give prominence to creativity, criticism and reflection.

Introduction

In its thirty-year history in British university departments of education, Curriculum Studies has experienced many attempts to recoup its losses, often in the face of critical commentators who periodically have judged its purposes to be overly and unhelpfully disparate (Reid, 1992). Other, less friendly, critics have simultaneously and negatively accused the field of being naively parasitical on better work underway in the more established 'foundation disciplines' in education, resulting, they conclude, in analyses that are frequently intellectually superficial, not to mention also too easy-going politically (Whitty, 1981). Critical dissidents operating within the field itself have also debated vigorously the prominence it should give to theory at the expense of practice. It was this dispute, everyone will recall, that led the US curriculum scholar, Joseph Schwab, to declare in 1970 that the field of Curriculum Studies had become excessively theoretical and lacking in vitality as a result – indeed, he argued it had become 'moribund' through its failure to connect with and meet adequately the concerns of educational practitioners and policy-makers anxious to find new ways of redefining and reforming the school curriculum.

Schwab went on to advise the field to transfer much of its energies from the theoretical to the practical. While I have always found this particular polarization unhelpful in my own writings about the curriculum, the idea that the field needs repeatedly to be rescued from itself appeals to me very much, suggesting an area of intellectual activity that is far from a near death experience. The recurrence of this phenomenon for me then is not without significance. For why is it, I ask myself, that the field's critics rarely finish up demanding its dismemberment and abandonment, least of all its 'burial', but rather its reinvention, including strong appeals to its core members, some-times co-members, to 'rethink' their objectives (Lawn and Barton, 1981), or to 'reconceptualize' their points of entry (Pinar, 1988), or, as with this collection, to identify 'new directions' for their work?

The answer to this question resides, I have concluded, in the fact that, however conducted, the academic study of the school curriculum is for many educationalists a central feature ultimately of any serious engagement with school policy, whether at state, local or immediately institutional level. For curriculum questions, when they are not narrowly focused on matters of how best technically to design and package a programme of study for a particular cohort of learners, get to the very heart of what schooling is about in terms of its overall aims and pedagogical imperatives and, relatedly, its role in cultural and social reproduction. Questions about the form and content of schooling, including, centrally, ones about its socializing and stratification functions in modern society, ultimately condense into questions about the curriculum – about its aims and the priorities it reflects, represents and recre-ates, including crucially what aspects of the culture of society it seeks to mediate, and in what ways, and to whom in particular.

No small wonder then that so many of us in the academy have sought intellectual asylum in the Curriculum Studies field which, historically, has acted as both the siphon for and the melting pot of our ideas about schooling, many of which were first developed within specialist areas of enquiry – particularly the sociology and philosophy of education – the abstract aspects of which are rendered practically significant in our work through their attachment to arguments about what subject matter schools should teach and how they should teach it, and to whom.

As such, Curriculum Studies, I have often felt, constitute a field of enquiry where educationalists can pursue their academic interests in a largely untrammelled fashion, unhindered by the protocols of any particular specialism. Thus defined, it is both an inter-disciplinary and an extra-disciplinary field of enquiry about the nature of schooling, without which, I want to insist, the study of education would not be complete. Certainly by allowing all manner of significant questions about education to be addressed, often at the same time, it represents one of the most inclusive of intellectual pursuits. This may frustrate the purists. But for those bent on looking at education from a multiplicity of angles, and at its constituent features, curriculum studies are a godsend. William Pinar and his colleagues, in their mammoth introduction to the field, understand this better than most, remarking:

> curriculum is intensely historical, political, racial, gendered, phenomenological, autobiographical, aesthetic, theological and international. [It is] the site on which generations struggle to define themselves and the world. [As such] curriculum ceases to be a 'thing', and it is more than a 'process'. It is [rather] a verb, an action, a social practice . . . and a *public hope*.
>
> (Pinar *et al.*, 2004: 848, my emphasis)

Elsewhere, they suggestively state that a key aspect of understanding the curriculum entails, centrally, studying it as 'text', the discourses of which require continuous 'reading', that is interpreting and reinterpreting (p. 49).

Curriculum as Utopian public hope

Following the lead of Pinar and his colleagues, my main purpose in this chapter is to recall and restore to importance a particular curriculum discourse about hope and curriculum design that presently is only residually apparent within the curriculum field. In the United States in the 1950s and 1960s this discourse exerted a powerful influence on the field. During this period studying the curriculum often entailed theorizing, frequently from within a 'reconstructionist' paradigm (Skilbeck, 1971), the form and content of a common or general education, the optimistic character of which prioritized the role of schooling in revitalizing civil society (see, for example, Smith *et al.*, 1950 and Broudy *et al.*, 1964).

In undertaking this exercise in excavation and restoration, I am motivated by the idea of bringing back into critical consciousness certain progressive ways of thinking and acting about the curriculum – and about the whole curriculum in particular – in order to challenge the hegemonic hold presently exerted on teaching and learning in our schools by particular retrogressive mechanical metaphors, of which 'performance', 'targets' and 'delivery' are the most dominant. These metaphors are not only retrograde in the manner in which they instrumentalize pedagogy, but also in the way they encourage an atomistic approach to the process of education that frustrates whole curriculum planning and reform, and thus deliberation of what an essential general education might consist. Such deliberation, I will argue in the rest of this chapter, can be helpfully kick-started by taking seriously that other observation of Pinar's – that curriculum is a form of public hope, which in my view is best understood in Utopian terms.

Such an association, I need quickly to stress, is not considered by me to be unique to specifically Utopian notions of the curriculum, for they find equally interesting and forceful expression in progressive traditions of educational thinking generally, notably 'child-centred' theories of teaching and learning. On the other hand, in what follows I will argue that certain positive aspects of the process of education in general and of curriculum practice in particular, which currently no longer are much to the fore, but deserve to be, are capable of being brought back to mind, either in memory or anticipation, by looking at them in a Utopian way.

While serving well my purposes here, mention of the utopian in that last sentence of mine is likely to confirm among particular readers of this chapter (especially ones under the influence of a naïve interpretation of Schwab's criticism) a worst expectation – specifically, that what follows will be for them yet another avoidable example of the kind of idealistic, impractical and fanciful theorizing about education that confounds the identification of realistic, pragmatic and workable proposals for what actually needs doing in the current juncture to make it more effective.

While such an expectation is partly a product of a certain restricted way of thinking about such matters that is not limited to educational issues, it is also an unconscious by-product of a particular historic understanding of 'Utopia' that strongly links it with a way of thinking, feeling and acting lacking in rigour and exactitude. Indeed, it is Utopia's contemporary colloquial interpretation that often gets in the way of more subtle and productive definitions. Where today it continues to operate as a verbal sign, it does so principally as a pejorative adjective, accentuating what its users consider are ideas about and proposals for society that are elysian, quixotic and paradisiacal. When it surfaces as the name of a literary form, it has a self-undermining status that 'risks being betrayed as soon as we speak it' (Eagleton, 2003: 24).

Such negative, elsewhere sometimes even maledictive, renderings of Utopia have their origins in Thomas More's short tract *Utopia* (1516), the title of which, like many of the other names it mentions, is a joke – specifically, a witty conflation of two Greek words: *eutopia*, a 'good place', and outopia, meaning 'no place' at all. 'Utopia' has thus always contained deliberate ambiguity: is it a good place or no place, and are these necessarily the same? More's joke, as Levitas (1990) says, has 'left a lasting confusion around . . . [utopia], and one which constantly recurs like a familiar but nonetheless troublesome ghost' (pp. 2f). The result is that today there remains a tendency to dismiss Utopias and Utopianism in equal measure, and for much the same reason – neither being judged to be sufficiently 'practical' to be adequately 'usable'. My aim is to show that this is a mistake where curriculum is concerned, for there are good Utopias that can be written about it that are profoundly 'practical' in their effects.

Promissary notes and curriculum Utopias

Of course, much depends upon what is meant by 'practical' in this context. As we learnt earlier, Schwab had a clear view about this, which he linked with the capacity successfully to 'deliberate'. For Schwab (1970), being a university-based curriculum specialist should be centrally about the skilful use of what he defined as the rhetorics of persuasion – that is to say, with finding ways better to enable school practitioners and policy-makers to judge the relative merits of different proposals for curriculum reform, including the detail of their implementation. Not wanting to be interpreted as being anti-intellectual in making this suggestion, Schwab insisted at the same time that curriculum expertize required also the ability to comment insightfully on the social injustices of the day that bear on education.

Whatever merits they might have in that direction, all curriculum proposals embody an implicit promissory note, to the extent that, in stipulating what should be taught, they pledge to those for whom they have been devised certain outcomes, often expressed at the outset in general terms as 'aims' or, more specifically, as 'objectives'. They also subsequently anticipate engagement with particular subject-matters, making them, like bank cheques, texts waiting to be 'cashed-in.' As such, curriculum proposals embody discourses of educational hope, though we might wish to argue of course with the sort of expectations they identify. It is at this point in the discussion, in the course of undertaking a Schwab-like evaluation, that exercises of the Utopian imagination might be both helpful and instructive.

For Utopianism is a distinctive and radically inflected vocabulary of hope. Indeed, if we ask where and what kind of place is the place of progressive hope, then one answer might be Utopia. Although every expression of this sort of hope does not require the exercise of the Utopian imagination, all Utopias are driven by it: that is to say, they express the dreams of an age, and they say something about its capacity for change. Indeed, to the extent that the power of Utopian thinking derives from its inherent ability literally to visualize the future in terms of radically new ways, Utopianism in the curriculum field holds out the promise to its university-based experts of their being able better to reconsider and share their opinions about the most desirable ways of developing programmes of study that effectively assist pupils to make more of themselves than is immediately apparent. So, while curriculum Utopias may come in all shapes and sizes, being vastly different in their pedagogical reach and scope, they all seek to identify a normatively appealing kind of education. My personal favourites, however, as will become apparent, are those that visualize a design for the school curriculum as a whole.

Although motivated by quite different purposes, which in his case were about societal rather than curriculum reform, this is what More sought to achieve in writing *Utopia*. It is also, more recently, what the 'Real Utopias Project', based at in the United States at the University of Wisconsin in

Madison, has been working at for nearly eleven years since 1994. This initiative, which is built around a series of workshop conferences, involving philosophers, political scientists, economists, educationalists and sociologists, has dealt with, and subsequently published books about, a range of big social issues, including how best to reform the welfare state, the potential of quasi-voluntary secondary associations for the renewal of social democracy, the viability of market forms of socialism, the future of family life, making the transition to environmentally sustainable development and creating institutions for global equality.

While the details of these debates and publications are not relevant here, the point behind them is. Essentially, they are about taking seriously and deliberating the relative merits of radical alternatives to existing institutions which, by common agreement, are not functioning well in the current juncture or even in their own terms. The 'Real Utopias Project', however, is not interested in providing detailed blueprints for reform. Rather, what it seeks to do is to identify particular practical embodiments of desired futures, in each case based upon 'clear elaborations of the *institutional principles* that inform progressive alternatives to the existing world' – an objective that 'falls between a general discussion of the moral values that motivate the enterprise and the fine-grain detail of institutional characteristics' (Wright, 1995: xii).

This particular appreciation of Utopianism leads me to think of the process of constructing curriculum Utopias as a form of practical, political and moral philosophy, in the course of which one explores and exercises judgement about valued ends, appropriate means and existing conditions in order to encourage effective activity, not only, but ultimately at the level of the school. What distinguishes curriculum Utopias from other writings of political and moral philosophy, however, is that their principles are not abstracted from, but rather displayed in, practice. On this understanding, curriculum Utopias are best conceived of as operational images or speaking pictures of what schooling would be like if it was based upon certain progressive educational principles.

The very positive account of the Utopian impulse I have so far provided helps partly to explain why I am always a bit taken aback by the objections some of my colleagues and friends express at the level of principle about my advocacy of Utopianism in the curriculum field. To be sure, some people's Utopias – notably those advocated by dictators and megalomaniacs – turn out to be living nightmares or dystopias for the rest of us. Equally, some Utopias are so naively expressed as not to be worth the paper they are printed on. Quite rightly, they are criticized for eschewing complex notions of hope in favour of wistful yearnings – a 'wouldn't it be nice if' approach – that have no basis in the actual.

But this surely is not a good reason to oppose all visionary analysis and all Utopian examples of it. Indeed, it seems to me that on those occasions when it is not a means of legitimizing satisfaction with the social and political status quo, attacks on Utopianism, in the curriculum field and generally, are about as meaningful as denunciations of dreaming. The sociologist Krishan Kumar goes further, arguing that Utopian conceptions are 'indispensable to politics and to progress; without them, politics would be a soulless world, a mere instrumentality without purpose or vision' (1991: 95). Allan Bloom, the cultural critic, says much the same, suggesting that

> [to] suppress this most natural of inclinations because of possible abuses... is to throw the baby out with the bath water. Utopianism is the fire with which we must play because it is the only way we can find out what we are. We need to criticise false understandings of utopia, but the easy way out provided by realism is deadly.
>
> (1987: 67)

The much harder thing to achieve is to identify and describe a curriculum vision that is based upon a perceptive understanding of the forces and resources within the present order that are capable of transforming it for the better, so as to provide a significant dynamic for action in the here and now: to discern, in other words, the unrealized opportunities which lie dormant or unfulfilled in the recesses of the present, and maybe the past too. Anthony Giddens labels this effort 'Utopian realism' (1994: 101); Pierre Bourdieu defines it as the 'political task of social science' (Bourdieu and Wacquant, 1992: 197). Thus conceived, a realistic curriculum Utopian in my scheme is defined as a kind of 'intellectual lookout', someone who (in Said's words) 'hypothesizes a better situation from the known historical and social facts... [in order to] discern the possibilities for future action' (2004: 140).

Curriculum Utopias as rhetorics of persuasion

One of the best examples of the sort of curriculum Utopianism I have in mind here is that provided by the Australian curriculum analyst, Malcolm Skilbeck, although I dare say he would be surprised to have his work described as such. Arising out of a series of empirical and conceptual studies organized by the Australian Curriculum Development Centre between 1977 and 1981, Skilbeck has set down the outlines of a design for a radical kind of common core curriculum (see Skilbeck, 1984: 175–203 for details), requiring teachers, at the level of the school, to undertake a 'mapping' exercise in which they deliberate the foundations of contemporary social and cultural life as the basis subsequently for providing a general education for pupils.

In ways of which one suspects Schwab would very much approve, Skilbeck offers assistance in this task by providing a progressive (I think, Utopian) three-dimensional heuristic to guide teachers through the practical process of planning, designing and implementing the kind of core curriculum he has in mind. The 'dimensions' include various 'areas of [worthwhile] knowledge and experience', a set of 'learning processes' to help interrelate them, and a selection of 'learning environments' within which desirable teaching will be provided and effective learning promoted. Working with this heuristic, teachers, Skilbeck envisages, will be better able than hitherto to develop a core curriculum for their pupils that reconstructs rather than reproduces experience and culture, and in ways that give prominence to creativity, criticism and reflection.

Skilbeck's approach has a number of Utopian characteristics. It is noticeably different, for a start, despite using familiar labels. So, his 'areas of worthwhile knowledge' are not interpreted by him in ways that reproduce the sort of subject curriculum with which the majority of teachers in English schools are currently most familiar. Skilbeck is not remotely interested in reinforcing such a curriculum model, but rather in identifying a method to encourage teachers to identify and then represent in their work with pupils all of the major domains through which human experience is presently organized. This is quite a different matter from pressurizing them to 'delivering' a prescribed set of subjects alongside the setting of targets to be met and assessments to be undertaken. Relatedly, unlike much of current curriculum policy for schools, Skilbeck's Utopian model does not favour learning content over learning processes and learning situations, preferring instead to insist on their necessary articulation. But, more than that, his schema reminds us of the variety of contexts in which learning can take place, which go well beyond the confines of the classroom, and of the different ways in which learning can be promoted within them, which exceed approaches that emphasize instruction and didacticism.

Skilbeck's schema has other Utopian features, each of which connects more directly with the ones I identified earlier when describing some of the general characteristics of Utopianism. While it takes the form of an invitation to its users to work with the grain of an approach to curriculum reconstruction that, for sure, is out of the ordinary, Skilbeck's model manages equally to promote a new vision of curriculum reality that articulates sensitively with what is known already, if only partially. To that extent, there is nothing in it that should overly surprise anyone. Even so, his version of Utopian realism in the curriculum field, which (to re-quote Said) 'hypothesizes a better situation from the known historical and social facts', manages also to relativize what is presently assumed by promoting an alternative curriculum schema that points towards educational change. Indeed, Skilbeck's heuristic provides teachers with a means to distance themselves from their existing states of affairs, allowing them to judge what they are presently doing in the light of what they could or should do. This is exactly what More was up to in his *Utopia*, though of course for quite different purposes, inasmuch as he was anxious to encourage reflection on the social and political circumstances of his day in order to promote ways of improving them.

Thus understood, and to again repeat something I wrote earlier, Skilbeck's schema offers teachers an operational image of what a core curriculum would be like if it was based upon certain progressive educational principles.

So, while his curriculum vision has content, it is its function in promoting the consideration of an imaginative curriculum alternative that, in the final analysis, makes it Utopian. As Terry Eagleton says, 'in a great deal of utopian writing, alternative worlds are simply devices for embarrassing the world we actually have. The point is not to go elsewhere, but to use elsewhere as a reflection on where you are' (2000: 33). This is what Skilbeck helps his readers to achieve.

'Good' Utopias in the curriculum field, Skilbeck also teaches us, are always future-oriented, and thus contrast with the utopian veneer projected by conservative images of a desired curriculum in which traditions that assume old hierarchies and seek to preserve antiquated modes of deference and control are given priority. Curriculum utopias are about offering radical challenges to the educational status quo, not reinforcing or reconstructing it. As Eileen Hogan says, 'utopia cannot be "what was" – it is, by definition, progressive' (n.d.: 28), a view which helps to explain Ruth Levitas' claim that utopianism should be considered as 'the necessary starting point for a critical social policy' (2001: 463), and maybe one starting point, among others, for a critical theory of the curriculum.

This is not to say the past has nothing to contribute to Utopian thinking about the curriculum. On the contrary, certain kinds of nostalgia can contribute a great deal to it. The unfulfilled desires of the past, for example, may act as a resource in contemplating an improved immediate present in education and better long-term future for it. As Raymond Williams's discussion of 'heuristic Utopias' suggests, nostalgia of this sort can assist educationalists to reflect on the current standing of esteemed 'structures of feeling' in existing curricula. Heuristic Utopias, he says, are ones that encourage the facility 'to strengthen and confirm existing feelings and relationships which are not at home in the existing order and cannot be lived through in it' (1983: 13). David Harvey, echoing these sentiments, considers that particular forms of Utopia are capable of 'opening up ways of thinking that have for too long remained foreclosed' (2000: 17). Thus understood, curriculum Utopias encourage us to ask and answer the question, 'for what may I hope educationally?' They tell us (in Ruth Levitas's words) 'where the felt absences are in [teachers'] lives – the spaces, that is, that Utopia offers to fill, whether in fantasy or reality' (1990: 189). Similarly, in her review of feminist Utopias, the political scientist, Lucy Sargisson, observes that Utopian texts 'break and transform societal and cultural rules. In so doing...they create new conceptual spaces in which radically different ways of being can be imagined' (1996: 2). They achieve this by encouraging the perception that social reality is neither static nor unchangeable. This perception in turn realizes a form of estrangement whereby the commonplace is rendered unusual and unfamiliar, serving to distance us from social reality, while at the same time engendering the idea that it could be changed for the better and in particular ways.

In developing operational images of better alternatives for the curriculum, there is need, I readily concede, for educational Utopians to be cautious, provisional and reflexive in order to fend off charges of being exclusive, unilateral and uncompromising in their thinking. Accordingly, while More had very strong views about most things, and was rarely, even unto death, fearful of expressing them, his ideas about an ideal commonwealth were written up by him to promote debate among the intellectual elite of his time about the principles that should inform the ways in which people should live together and govern their affairs. His was not a blueprint for the future development of Tudor England, to be imposed on its citizens whether they liked it or not, but rather a fictional heuristic designed to foster reflection and discussion about the nature of society and its basic institutions.

Much the same, minus the fictional element, can be said of Skilbeck's particular 'rhetoric of persuasion' (one of Schwab's key expressions, remember), which I outlined a moment ago, leading me to say now that we need more of such imaginings, not less of them, and especially at this time, given the demise of grand-scale thinking about society and the underplaying of the ideological frameworks within which it used to be conducted. In this connection, it strikes me as very odd that, apart from a few notable exceptions (e.g. Quicke, 1999), the field of Curriculum Studies in recent years has generally steered away from developing theories about the form, content and overall design of the whole curriculum. Personally, I think this is a shame, given the major challenges in this area we currently face and the availability and ascendancy of narrow government-provided solutions to them. To that extent, there is a sense in which the field has lost out, partly by leaving the debate to others less qualified to engage with it, and partly also through certain self-denying ordinances that have discouraged it from thinking that it has anything any longer worth saying in the area. On the other hand, it is, for me, both a curious and pleasing fact that, while it was produced over twenty years ago, Skilbeck's utopian rhetoric of persuasion still retains today considerable potential power to influence for the better teachers' thinking about curriculum design. Certainly, it is a million miles away from the conservative and retrogressive curriculum discourses that presently hold center stage.

Conclusion

Such schema may also help to fend off the worst effects of the kind of melancholia suffered by many teachers as they struggle to implement government policies for education that rub uneasily up against their personal pedagogic philosophies (see Moore *et al.*, 2002). I am thinking here of those teachers who, while wanting to do the best for their pupils, find themselves overly immersed in a regime of teaching and learning that stresses pupil performativity and curriculum target-setting, each of which frustrates their best efforts as a result.

The facility to be able to draw on the sort of optimistic discourses about teaching and learning that Utopianism encourages may act as a spur to teachers to undertake new action, promoting in its wake a better sense of professional well being. Accordingly, teachers should not underestimate the degree to which the adoption of Utopian-like perceptions of control and mastery over events might also contribute to their ability better to engage in productive and creative work, even in circumstances where this is ordinarily very difficult. As the psychologist Shelley Taylor writes: 'Normal human thought and perception is marked not by accuracy, but positive self-enhancing illusions about the self, the world, and the future. Moreover, these illusions appear actually to be adaptive, promoting rather than undermining mental health' (1989: 25).

The rhetorics of persuasion entailed in Utopianism ultimately have the power to encourage teachers to carry out thought experiments that assist both in the recovery of obscured, submerged and positive ways of thinking about the curriculum and in the reconceptualizing of different ways of designing it. This kind of restorative and anticipatory consciousness, if conducted publicly and with others, moreover, may provide one of the necessary conditions for initiating collective action for curriculum improvement. It also underscores the importance of keeping to the forefront of one's mind that, however difficult things appear to be, there is likely to be a way of making progress, providing one is prepared to make the effort to find and act upon it. As Raymond Williams once so tellingly remarked:

> It is only in a shared belief and insistence that there are practical alternatives that the balance of forces and chances begins to alter. Once the inevitabilities are challenged, we begin gathering our resources for a journey of hope. If there are no easy answers, there are still available and discoverable hard answers, and it is these that we can learn to make and share.
>
> (1983: 268–269)

It has been one of the premises of this chapter that such 'hard answers' within education generally, but in the curriculum in particular, are capable of being envisaged through exercises of the Utopian imagination. Such positive imaginings, which seek to relativize and offer a critique of present curricula, by conjuring images of alternative futures to them, provide both an antidote to depressive inaction in education and a prompt to think and act progressively about it.

11 Learning and curriculum
Agency, ethics and aesthetics in an era of instability

Gunther Kress

This final chapter begins with an acknowledgement, contextualized within memories of the author's own childhood, of the nature of the current 'generation gap', characterized by a less nostalgic, more present-oriented understanding of the social world on the part of young learners living in an era of rapid and unpredictable change. Part of that change is linked to the development of the World Wide Web, and to the ways in which information of all kinds is disseminated, accessed and read – a development which itself prioritizes and 'authorizes' the learner as agent, at the same time undermining the authority of more traditional texts and calling for new ways of assessing learning that do not rely on common outcomes. Changes in the nature and application of texts are linked by Kress to wider issues of authority and agency in learning and schooling, but also to the ways in which children's attitudes to and experiences of the social world shape their learning and help make them the kind(s) of learners they are. Returning to a key issue for current curriculum theory of considering the ways in which learner agency can be reconciled with predefined school curricula, Kress suggests a conceptualization of curriculum as 'promotion' (of learning) and, simultaneously as an ethical and aesthetic orientation, in which the body of knowledge, important though the selections are, may be considered less important than the intellectual, emotional and social learning that result from its consideration.

The present environment: matters of learning, teaching and authority

The last fifteen years or so have seen a shift from a focus on teaching to a now ubiquitous emphasis on learning. Where once teaching ruled, learning is now the focus. That itself is a matter inextricably wound into all aspects of the social, economic, political but also technological changes which characterize the present in the 'developed' world – all in their ways part of that vast and nebulous notion of globalization (Gee *et al.*, 1996). We can say that the shift from teaching to learning speaks about challenges to, and shifts in, authority and power. Wherever social and economic factors are involved we know that culture is implicated; this acts as a constant reminder that while global forces are at work, local factors will be at work in often equal measure. The shift from teaching to learning, and what has produced it, has profound implications for conceptions of curriculum.

In Western Europe the world is changing at a rate more pronounced than at any time over the last 800 years or so. This may seem wildly overstated, given the effects of nearly two and a half centuries of the Industrial Revolution, and given the cataclysms of two world wars. And yet, as a child growing up in a village in southern Germany, in the 1940s and 1950s, the shape of the fields I saw, the tools that were in use, the practices which I learned, were entirely those I would recognize later in Breughel paintings from 400 years earlier. In these paintings, the iron rims of the wooden carts were forged, as in my village, by the village smithy and, as in 'my' village, drawn by oxen. The tools to work our fields were still those used four centuries ago: the scythes, rakes, forks, ploughs, made of wood largely, or iron where that was essential. Over the succeeding thirty years all that was swept aside, earlier in the north and west of Europe and later in the south, where that era persisted well into the 1970s. I imagine that similar stories can be told about other parts of the world.

My point is that our present is the culmination of two cycles: one, the agricultural, of more than a thousand years' duration; the other, the industrial, of some two and a half centuries. The potent myths and metaphors which shape, still, the imagination and the practices of the present, come from those two long-lasting, distinct and yet connected cycles. Two of the persistently dominant conceptions (as myth or as metaphor) are those of stability and of a homogeneous society. The former offered a relative certainty that whatever cataclysmic events, natural or social, might befall, the world, tomorrow would recognizably and in all essential ways be much as the world of yesterday. The latter offered the promise that all those who belonged in my community were in all essential respects like me. Of course the notion of stability is always a myth: there was the Reformation, the Renaissance, the Enlightenment, the developments of mercantile capitalism and later of the nation-state. Yet while all these had profound effects on notions of authority and on the realities of the relation of the individual to power – whether secular or divine – the deeper metaphors remained intact enough to be used, still, as points of reference and 'appeal'.

The present is marked by a new revolution, a revolution in the meanings, effects and uses of time and space. Now, for information of all kinds, the ruling sense of time is that of the speed of light; the relevant unit of space that of the globe. The effect of these two together, in political, social and economic terms, in terms of the impact of technologies of all kinds, whether of transport of information or of people, is to unmake all former framings and with that all former certainties, in all domains. That is so whether it is the frame of the nation state, with its imagined homogeneous citizenry (I am speaking of Europe); of the (formerly) nationally controlled economy and its local labour force; of framings around knowledge; of forms and means of communication; or of authority and authorized individuals in different domains – whether the political, the social, the ethical, the intellectual, the economic or, by no means last, the personal/individual.

The school of the 'West' has a history roughly speaking co-extensive with the cycle of industrialization. It was established in response to the needs of that period – socially and politically, to produce 'citizens', and economically to produce the nation's labour force. There was a tight link between the needs of the state and its economy and the expectations held of the school. The tight framings of the society in all its forms became the framings of the school, and both together provided a tight, close, relatively well-functioning – from a perspective from 'above' – and motivated fit. Curriculum could be founded on authoritative knowledge, and on the utility of the knowledge in relation to the social and economic givens. Pedagogies – the instantiation of social forms, relations and processes in the classroom – could make appeal to ethical, political and social authority (Bernstein, 2000). Conceptions of the individual, of subjectivity, of the extent, possibilities and limits of agency, but also of duties, obligations and responsibilities could be derived from a stable and known ethical, social, economic and political environment. These gave meaning and legitimation to the structures, processes and practices of the school, to teaching, learning and curriculum. In many ways they still do, though now in purely ideological form.

'Pace', stability/instability, homogeneity/diversity

Given my emphasis on change, it is worth reflecting on the question of 'pace' – the pace of human biological change on the one hand, and the pace of economic and technological change, of social and cultural change on the other – and how the two can be brought to 'mesh'. Here the myth of a stable world – whether divine, celestial, terrestrial, social, cultural – is crucial. The long cycle of medieval agrarian culture allowed for gradual adjustments by humans to the changes that always took place, but at a pace so slow as to be imperceptible to anyone living in the period. It was possible to believe that the economic world was stable. In the much shorter cycle of industrializing and industrialized Europe, the 'pace' had quickened, economically, technologically, socially and culturally. Yet while the speed of transport had increased enormously with the advent of steam and rail, as of electricity, that new pace still made it possible to construct stable institutions which would cope with economic, social and cultural upheaval.

At the same time, more than the vestiges of the former economy and its social and cultural forms carried on intact, relatively speaking. Anyone living in that period had relatives for whom the former period was vividly present still. I am shaped by my experience of my grandmother's values and practices, which connect me effortlessly to the middle of the nineteenth century. With these mythic, affective and intellectual resources I face a present in which the pace of technological, economic, social, cultural and political change is such as to make apt responses impossible, either at an institutional level (witness the constant restructurings of all kinds of institutions), or of myself as an individual. Of course, anyone under the age of thirty or so does not carry the baggage of the nineteenth century so tangibly; but for them too, the pace of change, technologically and culturally, is such that they can neither imagine nor construct appropriate institutional forms or individual responses which might bring human (biological) pace into some reasonable conjunction with the pace of the digitally globalizing world. This is a central problem for the school, as a social as much as a cultural institution.

If we ask 'How do we now imagine an apt curriculum?' our answers need to be set in the historical, social, economic, political and cultural environment where the question is posed. In the United Kingdom, as in other anglophone societies, that is shaped by instability where there had been stability; by multiplicity and diversity where there had been singularity and homogeneity. The effects of the shift from stability to instability are clear enough: in conditions of stability it is possible to predict; that is not the case now. Those who constructed curricula could anchor the curriculum to the stable givens of the society of their day and be certain that it would 'fit' the society of tomorrow. That is no longer so. The shift from teaching to learning is both symptom and response to that. The effect of the shift from homogeneity to diversity on curriculum is different: where before one could assume that one knew the audience, understood and shared its values and needs, that is absolutely not the case now. The re-emergence of the need for the concept of rhetoric (and, for me, of design) is one response to that.

To list some of the crucial differences: 'Then' work and leisure were distinct in site, in time, in tools; now these are blurred. 'Then' transport was slow; 'now' transport is fast – and in relation to information (including finance), instantaneous. 'Then' the major institutions of the state – social, economic, political – were stable; now they are unstable – often, they are ad hoc and short-term institutions formed by 'local communities'. 'Then' the state and its demands – producing citizens and a labour force for a local economy – were clear; now the state's demands and requirements have been displaced by those of the market – a market that is interested in consumers, not citizens as an economy based on production is displaced by an economy based on consumption. 'Then', the state spoke with a single voice in matters of ethics; now, the market asserts its cacophony of voices. While the ethics of state and market were (and still are, in some respects and differently in different places) distinct, now the state is increasingly the servant of the market: of its requirements, of its demands, of its values. (In all this, I am speaking principally about the United Kingdom; the situation is differentially so in different parts of Europe and elsewhere.)

Education and the market

The impact of market ethics and demands on education in general and the curriculum in particular merits a further word or two in light of what I shall argue later. Put bluntly, a state which is becoming the servant of the market, and an economy based on consumption, have an entirely different relation to the 'education system' than those of before. This needs more sustained exploration than I can provide, but: the market is not interested in citizens, its needs are for consumers; the subjectivities of citizens and consumers are differently formed, and are ruled by a different ethos; the market is not interested in the training, development, production and sustaining of a differentiated, skilled and professional labour force, nor is it interested in homogeneity of any kind: under contemporary forms of consumption, it is the strategy of the niche market which offers most return and reward. This, however, is a strategy for social fragmentation. The curricula of the nation-state, with its mass institutions – whether of transport, the military, hospitals, schools – and its mass market were a means for producing social cohesion.

To restate, the school was founded on the givens of the former environment: stable/predictable needs and requirements; stable sites of learning; stable (canonical) forms of knowledge; stable (canonical) media of dissemination and modes of representation; clear frames and boundaries 'between' sites and times of work and leisure; between the knowledges of school and work versus those of the home and of leisure. Now there are no agreed needs; nor are needs either knowable or stable over a longer term. Without social stability, without a knowable and stable economy, in the presence of intense diversity, there can be no stable and legitimated forms of power; there is neither authoritative knowledge nor are there shared values. Without these there can be no legitimated stable curriculum nor a secure, stable pedagogy.

Those who can consume enjoy both the reality and the illusion of choice: subjectivity and identity are now shaped and defined in consumption where once they were shaped through the meanings of social roles and structures, and of those of participation in an economy of production. The analogue in education is the niche education of 'personalized' learning and curricula. At a more profound level the effect on learners is their taken-for-granted assumption that they have power, that they are agentive in their own learning, that they choose that with which they wish to engage on the basis of their interest, and that in their actions they remake their world in their image. That presents a deep paradox for the school, which may wish to say 'yes' to the learner's agency, but 'no' to the personalized curriculum.

The school has no answer. Indeed, it has barely begun to realize the causes of its problems. One major – even if transitional – problem for education systems now is the generation gap in the sense that dispositions and subjectivities shaped by the myths, metaphors and ideologies (as well as the realities) of the preceding era come up against not just the absence of those myths, metaphors and ideologies, but the absence of any compelling, newly legitimated myths, metaphors and ideologies. Conventional power still lies with the school; yet it is becoming increasingly clear where alternative power is beginning to assemble: in forms of often outright refusal, avoidance, alternative routes, truancy, and so on.

And there is a deep problem of 'recognition': the generation now undergoing schooling simply does not recognize the accounts of the present given by their elders. To the young the present is what is; it is not some changed or lesser form, with lesser potential and possibilities, a constant cause for nostalgia. It is what it is, and is taken as what it is. In that perspective notions of instability and change are perplexing. Whose problems, whose perceptions are these? Mine? Theirs? Here lies another problem of generation, which will be with us for another twenty years or so: everyone over the age of thirt-five, more or less, went to school before the real impact of the digital technologies and of the multiple factors of globalization had begun to bite, in irrefutable ways. But for anyone whose schooling started in the early 1990s, these are quite simply how things are.

All this leads to intractable problems. Reproduction, whether of society and its culture(s), of making the young in the image of a former society, with its valued knowledges and value-systems, is no longer a possible agenda for education. The task now is to understand the new, constantly changing environments, to try to grasp clearly what the new conditions of learning are, and out of such understanding to design curricula and pedagogies which are suited for a future which we may guess at but cannot know.

Whose perspective should rule? It is my generation (and that following mine) which still sets the educational agendas. The young want to get to grips with the world as it is, and they do: but in the United Kingdom, by and large, the place to do so is outside of school. In this context the most urgent question is how to re-make and re-think the school as a relevant, significant site of learning, alert and responsive to the shape, environments and demands of the contemporary world.

Power versus interest and consent: learner-transformers versus authoritative curriculum

In the least mythically stable societies of earlier times, the directionality of authority was clear: state power supported the school, the school had clear purposes, its links with state, society and economy were clear and in some ways worked with some benefit for most, even if with huge differentials, and so its values, principles, resources, among them its curricula, were clear and legitimate. They might be rejected (Willis, 1977), but they were not challenged. The gap, a chasm nearly, that exists now between the school and the world around the school did not exist then: the school promised, and by and large could keep its promises; though it promised differentially. There was a unidirectionality of power and authority, and there was a unidirectionality of the problems the school was there to solve. The school knew the constitution of the life-worlds of its students, and its curricula promised and provided the resources for their solution.

But that relation of authority was homologous with that of society at large; it was there in all forms of communication around authoritative knowledge, with the same directionality. Figure 11.1 is an (entirely banal) example: *The Boy Electrician* was first published in 1920 (Sims, 1920); my copy (the sixth edition) was reprinted in 1946. As I said, the world of the industrial cycle too had great stability. In the Preface to the book the author states: 'The prime instinct of almost any boy at play is to make and to create. If left to himself he will make things of such material as he has at hand . . . .The four-year old will lay half-a-dozen wooden bricks end on, put a cotton reel on one end, and tell you it is a "puff-puff" . . . .At seven he will wire the whole house with his telephone system . . . His elder brother will improve on this by purchasing a crystal, a telephone receiver . . .' (Sims, 1920: 5). This author was an expert as much on electricity as his readers: he knew their world, understood his readers' needs; he laboured to provide the knowledge-as-tool that would solve the problems in their life-world. The readers' task was to 'acquire' that knowledge in the form that the author had assembled and presented here.

The forms of representation and communication fitted that task exactly. The contents pages set out the chapter descriptions in stately order; each chapter comprising carefully packaged knowledge, each to be acquired in the set order so as to gain access to the whole 'body of knowledge'. This was also so for the order of each page; the order of reading was fixed: from top left-hand corner to bottom-right; each line read from left to right, each syntactic unit read in the sequence given, and each element within these units read in the order laid out. The author established the order of the world, and the reader's task was to fit into the order established by the author. This order was that of the social world, everywhere insistently present, through the power of the author inscribed into the very forms of representations and the media of communication. This ordering was readily translatable – and not just as a metaphor – for the school, its curricula, its syllabi, its timetables and as the calendar for the year. There was a homology between all aspects of cultural, social, economic, political life, and expressed in all forms and processes of representation and communication.

My next example (Figure 11.2), from the contemporary world of representation, shows a situation which is entirely different. It is the homepage of the Institute of Education, University of London.

This homepage neither offers 'knowledge' nor an order in which it should be read. Where the traditional page had one 'entry point' – in the case of an English-language text, the top left hand corner – and a set reading path, this 'page' has twelve or thirteen entry points. What it offers is 'information', as does the rest of the website. If the author of the traditional page we looked at above knew his audience – a myth, though a potent one – the authors/designers of this page do not. They have hunches about who might

In the eighteenth century, when Benjamin Franklin performed his famous kite experiment, electricity was believed to be a sort of fiery atmospheric discharge which could be captured in small quantities and stored in receptacles known as Leyden jars.

Franklin was the first to prove that the lightning discharges taking place in the heavens are electrical.

The story of his experiment is very interesting.

He secured two light strips of cedar-wood, placed crosswise and covered with a silk handkerchief for a kite. To the top of the upright stick of the kite was fastened a pointed wire about a foot long. The twine was of the usual kind, but was provided with a short piece of silk ribbon and a key. The purpose of the ribbon was possibly to prevent the lightning's running through his body, silk being a ' non-conductor,' as will be explained a little farther on. The key was secured to the junction of the silk ribbon and the twine, to serve as a convenient conductor from which to draw the sparks—if they came. He did not have to wait long for a thunderstorm, and as he saw it gathering he went out with his son, then a young man twenty-two years of age. The great clouds rolled up from the horizon, and the gusts of wind grew fitful and strong. The kite felt a swishing blast and began to rise steadily, swooping this way and that as the breeze caught it. The thunder muttered nearer and nearer and the rain began to patter on the grass as the kite flew higher.

The rain soon began to fall heavily, compelling Franklin and his son to take refuge under a near-by shed. The heavy kite, wet with water, was sailing sluggishly, when suddenly a huge low-lying black cloud travelling overhead shot forth a forked flame, and the crash of thunder shook the very earth. The kite moved upward, soaring straight into the black mass, from which the flashes began to come rapidly.

Franklin watched the silk ribbon and the key. There was not a sign. Had he failed ? Suddenly the loose fibres of the twine erected themselves. The moment had come. Without a tremor he advanced his knuckle to the key, and between his knuckle and the key passed a spark ! then another and another. They were the same kind of little sparks that he had made hundreds of times with a glass tube.

Then as the storm abated and the clouds swept off towards the mountains and the sun came lazily in the blue, the face of Franklin gleamed in the glad sunshine. The great discovery was complete, his name immortal.

The cause of lightning is the accumulation of the electric charges

in the clouds, the electricity residing on the surface of the particles of water in the cloud. These charges grow stronger as the particles of water join together and become larger. As the countless multitude of drops grows larger and larger the *potential* is increased, and the cloud soon becomes heavily charged.

Through the effects of a phenomenon called *induction*, and which we have already stumbled against in the experiment with the tacks and the magnetic chain, the force exerted by the charge grows stronger because of a charge of the opposite kind on a neighbouring cloud or some object on the earth beneath. These charges continually strive to burst across the intervening air.

As soon as the charge grows strong enough, a vivid flash of lightning, which may be from one to ten miles long, takes place. The heated air in the path of the lightning expands with great force : but immediately other air rushes in to fill the partial vacuum, thus producing the terrifying sounds called ' thunder.'

In the eighteenth century electricity was believed to be a sort of fiery atmospheric discharge, as has been said. Later it was discovered that it seemed to flow like water through certain mediums, and so was thought to be a fluid. Modern scientists believe it to be simply a vibratory motion, either between adjacent particles or in the ether surrounding those particles.

It was early discovered that electricity would travel through some mediums but not through others. These were termed respectively ' conductors ' and ' non-conductors,' or *insulators*. Metals such as silver, copper, gold, and other substances like charcoal, acidulated water, etc., are good conductors. Glass, silk, wool, oils, wax, etc., are non-conductors, or insulators, while many other substances, like wood, marble, paper, cotton, etc., are partial conductors.

There seem to be two kinds of electricity, one called ' static ' and the other ' current ' electricity. The former is usually produced by friction, while the latter is generated by chemical or mechanical action, which we shall deal with in a later chapter.

A list of materials will be found in the Appendix placed in order of merit as insulators or conductors.

Warm a piece of writing-paper, then lay it on a wooden table and rub it briskly with the hand. It soon will become stuck to the table and will not slide along as it did at first. If one corner is raised slightly it will tend to jump right back. If the paper is lifted off the table it will tend to cling to the hands and the clothing. If held near the face it will produce a tickling sensation. All these things happen because the paper is electrified. It is drawn to the

Figure 11.1 The Boy Electrician.

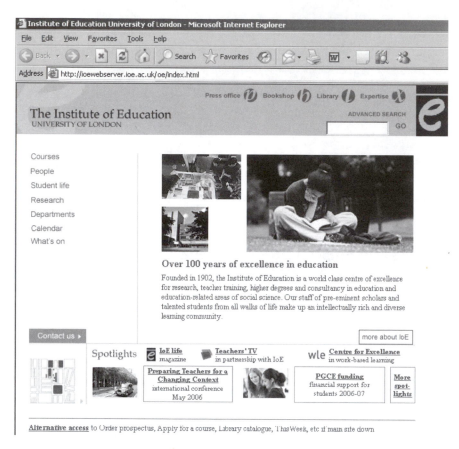

Figure 11.2 Institute of Education University of London 'Home Page'.

wish to visit (not read) the site; and the homepage is organized according to the assumed interests of the visitors who might come to the site. These visitors will navigate the site in accordance with their interests and the facilities offered by the site.

Responsibility for constructing knowledge from the information that the visitors gather here rests with them. As Boeck puts it: 'Information is material which is selected by individuals to be transformed by them into knowledge to solve a problem in their life-world' (Boeck, 2004). The visitors make their knowledge out of the resources offered by the site and with the principles derived from their own interests.

Mr Sims had certainty, the designers of this page do not. Where he had authoritative knowledge, they have hunches about what might be useful information. Where the traditional author knew the life-world of his audience, expressed in every aspect of the ordering of his materials and of the medium, the designers of the website have informed guesses, expressed in the thirteen 'entry-points' to this page. Mr Sims could offer knowledge as a tool; this site offers information to be shaped into the tool needed by the visitors.

This is is an example of the shift from the power/authority of the author (and the institution) to the power/agency and interest of the reader, as of the child/student. Children in school are users of these media, they have become subjects with the implied habitus of relation of their power/authority to knowledge and interest, shaped by that use (Bourdieu, 1984). This provides an apt and essential metaphor for (re)thinking school, curriculum and learners, and their relation. Equally, it indicates the habitus with which children now come to school, only to meet there an entirely different model of that relationship. This poses the problem that the school faces in sharp relief: that of the power of institutional authority versus the interest of the learners, and the need for their consent, in a world where, ideologically at least, the directionality of power, authority and knowledge to learner and life-world has been inverted.

'What is learning?', 'what is to be learned?' and 'what are the environments of learning?'

What is learning? Here are two examples. Figure 11.3 shows the engagement by two girls (both three and a half years at the time) with the script-systems of their cultures.

How can we attempt to understand and uncover the meanings which might inhere in these marks? How are these two examples evidence of learning? While seeing just the one – the 'squiggles on the lines' – might lead to the assumption that what was going on here was 'merely scribble' (a response I have frequently encountered), the contrast between the two forces one into a different stance. It allowed me to speculate that each is shaped by the characteristics of the world which these learners engaged with, in this case the script systems, shaped by principles, which their makers each brought to and developed out of their engagement with that bit of the world. In the interaction of principles and world each is transformed: the girls' understanding of the world they have engaged with, and the principles which were brought to that engagement. The two learners too are transformed: their capacities, their resources for engaging with the world, both semiotic and conceptual, are now not as they had been before. The writer of the alphabetic lines seems to have deduced the following principles about alphabetic script: it is linear, it is directional (in this case written from right to left), the elements are simple, the elements are (relatively) alike, they are usually connected, and they are repeated. In the other case the principles seem to include: the script is linear, it is directional, the elements are (highly) complex, each element is different, the elements are not connected, they are not repeated. Both 'writers' apply and uncover principles and these are

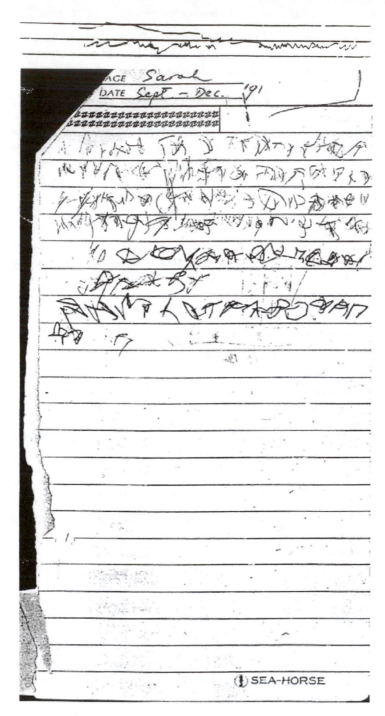

Figure 11.3 Learning script-systems.

represented in their drawing/sign. Some of the principles are shared (linearity, directionality, connectedness, complexity/simplicity); what differs is how the principles are realized in each of the script-systems.

The examples are evidence of learning; we can ask 'what has been learned?' and put develop a plausible account. This is learning without a (pre-existing) curriculum; there is no overt pedagogy or assessment. The curriculum that is present – if we wanted to use that term – is of the children's own making, likely to have been fostered (explicitly or implicitly) by their parents' interest. However, the motivation to *materialize* that learning comes from them. There is no overt teaching; if there had been, the results shown here might well have been regarded by their 'teachers' as failures. The children's learning does not stop here, it is ceaseless; at times visible, at other times not. The general point that I derive from this example is that *learning is the transformative engagement by the learner with an aspect of the world on the basis of principles brought by them to that engagement, leading to a change in the learner's conceptual resources.*

The next example (Figure 11.4) shows the relation between two occasions of learning: one in school and the other, following that, the result of continuing (inner) semiotic activity, done out of school.

The second image shows a page made by me from six small square pieces of note-paper. One summer afternoon, while we had been entertaining friends in our garden, our then five-year-old son had busied himself, unnoticed by us, in drawing images on square bits of notepaper kept by the telephone. When I encountered him later, in the hallway, laying them out in pairs, as on the sheet here, I asked him what he was doing; he gave me the glosses written on the sheet. Some three weeks later, at the end of the summer term, he came home from school with all his exercise books, among them the one with the page which is reproduced here as the first image. From the date on that page it is clear that the exercise had been done some three weeks before the drawings made in the garden.

The exercise in the school-book was within an explicit curriculum, broadly around the issue of 'classification' – 'matching like with like' – in the context of a pedagogy. But the meaning-making engendered by this exercise did not stop once the book had been closed and put away; it continued 'internally' and ceaselessly. When it 're-emerged' in outward sign-making some three weeks on, the issue of classification had become considerably more complex than it had been on the first occasion in school: categories such as 'animateness' ('being in life') are there, even though the child does not have the words for them. The absence of an explicit curriculum or pedagogy did not impede the ongoing semiosis, the continuing inner transformative work, the continuing learning. The school's role had been to 'propose' an issue – what is to be learned – as part of its curriculum; the child used that as a resource for further semiotic work, to 'take it further' on the basis of his interest. We might note the connected yet different tasks and roles of school, curriculum and learner: for the school *proposing what is to be learned* (the curriculum),

Figure 11.4 'Classification' in school and out of school.

and for the student *taking it further in transformative work* on the basis of this learner's interest. These two together might constitute a useful schema and principle for imagining a differently conceived role for the school with its resources, for teachers and their expertise, and for learners as agentive in their own interests.

What is to be learned points to a continuing significant function for the school in any society that wishes to maintain a sense of cohesion, in this case around a core of shared knowledge, values and dispositions. We might assume that the school selects on the basis of such criteria of relevance and significance as can be established as socially / culturally legitimate and as economically desirable (this might be at the level of a local community, or of larger level social groupings), and presents that as the world to be engaged with, that is, the curriculum for students in school. This acknowledges and values past and present cultural work, the expertise of those engaged in that, and the concerns of the social group for the maintenance of grounds and principles for continued sociality. Given the definition of learning as *the transformative engagement by the learner with an aspect of the world on the basis of principles brought by them to that engagement, leading to a change in the learner's conceptual resources*, it also acknowledges the real agency of learners.

In this shift there are consequences of a profound kind for authority and power: in the past it was the power of society, vested in the school, which decided what was to be learned. Now with social power much more in question, and with a wide gap between the world as it appears in the school, and as it appears to those who are students in the school, with their experience of that world, there is a need for searching debate, for a reconsideration of power, for the recognition and affirmation of the interests of the students. The compromise that might be reached would affirm both the school's expertise and the students' interest. It would be based on a transformative view of learning, in which the students' agency would be in the centre. This abandons in no way the central social and cultural role of the school, the legitimacy of the knowledge and values of the community, or the expertise of teachers. It attempts to find a means of valuing those as necessary resources, and to accord appropriate recognition to the transformative action of learners.

What are the environments of learning? Power and authority provide the most significant aspects of any environment of learning: whose authority? in what domains? whose power? how exercised? In this conception the school provides the environment for engagement with a socially essential and legitimated curriculum, together with ethical, intellectual and conceptual principles for navigating the world. The school takes responsibility for providing the environment of learning: what social relations are imagined and projected in the pedagogies enacted in classrooms; what role power plays in relation to knowledge; what value is given to accuracy (an ethical issue, linked to truth) as against correctness (a social issue, linked to convention);

what modes for representation are admitted and which are marginalized or banished; and, above all, what forms of evaluation and assessment are used, and how do they respond to the transformative work of students.

Learning happens in many sites; though when it does – as in my example of the learning of the script systems – it happens in environments constituted with different authority, principles, power and values. These are sites that range from workplaces to leisure centres, from the play-station and the laptop at home to the visit to the museum, the supermarket or the art gallery. In each case the relevant questions are: whose interests, whose agency, whose power is active, constitutes the curriculum (implicitly or explicitly) and determines the pedagogy?

Two central features of the new media may serve as a guiding metaphor in this respect. Both circle around the user's activity seen as interactivity. In principle there are two distinctly different features: directionality and ordering. I have discussed this above, in relation to the traditional book, and the new website. With the media of the page the direction is from author to reader; the reader of course may do very many things with the text, from outright refusal to engage to intense opposition, to full 'alignment'. However, it is very difficult for the reader to 'write back' to the author; dialogue, as Barthes (1983: 38) has suggested, is hardly possible in this case. With the media of the screen the direction is always two ways: I can change the email that has been sent to me, or the text of the attachment that came with it. The possibilities of dissemination of my text-as-message are the same for me as they were for the person who had sent me their message. This has entirely changed the authority of authorship.

This is what is now normal for the young and is rapidly becoming normal for all. In contemporary multimodal (and not only screen-based) texts, it is readers who design the order of the text with which they engage. In the 'older' text, the reader was obliged both by the form of the text and by convention to read the text in the order set out by the author. Now it is the reader's interest which fixes the order of reading. For the young, this new mode of reading as design is one they bring even to traditionally constituted texts. In that sense all such readers have become authors/designers of the texts with which they engage. This has its analogue in composing (a general term I use, to include writing), a situation much lamented by teachers. Students who are on the Internet may go where they choose, constrained to some extent by the organization of choices in the architecture of sites. If I am thinking of composing a text, I can take the resources for my text from anywhere: usually described and misunderstood as cut and paste, as not real writing or composition.

These principles, taken together, are remaking the world of representation and communication; in that, they have the profoundest effects on arrangements of power in all domains. The recognition of the transformative agency of learners leads to a profoundly different conception of learning and learners, and acknowledges the effect of the learner in learning what is to be learned. It leads to the need for different metrics in assessment. But that is not the same as assuming that all learning and all curricula are personalized; rather it sees a balance between the legitimate desires of the community and the agency of learners, with a due valuation of both.

'Assessment'

Assessment in all of its forms provides the means and a metric for the process of policing of social practices around learning (and others). The example below is from a science classroom. The learners are thirteen-year-old girls. They have had four lessons on plant cells; now their teacher has asked them to prepare a slide of an onion's epidermis, and then view it under the microscope. The teacher has instructed them to 'write what you did' and to 'draw what you have seen'. He has told them to put the written report at the top of the page, and to place the drawing underneath, and not to use colour pencils. Groups of four girls work around one microscope, having previously made their one slide. Here are two of one group's texts.

Considering that the young women had sat through the same lessons, had prepared, looked at and discussed the same slide under the microscope, there are startling differences here, apart from Figure 11.5 having the drawing at the top (see Kress *et al.*, 2001).

Each of the four had made very different selections from the masses of material offered during the lessons and from the discussions between the girls during their joint work. Each had transformed the material in specific ways. They had 'selected out' and transformed elements, but they had also 'moved' material from one semiotic mode (writing or speech) to another (image). The move of material from one mode of representation to another – from writing say, to image – I call *transduction*, to mark it as different to the process in which elements are *transformed*, where there is no change in mode. What had appeared in writing on a handout-sheet ('the cells will look like bricks in a brick-wall') appears in Figure 11.5 in the mode of image; what had appeared in the mode of speech as talk around the microscope ('it looks like a wavy weave'), has similarly been *transducted* to the mode of image.

To get beyond current understandings of learning as acquisition and the forms of assessment which follow from that, we need to ask closely about the principles of selection, transformation and transduction which were applied here and which emerge in these texts, arising from the differing interest of the learners/sign-makers.

The teacher's instruction to 'write what you did' is realized once as the genre of recount (events in chronological order), and once as the genre of procedure (instructions for producing actions in sequence). The operations of transformation and transduction are complex: material presented by the teacher across the four lessons is selected from and re-presented in relation to each sign-maker's interest. For one girl 'write what you did' meant 'report accurately what you actually did'; for the other it meant 'present a regularized

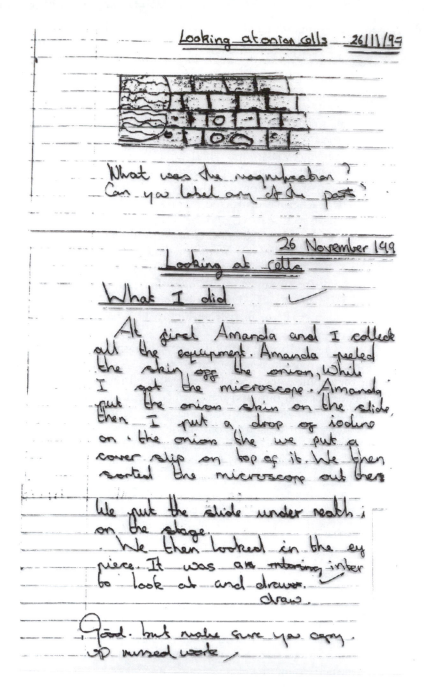

Figure 11.5 Onion cell/theory.

account of what should happen'. Each indicates their sense of what 'being scientific' means for her: in the recount, as the accurate recounting of all relevant events and actions in the chronological order in which they took place; in the procedure, as careful specification to ensure the replicability of actions.

The teacher had given a generically vague instruction '*write* what you did' (Figure 11.6); and he made no comment on the epistemological significance

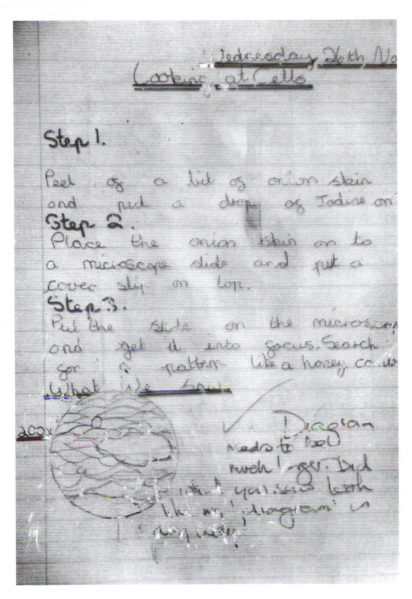

Figure 11.6 Onion cell/eye-piece.

of the different genres. That aspect of learning was not recognized, and therefore not assessed.

The images show significant differences: the writer of the recount stays close to the handout's statement: 'the cells will look like bricks in a brick-wall'. She transforms what she saw into a depiction 'predicted' by the 'theory' provided by the handout: 'theory tells us that it ought to look like this'. The writer of the procedure stays close to accurate visual recording, treating that principle as being essentially 'scientific'. Both drawings are signs of learning: they are precise accounts of the interest of each of the two young women, though resting on different principles. Each has led to distinct notions of 'being scientific'; from each we get a real sense – I would say *the* real sense – of their learning. Again, the teacher makes no comment relating to the epistemological difference in the two drawings: his comments are in one case 'Diagram needs to be much larger. Did what you saw look like my diagram in any way?' and 'What was the magnification? Can you label any of the parts?' in the other.

The texts overall – the combination of written genre and image – are precise and complex records of the principles applied in engaging with the curriculum. In the one text the written part suggests that being scientific is to adhere to strictly prescribed practices; while its image suggests that being scientific is to be accurate in the visual recording of the empirical world. In the other text the writing suggests that being scientific is about recording accurately what actions were actually performed and in what sequence; while the image suggests that being scientific is to uncover the truth of theory in the messiness of the empirical world.

These texts starkly pose the question: what forms of assessment of learning would be apt for a theory of learning as transformative action, within a curriculum of principles and contents. Can it be a metric of acquisition as conformity to the authority of the curriculum, or does it have to be a metric of the transformation of materials on the basis of the principles brought to the materials, which emerge in these signs. In my view, only the latter opens up the window on learning according to the description of learning that I have posited. From the position reached here, we can ask other crucial questions: Which view of learning responds to conceptions of creativity, of diversity, of change? Which view is apt for the givens and demands of the contemporary world? And from this position another bothersome question arises for me: What is not learning?

What is the curriculum for?

In the environment where the market is increasingly the dominant social, cultural and economic force, a no doubt old question needs to be posed newly and urgently: What is the curriculum for, and what is this subject for?

Most, maybe all the school subjects in the National Curriculum of England – and no doubt this applies in many places – are in profound crisis.

If in the past Science had had the dual function of acquainting a fraction of the school population with the means a culture has developed to gain a secure understanding of the natural world – that is, scientific method – and to provide a route into science as a profession, now the task of Science is less clear: more about providing all of the school population with some means of navigating an everyday world ever more insistently shaped by the impact of scientific/technological developments on the lives of consumers. Yet the earlier function remains, uneasily.

If I ask the question: 'What is English for?' it is not certain that despite years of policy and endless elaboration of the subject English in England, there is a clear or an agreed sense of what English is, never mind a sense of 'what it is for'. Yet what is needed are solid grounds for saying: This subject has to be in the curriculum because in a society dominated by the market and by consumption this subject provides absolutely indispensible resources. It is the subject in which the issue is meaning, in all forms and everywhere; how meanings are made and received in all the many ways and through all the many media of the society in which learners live. It provides, fully and explicitly, the means for making meaning, and for disseminating meanings as messages in communication. This subject provides the means for making principled judgements about choices in making meaning, whether in prod-uction of messages or in 'reading', viewing, learning. It provides principles which allow us to understand and judge how choices are made, and in this English becomes (and remains) the subject concerned with ethics; not as a subject purveying ethical systems, but as a subject that deals with how we might establish and assemble principles for making ethical judgements.

In a consumption-driven society these are essential navigational aids which the school needs to provide. From choice comes style, as the effect of the sum total of choices made in relation to particular actions or judgements, and via style English becomes the subject which deals with *aesthetics as the politics of style*, that is, aesthetics as the site where political and social power expresses itself in the production and evaluation of commodities. Such an aesthetic deals with all the practices and objects which are central in the cultural world encountered by the young, from the seemingly banal to the culturally salient to the socially and politically most valued.

This would be a curriculum both of *principles* and of *contents* through which the principles could be elucidated and sociality affirmed. If the school is to remain a site where community and sociality are affirmed then the prin-ciples have to be fit for that, and the contents have to be so, equally. So, for instance, the question of 'set texts' as the site where a society with its cultural groups affirms what is seen as useful, as necessary, as valuable, and why. Similarly with 'skills' which are regarded as essential for equitable participa-tion in society. Clearly such a curriculum of principles and contents needs careful, sensitive and detailed elaboration; the forms of pedagogy that accompany it would need to be compatible with the acceptance of the centrality of the transformative actions of learners, and forms of assessing principles of transformative engagement would need to be in entire harmony with these.

A curriculum rethought

In some ways my proposal for placing the learner and the learner's transforming agency at the centre of institutionalized education (the school, the workplace, the leisure centre, the vacation course, etc.) might seem just another version of 'personalized learning', or of the 'personalized curriculum'. I do not see it like that. On the one hand, 'personalized learning' and the 'personalized curriculum' are responses to the radical instability of contemporary economic and social givens; on the other hand they are manifestations of politically fragmenting forces: in the case of England, the end-point of the neo-liberal Thatcherite project. In any case I would wish the school to remain as special and essential in relation to maintaining and building sociality, social cohesion, the possibility of community and society. But in any instance of institutionalized education, the structure that I am advocating – a constellation where the learner and the learner's principled transformative engagement are at the centre, engaging with institutionally provided (navigational) principles and contents, and metrics of assessment of an apt form – would have these essential features. The purposes of the institution and of those who come to it, with the structures of power and interest that attend on that, would lead to the more specific articulations of curriculum *and* pedagogy.

References

Acker, S. (1994) *Gendered Education*, Buckingham: Open University Press.

Adams, N. and Bettis, P. (2003) 'Commanding the Room in Short Skirts: Cheering as the Embodiment of Ideal Girlhood', *Gender and Society*, 17(1): 73–91.

Aldrich, R. (1988) 'The National Curriculum: An Historical Perspective', in D. Lawton and C. Chitty (eds), *The National Curriculum*, London: Institute of Education, University of London.

Allen, J. (2002) 'Symbolic economies: The "Culturalization" of Economic Knowledge', in P. du Gay and M. Pryke (eds), *Cultural Economy*, London: Sage.

Apple, M. (1979) *Ideology and Curriculum*, London: Routledge and Kegan Paul.

——(1995) *Education and Power* (2nd edn), New York and London: Routledge.

——(1993) 'The Politics of Official Knowledge: Does a National Curriculum Make Sense?' *Teachers College Record*, 95(2): 222–241.

Apple, M. and Beane, J. (1999) *Democratic Schools*, Buckingham: Open University Press.

Assessment Reform Group (1999) 'Assessment for Learning: Beyond the Black Box', Cambridge: University of Cambridge, School of Education, http://www.assessment-reform-group.org.uk/publications.html

Attar, D. (1990) *Wasting Girls' Time: The History and Politics of Home Economics*, London: Virago Press.

Baker, E. (2003) 'Reflections on Technology-Enhanced Assessment', *Assessment in Education*, 10(3): 421–424.

Ball, S.J. and Lacey, C. (1980) 'Subject Disciplines as the Opportunity for Group Action: A Measured Critique of Subject Subcultures', in P. Woods (ed.), *Teacher Strategies*, London: Croom Helm.

Banks, J.A., Banks, C.A.M., Cortes, C.E., Hahn, C., Merryfield, M., Moodley, K.A., Murphy-Shigematsu, S., Osler, A., Park, C. and Parker, W.C. (2005) *Democracy and Diversity: Principles and Concepts for Educating Citizens in a Global Age*, Seattle, WA: Center for Multicultural Education, University of Washington.

Barnes, D. (1969) *Language, the Learner and the School*, Harmondsworth: Penguin.

——(1976) *From Communication to Curriculum*, Harmondsworth: Penguin.

Barthes, R. (1983) *Selected Writings*, Oxford: Fontana/Collins.

Bauman, Z. (1988) 'Sociology and Postmodernity', *Sociological Review*, 36(4): 790–814.

——(1998) *Globalization: The Human Consequences*, Cambridge: Polity Press.

——(2000) *Liquid Modernity*, Cambridge: Polity Press.

Beck, J. and Young, M.F.D. (2005) 'The Assault on the Professions and the Restructuring of Academic and Professional Identities – A Bernsteinian Analysis', *British Journal of Sociology of Education*, 26(2): 183–197.

Beck, U. (1998) *Democracy without Enemies*, trans. M. Ritter, Cambridge: Polity Press.

—— (2000) *The Brave New World of Work*, trans. P. Camiller, Cambridge: Polity Press.

Bell, R. and Prescott, W. (eds) (1975) *The Schools Council: A Second Look*, London: Ward Lock.

Bereiter, C. (2002) *Education and Mind in the Knowledge Age*, Mahwah, NJ and London: Lawrence Erlbaum Associates.

Bernstein, B. (1971a) *Class, Codes and Control, Vol.1*, London: Routledge and Kegan Paul.

—— (1971b) 'On the Classification and Framing of Educational Knowledge', in M.F.D. Young (ed.), *Knowledge and Control*, London: Collier-Macmillan.

—— (2000) *Pedagogy, Symbolic Control and Identity: Theory, Research, Critique*, Oxford: Rowman and Litttlefield.

Best, R. (1998) 'The Development of Affective Education in England', in P. Lang, Y. Katz and I. Menezes (eds), *Affective Education*, London: Cassell.

Beynon, J. and Mackay, H. (eds) (1993) *Computers into Classrooms: More Questions than Answers*, London: Falmer Press.

Bidwell, C.E. (2001) 'Analyzing Schools as Organizations: Long-Term Permanence and Short-Term Change', *Sociology of Education*, 74(Extra Issue: *Currents of Thought: Sociology of Education at the Dawn of the 21st Century*): 100–114.

Biggart, N.W. (1989) *Charismatic Capitalism: Direct Selling Organizations in America*, Chicago, IL: University of Chicago Press.

Binfield, C. (1977) *So Down to Prayers: Studies in English Nonconformity 1780–1920*, London: Dent.

Bloom, A. (1987) *The Closing of the American Mind*, New York: Simon & Schuster.

Board of Education (1929) *Handbook of Suggestions for the Consideration of Teachers and Others Concerned in the Work of Public Elementary Schools*, 6th impression, London: HMSO.

Boeck, M. (2004) 'Family Snaps: Life Worlds and Information Habitus', *Journal of Visual Communication*, 3(3): 281–293.

Boler, M. (1999) *Feeling Power: Emotions and Education*, London: Routledge.

Bork, A. (1980) 'Learning through Graphics', in R. Taylor (ed.), *The Computer in the School: Tutor, Tool, Tutee*, New York: Teachers College Press.

Bourdieu, P. (1971) 'Intellectual Field and Creative Project', in M.F.D. Young (ed.), *Knowledge and Control*, London: Collier-Macmillan.

—— (1977) *Outline of a Theory of Practice*, Cambridge: Cambridge University Press.

—— (1984) *Distinction: A Social Critique of the Judgement of Taste*, trans. R. Nice, London: Routledge and Kegan Paul.

Bourdieu, P. and Passeron, J.-C. (1977) *Reproduction in Education, Society and Culture*, London and Beverley Hills: Sage.

Bourdieu, P. and Wacquant, J.D. (1992) *An Invitation to Reflexive Sociology*, Chicago, IL: University of Chicago Press.

Bowles, S. and Gintis, H. (1972) 'IQ and the Social Class System', *Social Policy*, 3(4).

—— (1976) *Schooling in Capitalist America: Educational Reform and the Contradictions of Economic Life*, London: Routledge.

—— (1981) 'Contradiction and Reproduction in Educational Theory', in L. Barton, R. Meighan and S. Wallis (eds), *Schooling, Ideology and the Curriculum*, London: Falmer Press.

Brice Heath, S. (1983) *Ways with Words: Language, Life and Work in Communities and Classrooms*, Oxford: Oxford University Press.

Brighouse, T. (2000) *Passionate Leadership*, Nottingham: National College for School Leadership, http://www.ncsl.uk/index.cfm?pageid = ev_auth_brighouse

Britton, J. (1972) *Language and Learning*, Harmondsworth: Penguin.

Britzman, D. (1989) 'Who has the Floor? Curriculum, Teaching, and the English Student Teacher's Struggle for Voice', *Curriculum Enquiry*, 19(2): 143–162.

Broudy, H.S., Smith, B.O. and Burnett, J.R. (1964) *Democracy and Excellence in Secondary Education*, New York: Rand McNally.

Brown, J.S., Collins, A. and Duguid, P. (1989) 'Situated Cognition and the Culture of Learning', *Educational Researcher*, 32: 32–42.

Bruner, J. (1960) *The Process of Education*, Cambridge, MA: Harvard University Press.

Burbules, N. (1995) 'Postmodern Doubt and Philosophy of Education', unpublished paper, Philosophy of Education Society Annual Conference, San Francisco.

Burke, J. Edwards, J.A., Jeffries, J., Jones, K., Miln, J., Montgomery, M., Perkins, B., Seager, A. and Wright, H. (1988) 'My Mum Uses a Computer, Too', in C. Hoyles (ed.), *Girls and Computers: General Issues and Case Studies of LOGO in the Mathematics Classroom*, Bedford Way Papers 34, London: Institute of Education, University of London.

Burns, T.C. and Ungerleider, C.S. (2002) 'Information and Communication Technologies in Elementary and Secondary Education', *International Journal of Educational Policy, Research and Practice*, 3(4): 27–54.

Burton, L. (1986) *Girls Into Maths Can Go*, Eastbourne: Holt, Rinehart and Winston.

Burton, L. and Weiner, G. (1990) 'Social Justice and the National Curriculum', *Research Papers in Education*, 5(3): 203–227.

Cairns, J., Gardner, R. and Lawton, D. (2000) *Values and the Curriculum*, London: Woburn Press.

Callan, E. (1988) *Autonomy and Schooling*, Kingston, Ontario: McGill-Queen's University Press.

Campbell, C. (1989) *The Romantic Ethic and the Spirit of Modern Consumerism*, Oxford: Blackwell.

Castells, M. (1998) *The Information Age: Economy, Society and Culture*, vol. 3, Oxford: Blackwell.

Castles, S. and Davidson, A. (2000) *Citizenship and Migration: Globalization and the Politics of Belonging*, London: Macmillan.

Chitty, C. (2002) *Understanding Schools and Schooling*, London: RoutledgeFalmer.

Clark, M. (1985) 'Young Writers and the Computer', in D. Chandler and S. Marcus (eds), *Computers and Literacy*, Milton Keynes: Open University Press.

Clarke, D. and Peter, A. (1993) 'Modelling Teacher Change', in B. Atweh, C. Kanes, M. Carss and G. Booker (eds), *Contexts in Mathematics Education: Proceedings of the Sixteenth Annual Conference of the Mathematics Education Research Group of Australasia*, Brisbane: MERGA.

Clarke, F. (1923) *Essays in the Politics of Education*, Oxford: Oxford University Press.

—— (1940) *Education and Social Change: An English Interpretation*, London: The Sheldon Press.

Clayton, M. (1993) 'White on Autonomy, Neutrality and Well-being', *Journal of Philosophy of Education*, 27: 101–112.

Comenius, J.A. (1907) *The Great Didactic*, trans. M.W. Keatinge, London: Adam and Charles Black.

Connolly, P. (2000) 'Racism and Young Girls' Peer-Group Relations: The Experience of South Asian Girls', *Sociology*, 34(3): 499–519.

Council of Europe (1985) *Recommendation No. R(85)7 of the Committee of Ministers to Member States on Teaching and Learning about Human Rights in Schools*, Strasbourg: Council of Europe.

—— (2000) *All Different All Equal: From Principle to Practice*, European COE Conference, Strasbourg, October 2000.

Cox, G., Carr, T. and Hall, M. (2004) 'Evaluating the Use of Synchronous Communication in Two Blended Courses', *Journal of Computer Assisted Learning*, 20(3): 183–192.

Crook, C.K. and Light, P. (2002) 'Virtualisation and the Cultural Practice of Study', in S. Woolgar (ed.), *Virtual Society? – Technology, Cyberbole Reality*, Oxford: Oxford University Press, pp. 153–175.

Crouch, C. (2004) *Commercialisation or Citizenship*, London: Fabian Society.

Csikszentmihalyi, M. (1996) *Creativity: Flow and the Psychology of Discovery and Invention*, New York: Harper Perennial.

Cummins, J. (1984) *Bilingualism and Special Education: Issues in Assessment and Pedagogy*, Clevedon England: Multilingual Matters.

Deal, T. and Peterson, K. (1994) *The Leadership Paradox: Balancing Logic and Artistry in Schools*, San Francisco, CA: Jossey Bass.

Debarbieux, E. (1999) *La violence en milieu scolaire T.1 Etat des lieux* (2nd edn), Paris: ESF.

DEE/QCA (Department for Education/Qualifications and Curriculum Authority) (1999) *The National Curriculum Handbook for Secondary Teachers in England*, London: DFE/QCA.

Deem, R. (1978) *Women and Schooling*, London: Routledge and Kegan Paul.

Delamont, S. (1994) 'Accentuating the Positive: Refocusing the Research on Girls and Science', *Studies in Science Education*, 23: 59–74.

DES (Department of Education and Science)/Welsh Office (1990) *Technology in the National Curriculum*, London: Her Majesty's Stationery Office.

Descartes, R. (1637/1641/1968) *Discourse on Method and the Meditations*, trans. F.E. Sutcliffe, Harmondsworth, Middlesex: Penguin.

DFE (Department for Education) (1995) *English in the National Curriculum*, London: HMSO.

—— (1999) *Design and Technology*, London: Department for Education and Employment/Qualifications and Curriculum Authority.

DfEE/DMCS (Department for Education and Employment & Department of Media, Culture and Sport) (2000) Government Response to *All Our Futures: Creativity, Culture and Education*, http://www.culture.gov.uk/role/index_flash.html

DfES (Department for Education and Skills) (2000) *The National Curriculum*, London: DfES.

—— (2002) *Transforming the Way We Learn*, http://www.dfes.gov.uk/ictfutures

—— (2004a) *Final Report of Working Group on 14–19 Reform* (*aka The Tomlinson Report*), London: DfES.

—— (2004b) *GCSE and Equivalent Results for Young People in England*, 2003/04 (Provisional), http://www.dfes.gov.uk/rsgateway/DB/SFR/s000528/index.shtml

Dillon, D. (1985) 'The Dangers of Computers in Literacy Education: Who's in Charge Here?' in D. Chandler and S. Marcus (eds), *Computers and Literacy*, Milton Keynes: Open University Press.

DMCS (Department of Media, Culture and Sport) (1999) *All Our Futures: Creativity Culture and Education* (Report of the National Advisory Committee on Creative and Cultural Education), London: DCMS.

Dryden, C. (1999) *Being Married, Doing Gender*, London: Routledge.

DTI (Department for Trade and Industry) (1998) *Our Competitive Future: Building the Knowledge-Driven Economy*, London: DTI, http://www.dti.gov.uk/comp/competitive/an_report.htm

Du Gay, P. and Pryke, M. (2002) *Cultural Economy*, London: Sage.

Durkheim, E. (2001) *The Elementary Forms of Religious Life*, Oxford: Oxford University Press.

Dyhouse, C. (1976) 'Social Darwinistic Ideas and the Development of Women's Education 1880–1920', *History of Education*, 5(1): 41–58.

Eagleton, T. (2000) 'Utopia and its Opposites', in L. Panitich and C. Ley (eds), *Necessary and Unnecessary Utopias*, Rendlesham: Merlin Press.

——(2003) *Figures of Dissent: Critical Essays on Fish, Spivak, Zizek and Others*, London: Verso.

Edwards, D. and Mercer, N. (1987) *Common Knowledge: The Development of Understanding in the Classroom*, London: Routledge.

Eisner, E.W. (1979) 'Humanistic Trends and the Curriculum Field', in P.H. Taylor (ed.), *New Directions in Curriculum Studies*, Lewes, Sussex: Falmer Press.

Elias, N. (1994) *The Civilising Process*, trans. Edmund Jephcott, Oxford: Blackwell.

The English Centre (1981) *The Language Book*, London: The English Centre, Inner London Education Authority.

Equal Opportunities Commission (1999) 'Gender Issues in Vocational Training and Workplace Achievement of 14–19 year olds: An EOC Perspective', *The Curriculum Journal*, 10(2): 209–229.

——(2001) *Sex Stereotyping: From School to Work*, Manchester: Equal Opportunities Commission.

——(2003) *Key Statistics Education and Training Employment Equal Pay Public and Political Life Work/Life Balance*, Manchester: Equal Opportunities Commission.

Facer, K., Furlong, J., Furlong, R. and Sutherland, R. (2003) *ScreenPlay: Children and Computing in the Home*, London and New York: RoutledgeFalmer.

Figueroa, P. (2000) 'Citizenship Education for a Plural Society', in A. Osler (ed.), *Citizenship and Democracy in Schools: Diversity, Identity, Equality*, Stoke-on-Trent: Trentham.

Flintoff, A. (1993) 'Gender, Physical Education and Initial Teacher Education', in J. Evans (ed.), *Equality, Education and Physical Education*, London: Falmer Press.

Foucault, M. (1977) *Discipline and Punish*, trans. A. Sheridan, London: Penguin.

——(1978) *The History of Sexuality Volume One*, trans. R. Hurley, London: Penguin.

——(1980) *Power/Knowledge: Selected Interviews and Other Writings 1972–1977*, Hemel Hempstead, Herts: Harvester Press.

——(1982) 'The Subject and Power', in H.L. Dreyfus and P. Rabinov (eds), *Michel Foucault: Beyond Structuralism and Hermeneutics*, Brighton: Harvester Press.

French, M. (1994) 'Power/Sex', in H.L. Radtke and H.J. Stam (eds), *Power/Gender*, London: Sage.

Friedman, J. (1992) 'Narcissism, Roots and Postmodernity: The Constitution of Selfhood in the Global Crisis', in S. Lash and J. Friedman (eds), *Modernity and Identity*, Oxford: Blackwell.

Fullan, M. (1991) *The New Meaning of Educational Change* (2nd edn), London: Cassell.

Gallie, D., White, M., Cheng, Y. and Tomlinson, M. (1998) *Restructuring the Employment Relationship*, Oxford: Clarendon.

Gardner, H. (1983) *Frames of Mind: The Theory of Multiple Intelligences*, New York: Basic Books.

——(1999) *The Disciplined Mind: Beyond Facts and Standardized Tests, The K-12 Education That Every Child Deserves*, New York: Simon and Schuster.

Garrett, R. (2004) 'The Real Story Behind the Failure of the UK eUniversity', *Educause Quarterly* (4), http://www.educause.edu/ir/library/pdf/eqm0440.pdf

Gee, J.P., Hull, G. and Lankshear, C. (1996) *The New World Order: Behind the Language of the New Capitalism*, Sydney: Allen and Unwin.

Geyer, M. (1993) 'Multiculturalism and the Politics of General Education', *Critical Inquiry*, 19: 499–533.

Giddens, A. (1991) *Modernity and Self Identity*, Cambridge: Polity Press.

——(1994) *Beyond Left and Right: The Future of Radical Politics*, Cambridge: Polity Press.

Gilroy, P. (1997) 'Detours of Identity', in S. Hall and K. Woodward (eds), *Identity and Difference*, London: Sage.

Goldberg, D.T. (1994) 'Introduction: Multicultural Conditions', in D.T. Goldberg (ed.), *Multiculuralism: A Critical Reader*, Oxford: Blackwell.

Goleman, D., McKee, A. and Boyatzis, R.E. (2002) *Primal Leadership*, Cambridge, MA: Harvard Business School Press.

Goodson, I. (1983) *School Subjects and Curriculum Change*, Beckenham: Croom Helm.

Goodson, I., Cookson, P.J. and Persell, C. (1997) 'Distinction and Destiny: The Importance of Curriculum Form in Elite American Private Schools', *Discourse*, 18(2): 173–183.

Goodyear, P. (2001) *Effective Networked Learning in Higher Education: Notes and Guidelines*, http://csalt.lancs.ac.uk/jisc/Guidelines_final.doc

Grafton, A. and Jardine, L. (1986) *From Humanism to the Humanities: Education and the Liberal Arts in Fifteenth- and Sixteenth-Century Europe*, London: Duckworth.

Gramsci A. (1971) *Selections from the Prison Notebooks*, ed. and trans. Q. Hoare and G.N. Smith, London: Lawrence and Wishart.

Greaves, R.L. (1969) *The Puritan Revolution and Educational Thought: Background for Reform*, New Brunswick, NJ: Rutgers University Press.

Green, L. (1997) *Music, Gender, Education*, Cambridge: Cambridge University Press.

Griffin, C. (1993) *Representations of Youth: The Study of Youth and Adolescence in Britain and America*, Cambridge: Polity Press.

The Guardian newspaper (2003, 21 August 2003, p. 15) 'GCSE Grades by Subject', London and Manchester: *The Guardian* newspaper.

Gunn, S. and Bell, R. (2002) *Middle Classes: Their Rise and Sprawl*, London: Cassell.

Habermas, J. (1996) *Between Facts and Norms: Contributions to a Discourse Theory of Law and Democracy*, Cambridge, MA: Polity.

Hacking, I. (1999) *The Social Construction of What?* Cambridge, MA and London: Harvard University Press.

Hahn, C. (1998) *Becoming Political: Comparative Perspectives on Citizenship Education*, Albany, NY: SUNY Press.

Hall, S. (2000) 'Multicultural Citizens: Monocultural Citizenship', in N. Pearce and J. Hallgarten (eds), *Tomorrow's Citizens: Critical Debates in Citizenship and Education*, London: Institute for Public Policy Research.

Hamilton, D. (1990) *Curriculum History*, Geelong: Deakin University.

Hans, N. (1951) *New Trends in Education in the Eighteenth Century*, London: Routledge and Kegan Paul.

Hargreaves, A. (1997) *Rethinking Educational Change with Heart and Mind* (The Association for Supervision and Curriculum Development Yearbook), Alexandria, VA: ASCD.

Harris, J. and Penney, D. (2002) 'Gender, Health and Physical Education', in D. Penney (ed.), *Gender and Physical Education: Contemporary Issues and Future Directions*, London: Routledge.

Harrison, C., Comber, C., Fisher, T., Haw, K., Lewin, C., Lunzer, E., McFarlane, A., Mavers, D., Scrimshaw, P., Somekh, B. and Watling, R. (2002) *ImpaCT2 The Impact of Information and Communication Technologies on Pupil Learning and Attainment. ICT in Schools Research and Evaluation Series no 7*, Coventry: BECTA, http://www.becta.org.uk/research

Hartley, D. (1999) 'Marketing and the "Re-Enchantment" of School Management', *British Journal of Sociology of Education*, 20(3): 309–323.

Harvey, D. (2000) *Spaces of Hope*, Edinburgh: Edinburgh University Press.

Head, J. (1985) *The Personal Response to Science*, Cambridge: Cambridge University Press.

——(1997) *Working with Adolescents: Constructing Identity*, London: Falmer Press.

Held, D. (1995) 'Democracy and the New International Order', in D. Archibugi and D. Held (eds), *Cosmopolitan Democracy*, Cambridge: Polity Press.

——(1996) *Models of Democracy* (2nd edn), Cambridge: Polity Press.

——(2001) 'Violence and Justice in a Global Age', paper published at http://www.opendemocracy.net/forum/strands_home.asp on 14 September 2001.

Hewitson, R. (2004) 'A Critical Ethnographic Account of Teacher Professional Development in a Devolved High School Setting', PhD thesis, Flinders University, Adelaide, South Australia.

Hirst, P.H. (1965) 'Liberal Education and the Nature of Knowledge', in P.H. Hirst (ed.) (1974), *Knowledge and the Curriculum*, London: Routledge and Kegan Paul.

——(1974) *Knowledge and the Curriculum*, London: Routledge and Kegan Paul.

——(1993) 'Education, Knowledge and Practices', in R. Barrow and P. White (eds), *Beyond Liberal Education: Essays in Honour of Paul H. Hirst*, London: Routledge.

Hirst, P.H. and Peters, R.S. (1970) *The Logic of Education*, London: Routledge and Kegan Paul.

Hochschild, A. (1983) *The Managed Heart*, Berkeley, CA: University of California Press.

Hogan, E. (n.d.) 'Women on the Edge of Genre: Making Utopian Fiction Work in Feminist Theory and Practice', unpublished paper, Oxford: Templeton College, University of Oxford.

Hunt, F. (1987) 'Divided Aims: The Educational Implications of Opposing Ideologies in Girls' Secondary Schooling 1850–1940', in F. Hunt (ed.), *Lessons for Life*, Oxford: Basil Blackwell.

Illich, I.D. (1973) *Deschooling Society*, Harmondsworth: Penguin.

International Bureau of Education (IBE) (2004) *Message from the 47th Session of the UNESCO International Conference on Education and Proposed Priorities for Action to Improve the Quality of Education for All Young People*, Geneva: International Bureau of Education.

Isaacson, Z. (1986) 'Freedom and Girls' Education: A Philosophical Discussion with Particular Reference to Mathematics', in L. Burton (ed.), *Girls Into Maths Can Go*, Eastbourne: Holt, Rinehart and Winston.

Jacques, R. (1996) *Manufacturing the Employee*, London: Sage.

Jeffrey, B. and Craft, A. (2001) 'The Universalization of Creativity', in A. Craft, B. Jeffrey and M. Leinbling (eds), *Creativity in Education*, London: Continuum.

Jones, K. (ed.) (1992) *English and the National Curriculum: Cox's Revolution*, London: Kogan Page in association with the Institute of Education, University of London.

Jones, A. and Kirk, C.M. (1990) 'Gender Differences in Students' Interests in Applications of School Physics', *Physics Education*, 25: 308–313.

Kamin, L. (1974) *The Science and Politics of IQ*, London: Lawrence Erlbaum.

Kelly, A.V. (1991) *The Curriculum: Theory and Practice*, London: Paul Chapman Publishing.

——(1999) *The Curriculum: Theory and Practice* (4th edn), London: Paul Chapman Publishing.

Kenway, J., Willis, S., Blackmore, J. and Rennie, L. (1998) *Answering Back: Girls, Boys and Feminism in Schools*, London: Routledge.

Kerr J.F. (ed.) (1968) *Changing the Curriculum*, London: University of London Press.

Knox, H.M. (1953) *Two Hundred and Fifty Years of Scottish Education*, Edinburgh: Oliver and Boyd.

Kress, G. (1982) *Learning to Write*, London: Routledge and Kegan Paul.

Kress, G.R., Jewitt, C., Ogborn, J. and Tsatsarelis, C. (2001) *Multimodal Learning and Teaching: The Rhetorics of the Science Classroom*, London: Continuum.

Kumar, K. (1991) *Utopianism*, Milton Keynes: Open University Press.

Kymlicka, W. (2001) *Politics in the Vernacular: Nationalism, Multiculturalism and Citizenship*, Oxford: Oxford University Press.

Labov, W. (1972) 'The Logic of Non-Standard English', in P.O. Giglioli (ed.), *Language and Social Context*, Harmondsworth: Penguin.

Landow, G. (1992) *The Convergence of Contemporary Critical Theory and Technology*, Baltimore, MD and London: The John Hopkins University Press.

Lankshear, C., Peters, M. and Knobel, M. (1996) 'Critical Pedagogy and Cyberspace', in H.Giroux with C.Lankshear, P.McLaren and M.Peters (eds), *Counternarratives: Cultural Studies and Critical Pedagogies in Postmodern Spaces*, New York and London: Routledge.

——(2000) 'Information, Knowledge and Learning: Some Issues Facing Epistemology and Education in a Digital Age', *Journal of Philosophy of Education*, 34(1): 17–40.

Laqueur, T. (1990) *Making Sex: Body and Gender from the Greeks to Freud*, Cambridge, MA: Harvard University Press.

Lather, P. (1991) *Feminist Research in Education*, Geelong: Deakin University Press.

Lave, J. (1993) 'The Practice of Learning', in S. Chaiklin and J. Lave (eds), *Understanding Practice: Perspectives On Activity and Context*, Cambridge and New York: Cambridge University Press.

Lave, J. and Wenger, E. (1991) *Situated Learning: Legitimate Peripheral Participation*, Cambridge, New York and Melbourne: Cambridge University Press.

Lawn, M. and Barton, L. (eds) (1981) *Rethinking Curriculum Studies*, London: Croom Helm.

Lawton, D. (1968) *Social Class, Language and Education*, London: Routledge and Kegan Paul.

—— (1975) *Class, Culture and the Curriculum*, London: Routledge and Kegan Paul.

—— (1989) *Education, Culture and the National Curriculum*, London: Hodder and Stoughton.

Leadbeater, C. (1999) *Living on Thin Air: The New Economy*, London: Viking.

Levine, J. (ed.) (1990) *Bilingual Learners in the Mainstream Curriculum*, London: Falmer.

Levitas, R. (1990) *The Concept of Utopia*, London: Philip Allan.

—— (2001) 'Against Work: A Utopian Incursion Into Social Policy', *Critical Social Policy*, 21(4): 449–465.

Lloyd, B. and Duveen, G. (1992) *Gender Identities and Education: The Impact of Starting School*, Hemel Hempstead, Herts: Harvester Press.

Lucey, H. and Reay, D. (2002) 'Carrying the Beacon of Excellence: Social Class Differentiation and Anxiety at a Time of Transition', *Journal of Education Policy*, 17(3): 321–336.

Lyotard, J.-F. (1984) *The Post-Modern Condition: A Report on Knowledge*, trans. J.B. Thompson, Minneapolis, MN: University of Minnesota Press.

McFarlane, A.E. (2001) 'Perspectives on the Relationships between ICT and Assessment', *Journal of Computer Assisted Learning*, 17(3): 227–235.

—— (2003) 'Learners, Learning and New Technology', *Educational Media International*, 40(3–4): 219–227.

McFarlane, A., Bradburn, A. and McMahon, A. (2003) 'E-learning for Leadership; Emerging Indicators of Best Practice: Literature Review', National College for School Leadership, http://www.ncsl.org.uk/literaturereviews

Mack, P. (1998) 'Ramus, Petrus 1515–1572', in E. Craig (ed.), *Routledge Encyclopaedia of Philosophy Vol. 8*, London: Routledge.

McKibbin, R. (1998) *Classes and Cultures in England 1918–1951*, Oxford: Oxford University Press.

McKnight, D. (2003) *Schooling, the Puritan Imperative and the Moulding of an American National Identity*, Mahwah, NJ: Lawrence Erlbaum.

McLachlan, H. (1931) *English Education under the Test Acts: Being the History of Nonconformist Academies 1660–1820*, Manchester: Manchester University Press.

McLaren, P. (1989) *Life in Schools*, New York: Longman.

McLuhan, M. (1964) *Understanding Media*, London and New York: Routledge and Kegan Paul.

Melucci, A. (1989) *Nomads of the Present*, London: Hutchinson.

—— (1996a) *Challenging Codes: Collective Action in the Information Age*, Cambridge: Cambridge University Press.

—— (1996b) *The Playing Self: Person and Meaning in the Planetary Society*, Cambridge: Cambridge University Press.

Mercer, M. (2001) 'Dissenting Academies and the Education of the Laity, 1750–1850', *History of Education*, 30(1): 35–58.

Mestrovic, S. (1997) *Postemotional Society*, London: Sage.

Meyer, J., Kamens, D. and Benavot, A. (1992) *School Knowledge for the Masses: World Models and National Primary Curricular Categories in the Twentieth Century*, London: Falmer.

Miles, S. (1998) *Consumerism as a Way of Life*, London: Sage.

Miller, D. (1999) 'Bounded Citizenship', in K. Hutchings and R. Dannreuther (eds), *Cosmopolitan Citizenship*, London: Macmillan.

Miller, P. (1939) *The New England Mind: The Seventeenth Century*, New York: Macmillan.

Mills, C.W. (1951) *White Collar: The American Middle Class*, New York: Oxford University Press.

Moore, A. (1993) 'Siuli's Maths Lesson: Autonomy or Control?' in J. Beynon and H. Mackay (eds), *Computers into Classrooms: More Questions Than Answers*, London: Falmer Press.

——(1998) 'English, Fetishism and the Demand for Change: Towards a Postmodern Agenda for the School Curriculum', in G. Edwards and A.V. Kelly (eds), *Experience and Education*, London: Paul Chapman.

——(2000) *Teaching and Learning: Pedagogy, Curriculum and Culture*, London: RoutledgeFalmer.

——(2005) 'Culture, Knowledge and Inclusion. What place for Pluralism in the Common Curriculum?' in D. Halpin and P. Walsh (eds), *Educational Commonplaces: Essays to Honour Denis Lawton*, London: Institute of Education, University of London.

Moore, A., Edwards, G., Halpin, D. and George, R. (2002) 'Compliance, Resistance and Pragmatism: The (Re)Construction of Schoolteacher Identities in a Period of Intensive Educational Reform', *British Educational Research Journal*, 28(4): 551–565.

Moore, A. and Klenowski, V., with Askew, S., Carnell, E., Larsen, J. and Jones, C. (2003) 'Revising the National Curriculum: Teachers' and Pupils' Perspectives at KS2 & 3', report of DfES-funded research study, *An Evaluation of Recent Changes to the National Curriculum London*, London: Institute of Education, University of London.

Moore, R. (2004) *Education and Society; Issues and Explanations in the Sociology of Education*, London: Polity Press.

Moore, R. and Muller, J. (1999) 'The Discourse of "Voice" and the Problem of Knowledge and Identity in the Sociology of Education', *British Journal of Sociology of Education*, 20(2): 189–206.

Moore, R. and Young, M.F.D. (2001) 'Knowledge and the Curriculum in the Sociology of Education: Towards a Reconceptualisation', *British Journal of Sociology of Education*, 22(4): 445–461.

Morgan, J. (1986) *Godly Learning: Puritan Attitudes Towards Reason, Learning and Education, 1560–1640*, Cambridge: Cambridge University Press.

Moss, G. and Attar, D. (1999) 'Boys and Literacy: Gendering the Reading Curriculum', in J. Prosser (ed.), *School Culture*, London: Paul Chapman Publishing.

Muller, J. (2000) *Reclaiming Knowledge: Social Theory, Curriculum and Education Policy*, London: RoutledgeFalmer.

Musgrove, F. (1979) 'Curriculum, Culture and Ideology', in P.H. Taylor (ed.), *New Directions in Curriculum Studies*, Lewes, Sessex: Falmer Press.

NACCCE (National Advisory Committee for Creative and Cultural Education) (1999) *All Our Futures: Creativity, Culture and Education*, London: HMSO.

Nardi, B.A. (ed.) (1997) *Context and Consciousness: Activity Theory and Human-Computer Interaction*, Cambridge MA and London: The MIT Press.

National Women's Law Center (2002) *Title IX and Equal Opportunity in Vocational and Technical Education: A Promise Still Owed to the Nation's Young Women*, Washington, DC: National Women's Law Centre.

NCC (National Curriculum Council) (1990) *Technology in the National Curriculum*, London: HMSO.

Noss, R. (1988) 'Geometrical Thinking and LOGO: Do Girls have More to Gain?' in C. Hoyles (ed.), *Girls and Computers: General Issues and Case Studies of LOGO in the Mathematics Classroom*, Bedford Way Papers 34, London: Institute of Education, University of London.

Nunes, C.A.A., Nunes, M.M.R. and Davies, C. (2003) 'Assessing the Inaccessible: Metacognition and Attitudes', *Assessment in Education*, 10(3): 375–388.

Oakeshott, M. (1971) 'Education, the Engagement and the Frustration', in R.S. Peters, P.H. Hirst and H.T. Sockett (eds), Proceedings of the Philosophy of Education Society of Great Britain Annual Conference, 5(1): 43–76, Oxford: Blackwell.

O'Hear, A. (1991) *Father of Child-Centredness: John Dewey and the Ideology of Modern Education*, London: Centre for Policy Studies.

Organisation for Economic Co-operation and Development (OECD) (2004) 'Raising the Quality of Education for All', Meeting of Ministers of Education, 18th–19th March 2004, Dublin.

Osler, A. (1994) 'Education for Development: Redefining Citizenship in a Pluralist Society', in A. Osler (ed.), *Development Education: Global Perspectives in the Curriculum*, London: Cassell.

——(2005) 'Looking to the Future: Democracy, Diversity and Citizenship Education', in A. Osler (ed.), *Teachers, Human Rights and Diversity: Educating Citizens in Multicultural Societies*, Stoke-on Trent: Trentham.

Osler, A. and Starkey, H. (1999) 'Rights, Identities and Inclusion: European Action Programmes as Political Education', *Oxford Review of Education*, 25(1–2): 199–215.

——(2001) 'Citizenship Education and National Identities in France and England: Inclusive or Exclusive?' *Oxford Review of Education*, 27(2): 287–305.

——(2002) 'Education for Citizenship: Mainstreaming the Fight Against Racism?' *European Journal of Education*, 37(2): 143–159.

——(2003) 'Learning for Cosmopolitan Citizenship: Theoretical Debates and Young People's Experiences', *Educational Review*, 55(3): 243–254.

——(2005a) *Changing Citizenship: Democracy and Inclusion in Education*, Maidenhead: Open University Press.

——(2005b) 'Violence in Schools and Representations of Young People: A Critique of Government Policies in France and England', *Oxford Review of Education*, 31(2): 195–215.

Osler, A. and Vincent, K. (2002) *Citizenship and the Challenge of Global Education*, Stoke-on-Trent: Trentham.

——(2003) *Girls and Exclusion: Rethinking the Agenda*, London: RoutledgeFalmer.

Osler, A., Rathenow, H.F. and Starkey, H. (eds) (1996) *Teaching for Citizenship in Europe*, Stoke: Trentham.

O'Sullivan, M., Bush, K. and Gehring, M. (2002) 'Gender Equity and Physical Education: A USA Perspective', in D. Penney (ed.), *Gender and Physical Education: Contemporary Issues and Future Directions*, London: Routledge.

Paechter, C. (1993) 'What Happens when a School Subject Undergoes a Sudden Change of Status?' *Curriculum Studies*, 1(3): 349–364.
—— (1998) *Educating the Other: Gender, Power and Schooling*, London: Falmer Press.
—— (2000) *Changing School Subjects: Power, Gender and Curriculum*, Buckingham: Open University Press.
—— (2003a) 'Learning Masculinities and Femininities: Power/Knowledge and Legitimate Peripheral Participation', *Women's Studies International Forum*, 26(6): 541–552.
—— (2003b) 'Power/Knowledge, Gender and Curriculum Change', *Journal of Educational Change*, 4(2): 129–148.
—— (2004) 'Mens sana in corpore sano: Cartesian Dualism and the Marginalisation of Sex Education', *Discourse*, 25(3): 309–320.
—— (2005) 'Power/Knowledge and the Academic Woman', paper presented at the International Conference, Gender Studies in the Academia, University of Thessaly, Volos, Greece, 10–12 June 2005.
Papert, S. (1980) *Mindstorms – Children, Computers and Powerful Ideas*, Brighton: Harvester Press.
Parekh, B. (2000) *Rethinking Multiculturalism: Cultural Diversity and Political Theory*, London: Macmillan.
Parker, I. (1914) *Dissenting Academies in England. Their Rise and Progress and their Place Among the Educational Systems of this Country*, Cambridge: Cambridge University Press.
Penfold, J. (1988) *Craft, Design and Technology: Past, Present and Future*, Stoke-on-Trent: Trentham Books.
Peters, R.S. (1966) *Ethics and Education*, London: Allen and Unwin.
Phenix, P.H. (1964) *The Realms of Meaning*, New York: McGraw-Hill.
Pinar, W.F. (1979) 'The Reconceptualization of Curriculum Studies', in P.H. Taylor (ed.), *New Directions in Curriculum Studies*, Lewes, Sussex: Falmer Press.
—— (1988) 'The Reconceptualising of Curriculum Studies', *Journal of Curriculum and Supervision*, 3(2): 157–167.
Pinar, W.F., Reynolds, W.M., Slattery, P. and Taubman, P.M. (eds) (2004) *Understanding Curriculum: An Introduction to the Study of Historical and Contemporary Curriculum Discourses*, New York: Peter Lang.
Polanyi, M. (1958) *Personal Knowledge: Towards a Post-Critical Philosophy*, London: Routledge and Kegan Paul.
—— (1962) *The Republic of Science*, Chicago, IL: Roosevelt University.
Popper, K.R. (1972) *Objective Knowledge: An Evolutionary Report*, Oxford: Clarendon Press.
Power, M. (1997) *The Audit Society: Rituals of Verification*, Oxford: Oxford University Press.
Purvis, J. (1985) 'Domestic Subjects since 1870', in I.F. Goodson (ed.), *Social Histories of the Secondary Curriculum*, Lewes: Falmer Press.
QCA (Qualifications and Assessment Authority, England and Wales) (1998) *Education for Citizenship and the Teaching of Democracy in Schools: Final Report of the Advisory Group on Citizenship (aka The Crick Report)* London: QCA.
—— (2002) *Creativity: Find it, Promote it*, London: QCA.
Quicke, J. (1999) *Curriculum for Life: Schools for a Democratic Learning Society*, Buckingham: Open University Press.
Quine, W.V.O. (1953) *From a Logical Point of View*, New York: Harper and Row.

Reay, D. and Wiliam, D. (1999) ' "I'll be a Nothing": Structure, Agency and the Construction of Identity through Assessment', *British Educational Research Journal*, 25(3): 343–354.

Reid, W. (1992) 'The State of Curriculum Inquiry', *Journal of Curriculum Studies*, 24(2): 165–178.

Riddell, S. (1992) *Gender and the Politics of the Curriculum*, London: Routledge.

Ridgway, J. and McCusker, S. (2003) 'Using Computers to Assess New Educational Goals', *Assessment in Education*, 10(3): 309–328.

Ritzer, G. (2000) *The McDonaldisation of Society*, Thousand Island, CA: Pine Forge Press.

Roach, J. (1986) *A History of Secondary Education, 1800–1870*, London: Longman.

Rorty, R. (1979) *Philosophy and the Mirror of Nature*, Princeton, NJ: Princeton University Press.

Ross, A. (2000) *Curriculum: Construction and Critique*, London: Falmer Press.

Said, E.W. (2004) *Humanism and Democratic Criticism*, Basingstoke: Palgrave.

St John-Brooks, C. (1983) 'English: A Curriculum for Personal Development?' in M. Hammersley and A. Hargreaves (eds), *Curriculum Practice: Some Sociological Case Studies*, Lewes: Falmer Press.

Sargisson, L. (1996) *Contemporary Feminist Utopias*, London: Routledge.

Scardamalia, M. (2000) 'Can Schools Enter a Knowledge Society?', in M. Selinger and J. Wynn (eds), *Educational Technology and the Impact on Teaching and Learning*, Abingdon: RM, pp. 5–9.

Scase, R. (1999) *Britain towards 2010: The Changing Business Environment*, London: DTI, http://www.esrc.ac.uk/2010/docs/britain.html

Schwab, J. (1962) *Discipline and Schools: The Scholars Look at the Schools*, Washington, DC: National Educational Association.

——(1970) *The Practical: A Language for Curriculum*, Washington, DC: National Education Association.

Scraton, S. (1993) 'Equality, Coeducation and Physical Education', in J. Evans (ed.), *Equality, Education and Physical Education*, London: Falmer Press.

Seltzer, K. and Bentley, T. (1999) *The Creative Age: Knowledge and Skills for the New Economy*, London: DEMOS.

Sennett, R. (1998) *The Corrosion of Character: The Personal Consequences of Work in the New Capitalism*, New York and London: W.W. Norton & Co.

Sikes, P.J. (1988) 'Growing old gracefully? Age, Identity and Physical Education', in J. Evans (ed.), *Teachers, Teaching and Control in Physical Education*, Lewes: Falmer Press.

Simon, B. (1960) *Studies in the History of Education, 1780–1870*, London: Lawrence and Wishart.

Sims, J.W. (1920) *The Boy Electrician*, London: G.G. Harrap and Co.

Skelton, C. (2001) *Schooling the Boys: Masculinities and Primary Education*, Buckingham: Open University Press.

Skilbeck, M. (1971) 'Education and the Reconstruction of Culture: A Critical Study of 20th Century English and American Theories', unpublished Doctoral Thesis, London: Institute of Education, University of London.

——(1984) *School-Based Curriculum Development*, London: Harper and Row.

Smith, B.O., Stanley, W.O. and Shores, J.H. (1950) *Fundamentals of Curriculum Development*, New York: Harcourt, Brace and World.

Smith, J.W.A. (1955) *The Birth of Modern Education: The Contribution of the Dissenting Academies 1660–1800*, London: Independent Press.

SOLE (Student Online Learning Experience) (2004) *The Student Online Learning Experience Project*, http://sole.ilrt.org/findings.html

Soller, A. (2004) 'Understanding Knowledge-Sharing Breakdowns: A Meeting of the Quantitative and Qualitative Minds', *Journal of Computer Assisted Learning*, 20(3): 212–223.

Somekh, B. (2004) 'Taking the Sociological Imagination to School: An Analysis of the (Lack of) Impact of ICT on Education Systems', *Technology, Pedagogy and Education, Special Issue: Research into Information and Communications Technologies*, 13(2): 163–179.

Somekh, B. and Davies, R. (1991) 'Towards a Pedagogy for Information Technology', *The Curriculum Journal*, 2(2): 153–170.

Somekh, B., Lewin, C., Mavers, D., Fisher, T., Harrison, C., Haw, K., Lunzer, E., McFarlane, A. and Scrimshaw, P. (2002) *ImpaCT2 Final Report Part 3: Learning with ICT: Pupils' and Teachers' Perspectives*, London: DfES, http://www.becta.org.uk/research/reports/

Somekh, B., Mavers, D. and Lewin, C. (2002) *Using ICT to Enhance Home-School Links: An Evaluation of Current Practice in England*, London: Department for Education and Skills.

Somekh, B., Woodrow, D., Barnes, S., Triggs, P., Sutherland, R., Passey, D., Holt, H., Harrison, C., Fisher, T, Flett, A. and Joyes, G. (2002) Final Report, NGfL Pathfinders Programme, Coventry: Becta.

Somekh, B., Lewin, C., Mavers, D., Scrimshaw, Haldane, A., Levin, C. and Robinson, J. (2003) *Evaluation of the GridClub Educational Service: Final Report to the Department for Education and Skills, March 2003*, Manchester: Manchester Metropolitan University.

Sparkes, A., Templin, T.J. and Schempp, P.G. (1990) 'The Problematic Nature of a Career in a Marginal Subject: Some Implications for Teacher Education', *Journal of Education for Teaching*, 16(1): 3–28.

Spelman, E.V. (1982) 'Woman as Body: Ancient and Contemporary Views', *Feminist Studies*, 8(1): 109–131.

Spencer, B. (1997) *Utopian Writing: Its Nature and Historical Context*, http://oregonstate.edu/Dept/philosophy/club/utopia/utopian-visions/spencer-lec.html

Spender, D. (1980) *Man Made Language*, London: Routledge and Kegan Paul.

—— (1982) *Invisible Women: The Schooling Scandal*, London: Writers and Readers.

Stenhouse, L. (1975) *An Introduction to Curriculum Research and Development*, London: Heinemann Educational Books.

Strong, J. (1909) *A History of Secondary Education in Scotland*, Oxford: Clarendon Press.

Stubbs, M. (1976) *Language, Schools and Classrooms*, London: Methuen.

Suárez-Orozco, M.M. and Qin-Hilliard, D.B. (2004) 'Globalization: Culture and Education in the New Millennium', in M.M. Suárez-Orozco and D.B. Qin-Hilliard (eds), *Globalization: Culture and Education in the New Millennium*, Berkeley, CA: University of California Press with the Ross Institute.

Tawney, R.H. (1926) *Religion and the Rise of Capitalism*, West Drayton: Penguin.

Taylor, C. (1994) 'The Politics of Recognition', in A. Guttmann (ed.), *Multiculturalism: Examining the Politics of Recognition*, Princeton, NJ: Princeton University Press.

Taylor, P.H. (ed.) (1979) *New Directions in Curriculum Studies*, Lewes, Sussex: Falmer Press.

Taylor, S. (1989) *Positive Illusions*, New York: Basic Books.

Thomas, K. (1990) *Gender and Subject in Higher Education*, Milton Keynes: Society for Research into Higher Education and the Open University Press.

Thompson, E.P. (1982) 'Time, Work-discipline and Industrial Capitalism', in A. Giddens and D. Held (eds), *Classes Power and Conflict*, London: Macmillan.

Thomson, K.M. (1998a) *Emotional Capital*, Oxford: Capstone.

——(1998b) *Passion at Work*, Oxford: Capstone.

Thrift, N. (1999) 'Capitalism's Cultural Turn', in L. Ray and A. Sayer (eds), *Culture and Economy after the Cultural Turn*, London: Sage.

——(2002) 'Performing Cultures in the New Economy', in P. du Gay and M. Pryke (eds), *Cultural Economy*, London: Sage.

Tizard, B. and Hughes, M. (1984) *Young Children Learning*, London: Fontana.

Tomlinson, J. (1991) *Cultural Imperialism*, London: Pinter Publishers.

Torbe, M. (1986) 'Language across the Curriculum: Policies and Practice', in D. Barnes, J. Britton and M. Torbe (eds), *Language, the Learner and the School* (3rd edn), Harmondsworth: Penguin.

Triche, S. and McKnight, D. (2004) 'The Quest for Method: The Legacy of Peter Ramus', *History of Education*, 33(1): 39–54.

Trudgill, P. (1983) *On Dialect*, Oxford: Blackwell.

Turkle, S. (1984) *The Second Self: Computers and the Human Spirit*, London, Toronto and New York: Granada.

——(1995) *Life on the Screen: Identity in the Age of the Internet*, London and New York: Phoenix.

Turnbull, A. (1987) 'Learning Her Womanly Work: The Elementary School Curriculum 1870–1914', in F. Hunt (ed.), *Lessons for Life*, Oxford: Basil Blackwell.

Turner, A. (2001) *Just Capital: The Liberal Economy*, London: Macmillan.

United Nations Development Programme (2002) *Human Development Report 2002: Deepening Democracy in a Fragmented World*, Oxford: Oxford University Press.

United Nations Educational Scientific and Cultural Organisation (1995) *Declaration and Integrated Framework of Action on Education for Peace, Human Rights and Democracy*, Paris: UNESCO.

Usher, R., Bryant, I. and Johnstone, R. (1996) *Adult Education and the Post-Modern Challenge: Learning Beyond the Limits*, London: Routledge.

van Essen, M. (2003) 'No Issue, No Problem? Co-education in Dutch Secondary Physical Education during the Twentieth Century', *Gender and Education*, 15(1): 59–74.

Vygotsky, L. (1978) *Mind in Society: The Development of Higher Psychological Processes*, Cambridge, MA: Harvard University Press.

Walker, S.A. (2004) 'Socratic Strategies and Devil's Advocacy in Synchronous CMC Debate', *Journal of Computer Assisted Learning*, 20(3): 172–182.

Walkerdine, V. (1988) *The Mastery of Reason*, Cambridge: Routledge and Kegan Paul.

Walsh, P. (1993) *Education and Meaning: Philosophy in Practice*, London: Cassell.

Wartofsky, M. (1979) *Models: Representation and Scientific Understanding*, Dordrecht: Reidel.

Watts, I. (1792) *Logic: Or the Right Use of Reason in the Inquiry after Truth*, Edinburgh: J. Dickson; J and J Fairbairn.

Weber, M. (1930) *The Protestant Ethic and the Spirit of Capitalism*, London: Allen and Unwin.

Weiner, G. (ed.) (1985) *Just a Bunch of Girls*, Milton Keynes: Open University Press.

—— (1993) 'The Gendered Curriculum – Producing the Text: Developing a Poststructural Feminist Analysis', paper presented at the Annual Conference of the Australian Association for Research in Education, Perth, December 1993.

—— (1994) *Feminisms in Education: An Introduction*, Buckingham: Open University Press.

Wertsch, J.V. (1998) *Mind as Action*, New York and Oxford: Oxford University Press.

Wexler, P. (1992) *Becoming Somebody*, London: Falmer.

—— (1997) *Holy Sparks: Social Theory, Education and Religion*, London: Macmillan.

—— (2000) *The Mystical Society*, Boulder, CO: Westview Press.

White, J. (1982) *The Aims of Education Restated*, London: Routledge and Kegan Paul.

—— (1997) 'Effectiveness', in J.White and M.Barber (eds), *Perspectives on School Improvement*, London: Institute of Education, University of London.

—— (1998) *Do Howard Gardner's Multiple Intelligences Add Up?* London: Institute of Education, University of London.

—— (ed.) (2004) *Rethinking the School Curriculum: Values, Aims and Purposes* London: RoutledgeFalmer.

—— (2005) 'Reassessing 1960s Philosophy of the Curriculum', *London Review of Education*, 3(2): 131–144.

Whitty, G. (1981) 'Curriculum Studies: A Critique of Some Recent British Orthodoxies', in M. Lawn and L. Barton (eds), *Rethinking Curriculum Studies*, London: Croom Helm.

Williams, R. (1961) *The Long Revolution*, London: Chatto and Windus.

—— (1983) *Towards 2000*, London: Chatto and Windus.

Willis, P. (1977) *Learning to Labour*, Farnborough: Saxon House.

—— (1990) *Common Culture: Symbolic Work at Play in Everyday Cultures of the Young*, London: Open University Press.

Woodhead, C. (2004) *How to Lower School Standards: Mike Tomlinson's Modest Proposals*, London: Politeia.

Woolgar, S. (ed.) (2002) *Virtual Society? Technology, Cyberbole, Reality*, Oxford: Oxford University Press.

Wright, E.O. (1995) 'Preface: The Real Utopias Project', in J. Cohen and J. Rogers (eds), *Associations and Democracy*, London: Verso.

Yates, L. (1985) 'Is "Girl Friendly Schooling" Really What Girls Need?' in J. Whyte, R. Deem, L. Kant and M. Cruikshank (eds), *Girl Friendly Schooling*, London: Methuen.

Young, M.F.D. (1971) *Knowledge and Control: New Directions for the Sociology of Education*, London: Collier Macmillan.

—— (1991) 'Technology as an Educational Issue', in H. Mackay, M.F.D. Young and J. Beynon (eds), *Understanding Technology in Education*, Basingstoke: Falmer Press.

—— (2004) 'An Old Problem in a New Context: Rethinking the Relationship between Sociology and Educational Policy', *International Studies in Sociology of Education*, 14(1): 3–20.

Index

Note: Page numbers in italics indicate figures.